Music, Markets and Consumption

Daragh O'Reilly

Gretchen Larsen

Krzysztof Kubacki

(G) Goodfellow Publishers Ltd

W

780.
688
ORE

G) Published by Goodfellow Publishers Limited,
Woodeaton, Oxford, OX3 9TJ
http://www.goodfellowpublishers.com

British Library Cataloguing in Publication Data: a catalogue record
for this title is available from the British Library.

Library of Congress Catalog Card Number: on file.

ISBN: 978-1-908999-52-8

Design and typesetting by P.K. McBride, www.macbride.org.uk

Printed and bound in Great Britain by Marston Book Services Limited, Oxfordshire.

Cover design by Cylinder, www.cylindermedia.com

Dedications

For my family and friends. DOR

For all the wonderful people who have brought music into my life. GL

For Natalia. KK

Contents

List of abbreviations

A&R	Artists and repertoire
AIDS	Acquired immuno-deficiency syndrome
AMA	American Marketing Association
BBC	British Broadcasting Corporation
CCT	Consumer culture theory
CD	Compact disc
DAT	Digital audio tape
DJ	Disc jockey
DVD	Digital versatile disc
EP	Extended play record
FMCG	Fast-moving consumer good
IFPI	International Federation of the Phonographic Industry
LP	Long play record
MP3	Refers to a type of audio file format
R&B	Rhythm and blues
VJ	Video jockey
UNESCO	United Nations Educational Scientific and Cultural Organization
WHO	World Health Organization

Preface

Working in marketing groups within business/management schools, sharing a common research interest in music, and being conscious that a large part of human activity around music is described as the 'music business' or the 'music industry', we had been contemplating for some time how to apply marketing theory to this area. Through reading the many excellent insights provided by scholars in music, cultural, media, sociological and anthropological studies, and being active consumers of music ourselves, we were clear that a straightforward, instrumental application of classical, or so-called 'mainstream', marketing management ideas to the music business would have limited usefulness. Such ideas may be valuable when thinking about some of the marketing practices of major record labels when selling music as a packaged, tangible, fast-moving consumer good (FMCG), but are perhaps less relevant for musicians working independently or in less formally structured and market-oriented institutions, or indeed for artist managers or record label executives.

Much of the marketing literature around music has to do with either the commercial expediency or utility of music as a facilitator of the sales process in advertising and promotion, or its use in elevators and supermarkets. The question of music itself as the focus of exchange relationships, rather than as a promotional aid, is to our minds a far more interesting one.

Considering the major changes in the music business environment that began during the nineties, it seems that music marketing theory needs to become a fusion project which integrates insights from a range of disciplines into something more holistic and open than classical marketing theory allows. We were unable to find any books which examined how these ideas fuse together, so we decided to write one – and this is the result.

This book, then, is intended to shed more light on the relationship between music, markets and consumption, with music as the focal point of the exchange relationship. It is concerned with the connections that people in the business and their 'customers' make with one another.

Rather than writing a practical book on how to market music, of which there are several very good examples already in existence, we wanted to gather together in one volume a selection of theoretical perspectives which bear in different ways on the 'exchange' of music. This project represents an attempt to broaden the range of issues which marketers need to think about when considering how to market music. It is also an effort to join and contribute constructively to a conversation, which has been ongoing for a long time amongst different groups of scholars, about the ways in which music, markets and consumption interact. The book does not formally develop a new theory of music marketing, but we trust that it lays some essential groundwork for such a project.

Daragh O'Reilly, Gretchen Larsen and Krzysztof Kubacki

May 2013

Acknowledgements

We would like to take this opportunity to thank Sally North for her enthusiasm for this project and for her extremely patient shepherding of the book through the various stages of its writing. We also would like to thank the reviewers, who provided such helpful commentary at the mid-point of the writing, as well as on the final draft of the book. Special thanks also go to Panayiota Alevizou, Alan Bradshaw, Mark Bright, Robin Croft, Andreas Chatzidakis, Noel Dennis, Ian Fillis, Morris Holbrook, Finola Kerrigan, Rob Lawson, Dirk vom Lehn, Michael Macaulay, Geoff Nichols, Terry O'Sullivan, Ray Sylvester, Sarah Todd, Fraser Wilson, Cagri Yalkin, and Loo Yeo. Finally, many thanks also to the arts marketing community for being a wonderfully supportive, inspiring and enthusiastic group of scholars.

Part I
Introduction

1 Marketing and Music

Introduction

The purpose of this book is to contribute to discussions about the music business from a marketing point of view. Arts marketers have long argued that marketing thinking needs to be substantially adapted to deal with the complexities and particularities of the creative and cultural industries. There are a number of books which take a practical approach to the marketing of music (e.g. Baker's (2012) *Guerilla Music Marketing Online*), or provide an overview of the music industry (e.g. Kusek and Leonhard's (2005) *The Future of Music: A Manifesto for the Digital Music Revolution* and Wikstrom's (2009) *The Music Industry: Music in the Cloud*), or comment on economic aspects of the business from the point of view of popular music studies. This book, in contrast, deals with the application of marketing and consumer studies theory to the business. As far as the authors can establish, this has not been attempted before.

This project presents three challenges:

1 deciding what kind of marketing theory we are talking about (for there are different strands);

2 engaging with an appropriate selection of the relevant conceptual and empirical journal literature; and

3 applying it to the music business in a way which respects, and seeks to accommodate, the valuable insights generated by researchers in other areas, such as popular music, cultural, media and sociological studies.

The remainder of this introduction considers classical marketing and branding theory, and examines some of the difficulties in their application which, in our view, create the need for this book.

What's so special about music?

Music has been a notable part of human activity since prehistoric times. The precise origins of music have been discussed in such fields as evolutionary musicology (e.g. Wallin *et al.*, 2000), however the human significance of music has been recognized and debated since the earliest days of Western civilization, when philosophers such as Aristotle and Plato ruminated on the nature and value of music (Bowman, 1998). Music has always been fundamentally social. People share music with other members of their society – a practice which gives meaning not only to the music itself, but also to social interaction. Sounds are transformed into music through the meanings people imbue in them within a given social and cultural context (Hargreaves and North, 1997).

The sharing of music precedes any formal economic exchange, however the political economy has greatly influenced, and is influenced by, this fundamental, social human activity of music-making. Music as we know it now – as an 'autonomous production' – is an invention of only the past century or so, emerging out of Western capitalism. This represents a particular form of making and engaging in music, which, like any form, reflects the dominant structure of political power and social control (Attali, 1977/1985). Put simply, the market is a formalized way of regulating and capitalizing music-making, -sharing and engagement.

Marketing theory and practice provide a way of understanding and facilitating exchanges within the market (e.g. Bagozzi, 1975). Marketing as a discipline emerged in response to the physical separation between producers and consumers, which was a consequence of the Industrial Revolution. Driven by the tangible, physical nature of the manufactured goods of the times, marketers focused on the distributive function and sought to bring both products and consumers to the market in order to facilitate exchange. This emphasis remained and, despite the broadening of the scope of marketing into such functions as communications and branding, the formalization of the principles of marketing (Wilke and Moore, 2003) reflected an interest in physical products, such as consumer durables and FMCG (fast moving consumer goods). Therefore, marketers' initial interest in music was concentrated on how it could be used *in* the marketing of other products. The capability of music to evoke particular emotional and behavioural responses, and therefore to influence consumer decision-making and purchase intentions, was harnessed in an effort to increase the effectiveness of marketing practices (e.g. Smith and Curnow, 1966; Gorn, 1982; Park and Young, 1986).

The above point notwithstanding, this book is primarily concerned with the marketing of music. As a commodity, music is often converted into a physical form so that it can be captured, recorded, stored and reproduced within the market, but it can be argued that the core product itself – the sound – remains intangible and even ephemeral. These and other characteristics of music as a product (discussed in Chapter 3) mean that traditional marketing theory and practice cannot easily be transferred across to music markets. The point is that music problematises marketing. It is certainly not the only type of product to do so, but music does it in a way that is unique, and interesting enough to warrant careful examination. Many examples are discussed throughout this book of how music blurs the distinctions between categories that are foundational in marketing thinking and practice, such as producer/consumer, commerce/culture and amateur/professional.

The recognition of services as a type of market offering, and what is called the 'experiential turn' in marketing, opened the door for a greater interest in music markets, marketing and consumption. The marketing of music requires careful adaptation of customary marketing practices, or even the development of new approaches. From this, new ways of organizing music production, sharing and engagement have emerged. For example, there is an increasing proliferation of music genres which helps producers and consumers to communicate about the music and place it within the music market. An especially powerful and insidious mode of categorization is between high or elite music and low, mass or popular music. This distinction has had implications across the board, from determining and structuring music policy to underpinning the emergence of music-related subcultures. Frith (2007) argues that all of these categories are in fact part of a single musical culture that developed in response to the rise of liberal market capitalism, and that many categories, particularly the high/popular music distinction, might not even be helpful in terms of formulating a way of approaching the problem they emerged to resolve: making music in the marketplace. To illustrate this, Frith (2007) notes that the most successful music scenes actually blur the distinction between, for example, high and low art. Thus, just as it is claimed that music problematises marketing, so too can it be said that marketing (and markets) problematise music. It is precisely this complexity that makes the subject so fascinating. The intersection of music, marketplaces and consumption is one of the most potentially illuminating positions from which to understand contemporary issues surrounding music.

Mainstream managerial marketing

Within the academic marketing community, mainstream managerial marketing is a useful 'straw man' against which to position a range of more interesting theories of marketing. Yet there is a rump of basic or classical marketing theory which can be called mainstream managerial marketing. This is conventionally taught in business schools and is usually covered in two taught modules, firstly marketing principles and then marketing management. It is therefore worth examining what this theory contains so that the reader, who may be coming from a non-marketing background, can obtain an understanding of its main ideas.

The word 'market' may signify a place in which products or services are sold or exchanged, such as (a) the market area in a city, town or village; (b) the market for a particular product, which means the actual and/or potential demand for it; (c) a wider geographical area, such as the UK market; (d) a set of economic relations built around the exchange of a given offering; or (e) any kind of 'space', including cyberspace, in which commercial transactions take place.

Jobber and Ellis-Chadwick (2012:3) defined the marketing concept as:

> 'the achievement of corporate goals through meeting and exceeding customer needs and expectations better than the competition'.

They assert that there are three conditions for the realization of the concept, namely:

1   an organizational focus on providing satisfaction to customers;

2   integrated effort by the organization; and

3   a belief that organizational goals can be achieved through customer satisfaction.

This clearly locates marketing as a practice in the service of corporate goals, the most fundamental of which can be read as the return on capital, and as a specifically managerial practice. The marketer is a manager and, in the music business, there are many different kinds of organization.

According to the October 2007 definition of marketing by the American Marketing Association (AMA), marketing is 'the activity, set of institutions, and processes for creating, communicating, delivering, and exchanging offerings that have value for customers, clients, partners, and society at large'.

There is no mention here of marketing being a philosophy, a theory, or an academic discipline, much less an ideology (Marion, 2006). The AMA definition also assumes that marketing is the prerogative of the organization. The role of the consumer or customer in marketing is downplayed in this version. Given the almost religious-fundamentalist fervour with which some marketing academics and practitioners have talked up the authority and sovereignty of the customer or consumer, it seems odd that the 'king' of this economic process and of the exchange relationship is not honoured with a more central role in this official definition. The point that is being missed here is that markets only happen if there is a buyer and a seller. Therefore, markets are 'made' not just by business organizations, brokers or intermediaries, but also by consumers and customers. Marketing, in the sense of market-making, is, arguably, a consumer practice as much as an organizational one – no purchase = no sale = no market. However, this approach would not be explicitly considered in mainstream managerial marketing textbooks. The definition therefore functions as a version of 'marketing' which serves a particular view of the practice.

Marketing is a wide spectrum which includes many different positions, from 'hard left' critical marketing to far-right celebration of the triumph of marketing and capitalism. Mainstream managerial marketing is the kind which is generally spoken with differing degrees of fluency by marketing managers, salespeople and business people generally, and an increasingly common discourse by which consumers make sense of their exchange experiences. Since the early nineties, marketing has been one of the most highly subscribed subjects within business studies, itself one of the more popular subjects to study at undergraduate level. Marketing is now taught in thousands of business schools worldwide, at undergraduate and postgraduate levels. There are also many highly ranked academic journals which accept submissions on marketing topics. The consequence of this has been a considerable incremental increase in the development of theory, or ways of thinking about marketing. Marketing textbooks tend to be written from the managerial perspective, where the reader is assumed to be educating him/herself for a job or career in management. The textbooks are therefore written in order to help the prospective marketer better understand the world, using marketing concepts, constructs and frameworks or models. This is 'mainstream managerial marketing'. It includes analysis of the business environment; competitors; consumer behaviour; organizational buying behaviour; marketing research and information systems; market segmentation; targeting; positioning; the marketing mix (products/services, distribution, promotion/ marketing communications, pricing, business process, human resources, physical evidence); and marketing planning, strategy, objectives and implementation. Although marketing rhetoric insists that consumers and customers are the most important aspect of marketing, typically only two chapters out of 25 will be devoted to consumption issues, with the remainder being written from a firmly managerial perspective. Mainstream managerial marketing can be read as an instrumental body of theory in the service of capital.

The field of marketing, as conventionally understood, deals with the exchange relationship between two parties, one of which is categorized as the producer and the other as the consumer. Marketing includes the study of consumers and their behaviour, an area which draws heavily on insights and methods from economics, sociology, anthropology and psychology (of various kinds, though mainly cognitive and social psychology). The managerial side of marketing draws on various strands of thinking in macro- and microeconomics, organization and management theory, as well as sociological and psychological theory. Other disciplines upon which marketing scholars draw include, for example, media studies and communications studies in relation to marketing communications. In business schools, marketing students are taught how to develop enduring and profitable exchange relationships with customers or consumers in a competitive environment. As practitioners of marketing, marketers are expected to apply marketing principles in the service of their employers (or of themselves if they are entrepreneurs).

A complete marketing plan must include objectives for the recruitment and retention of customers, as well as a proposed strategy for achieving these objectives. When an organization such as a record label or a publisher is offering many products, a resource-balancing process such as a portfolio management strategy is called for. Many kinds of marketing strategies have been designed to help achieve the objectives of customer recruitment and retention. Generically, a marketing strategy is said to consist of segmentation, targeting, positioning, and management of the marketing mix.

Segmentation is the process of dividing the market (actual and potential demand) into different groups of consumers, called segments. Segmentation can be based on the benefits sought from products, or a combination of objective criteria such as age, gender, residential address, income, education and wealth. The benefit to the organization of segmenting its market is that it enables the organization to be selective about which segments or groups it wishes to do business with, and how it allocates its scarce investment resources. As organizational resources are typically limited or constrained, it is necessary from the perspective of corporate objectives to optimize the allocation of cash, time, technology, work and personnel. This construct 'segment' – meaning a group of consumers categorized in a certain way for the purposes of trading – is relevant to the fans' side of the exchange relationship. It represents the ascription of a common identity or attributes to a group of people by an organization.

Targeting means the prioritization of certain segments of consumers (e.g. young over old) according to their attractiveness as a 'target market' or segment. In turn, segments are based on the size, growth, wealth, degree of regulation and competitiveness of the segment. An organization needs to decide if it is going to target all of the segments it has identified, or select a few – or even just one – to focus on.

Positioning is the creation of an identity communicated to the consumer which identifies the marketer's product, service or 'offering' and distinguishes or differentiates it from competitors. This differentiation is centred on the functional, symbolic and expressive attributes built into the offering (Elliott and Percy, 2007). A key related concept is branding (see below), or the creation and management of meanings associated with the offering. Positioning is said to be 'in the mind of the consumer', not in the mind of the company, or the marketing manager. In this way, marketing respects the subjectivity and interpretive capability of the consumer. Segmentation and targeting are processes leading to decisions about how consumers are systematically categorized, often on the basis of marketing research. Positioning is a process of comparing and contrasting the organization's offerings with those of its closest competitors in order to identify areas of competitive advantage or product distinction. These three processes of segmentation, targeting and positioning are seen as being more important than the tactical decisions made about the marketing mix, and are categorized as strategic marketing.

Marketing mix issues such as product and process management are seen as tactical, and subject to planning in shorter time frames. This conceptual hierarchy places the customer at the beginning of the process and relegates many company-related issues to a less significant role. However, just to complicate the issue, marketers occasionally break the mould by making a tactical issue strategic, such as product variety (e.g. General Motors in the 1920s) or place/distribution (e.g. Dell Computers).

Positioning and branding

Positioning, one of the key strategic processes in marketing, bears directly on branding. An influential text relating to this idea of positioning is Ries and Trout's *Positioning: The battle for your mind* (1981). The authors' construction of the competitive relationships between suppliers as a war or battle for the consumer's mind is a staple cliché of strategic marketing management. The focus here is on the positioning of the offering in the mind of the consumer or fan (not in the mind of the marketer). Positioning is a simplistic spatial trope. Its key idea is that every consumer's mind is a kind of cognitive or mental 'space' which is divided by a set of cross-hairs, in relation to which competing products or brands can be represented on price and quality axes (the cross-hairs). On these axes, marketers can work out the position of their own brand, and the consumers' ideal positioning, as well as that of their competitors' brands. For example, a brand may be high price and high quality, or low price and high quality, and so on. Each of these positions has certain consequences for the marketing strategy of the brand. Marketing planning therefore requires the continual assessment (though market research) of a brand's position on consumers' perceptual maps. If the position of a brand on the price/quality axes (other axes may be added) is not considered sufficiently defensible, then the brand owner should attempt to 'reposition' the brand along the axes in such a way that it can offer greater competitive advantage and be closer to the target consumers' ideal.

Positioning generally means presenting the differential benefits the buyer will get from a particular offering over competitor offerings. These benefits are seen as being a three-fold combination of functional, emotional and self-expressive components. The self-expressive benefits of consuming music arise in its symbolic consumption. In other words, music consumers' listening choices and practices, and the ways in which they signal their allegiances to certain types of music and musical performers, are considered to be self-expressive. The functional benefits of music are closely associated with the emotional ones, in the sense of music used for mood regulation.

According to marketing principles, positioning should be clear, consistent, competitive and credible. However, these four 'Cs' were not developed with cultural offerings such as music in mind. Much of the discussion in Chapters 5 and 6 on branding is about a fifth 'C', namely culture. From a culturalist point of view, positioning is always already cultural. The positioning of cultural offerings therefore needs to take particular account of cultural dimensions of the industry, its players and their offerings, and also wider socio-cultural trends.

Services marketing and music

Economics tends to see market offerings as goods or services. The field of services marketing emerged in the 1980s (see, e.g., Zeithaml, Parasuraman and Berry, 1985), and is now an established part of the standard diet of most marketing degree programmes. Its relevance is that music can be considered as a service business, since a musical act provides a musical entertainment service. The need for a theory of services marketing emerged from marketing's inability to fully account for certain aspects of non-manufactured goods, e.g. the importance of the human dimension of the exchange (people!) and the often complex micro-processes that go into operationalising a service. Services are defined by Zeithaml et al. (2005) as 'deeds, processes and performances'. The service sector includes financial services, the retail and wholesale sectors, airlines, the hospitality industry, communications, utilities, charities, media, museums, professional services and public services.

An important services marketing concept is that of the 'service encounter', i.e. a point in time or episode during which the customer interacts with the firm. In the music business, these encounters could include a diverse range of situations, such as buying a product from a band website, attending a live concert, or trying to get an autograph from a band member. These encounters can be additional bases of favourable or unfavourable perceptions of the band. Different kinds of encounters also exist, including remote (e.g. via the Internet), phone (e.g. ticket bookings) and face-to-face (e.g. live concert). Some encounters are more important than others in building relationships. The face-to-face service encounter at a concert is a critical part of building band-fan dialogue and relationships.

Service offerings have four main characteristics which distinguish them from manufactured products.

1   They are intangible; they are not in themselves material objects, although the total service package may include some material element. A music performance is an intangible product, whereas a music CD is a tangible, manufactured product. The total offering of a musical act includes both products and services. In a service business intangibles abound, and therefore the managerial practice known as branding (see below) is of critical importance. Since music involves a significant experiential ('soft') dimension, as well as hard products, branding can be expected to be important.

2   Because services are delivered by human beings and involve human interaction, they are not standardized – each performance of a service will be different.

3   Whereas manufactured products can be stored and distributed for later purchase and consumption, services are often produced and consumed simultaneously – as in the case of a live music concert. This has implications in the event of service breakdown.

4   Service goods are perishable; for example, if a musical performer is appearing at a venue on a particular date and only half of the tickets have been sold, that particular opportunity to sell the performance is gone forever – it has perished, and the other half of the tickets will never be sold.

However, services marketing theory is weak when it comes to capturing the dimensions of consumption experiences. One response to this has been the attempt by some writers (e.g. Pine and Gilmore, 1999) to promote the idea of experiences and experiential marketing. This line of thinking borrows from dramaturgical theory to re-imagine market transactions as staged experiences or performances, and emphasizes the sensuous, or sense-related, and social aspects of consumption.

The marketing mix

The marketing mix (Borden, 1984) is a simple and popular conceptual marketing management framework. It is basically a kind of checklist for the tactical management of brand-consumer relationships. It consists of so called 'elements' (traditionally, for some unknown reason, beginning with the letter 'p') which can be said to include product, place, price, promotion, people, process and physical evidence (though their exact definition depends on the business context).

The **product** is, at a basic level, the music. Chapter 3 more fundamentally explores the framing of music as a product. Here, a number of basic issues relating to music as a product are discussed. In view of the possibility of recording music for replication and distribution for mass consumption, product format needs to be accounted for. Popular music is reproduced in various technical formats, such as: vinyl disc, minidisk, DAT (digital audio tape), video, audio cassette, MP3, CD, and Blu-ray disc. Musical genre is another way of classifying musical products — in the nineties and noughties, one had only to visit one of the dwindling number of retailers to see the changes in product category on the shop floor as a consequence of the emergence of newer genres, such as hip hop or R&B. Another product format, which is arguably the most important in terms of current business models, is live performance. In addition to the core product of music, ancillary products, such as t-shirts, exist. Other product varieties are release formats such as live albums, studio albums, singles, and EPs.

As far as **place** is concerned, music is distributed over the Internet in either buy-from-shop, streamed or downloadable format, from organizations like Amazon and iTunes, different kinds of e-tailers, or direct from the musical acts themselves. A large number of products are sold through high street music retailers, supermarkets, and motorway service forecourts, although the retailing of tangible products, such as CDs, DVDs and Blu-ray discs is under increasing threat from the Internet. From a popular music studies point of view, however, place relates to the places from which music originates and is heard. Certain types of music, and certain sounds, become associated with specific places, e.g.

Manchester (Haslam, 1999), Rio de Janeiro, Compton, Dakar, or even certain venues, e.g. CBGB's for punk and La Scala for opera. The places where live music is performed are often highly significant for consumers.

Promotion includes interviews with musicians, press releases, tour publicity, radio and TV promotion and performance, features, photographs, video clips, album trailers/teasers, web-based promotion (especially through the act's and the label's websites), merchandise, CD covers, artwork in general, music videos, live performance videos, and publicity photos. Music is heavily mediated – via TV, radio and the Internet. The playing of a song on the radio, TV or web can be read as both a 'delivery' of the product experience, and a promotion for the band or act. Promotional links between the mainstream non-music brands and popular music include celebrity endorsement (Erdogan, 1999), product placement and sponsorship.

In mainstream managerial marketing, the **people** element in the mix foregrounds those who deliver the service or salespeople who sell a product. In the music industry, this can include a wide range of people, from the band members, to the crew, tour managers, producers, freelance and label employees, session musicians, and a whole host of intermediaries involved in bringing the 'product' into being, including DJs in clubs and on the radio, as well as VJs. As far as process is concerned, most acts engage in five major or core processes: origination of material, rehearsal, recording, touring (e.g. Alan, 1992) and live performance. The first three of these tasks are back-office tasks with little customer exposure or contact. It is in live performance that the band's process interacts with those of the consumers or fans.

As far as **physical evidence** is concerned, the physicality, tangibility or materiality of the product is represented by the technological medium which carries it (e.g. CD, vinyl, DVD, computer file). But there is a much more important sense in which physicality is important – namely the so-called servicescape. This relates to where live music is performed, and can range from smoky jazz clubs, to dance venues (Garratt, 1998; Malbon, 1999), up to arena or stadia which can accommodate 100,000 people, as well as major open-air festivals, which can accommodate up to 200,000 attendees or more.

The final element of the mix, **price**, is basically the money charged for the recorded product or for entrance to see a live performance. Related to this is the question of perceived value for money, a factor which is not far from fans' minds. Pricing's ability to deliver sales revenue to the providers of musical offerings is constantly being challenged by such practices as illicit downloading, bootlegging and ticket touting.

Van Waterschoot and Van den Bulte (1992) argue for a more specific classification of the promotion element of the mix. Similarly, Harvey *et al.* (1996) argue that there is a need to add other elements to the mix, including publics, performance, politics, probability and planning. Constantinides (2006) reviews the critiques of the mix and concludes that there are two main flaws, namely, the model's internal orientation and focus on the mass market with a consequent lack of personalization. However, the major challenge to a managerial focus on the mix comes from relationship marketing (Grönroos, 1994), which has attempted to shift attention more clearly to the connection between the customer and the provider.

What is a 'brand'?

Branding is something which, on one level, everyone understands. Many things are commonly referred to as brands. Brands are marks of ownership, shortcuts to product recognition, resources for the construction of identity, means of differentiation, intangible and legal assets and signs of quality. All of these are communicative in some way, which returns us to the domain of communication and culture.

An extensive brand vocabulary has been developed by brand consultants, practitioners and scholars. From a strategic marketing point of view, branding is the practice of positioning the offering (functionally, competitively, and culturally), and brand identities are built through integrated marketing communications. Any communicative practice or behaviour contributes to brand-building or brand positioning, including advertising, personal selling, public relations, merchandising, sponsorship, point-of-sale materials, and consumer word-of-mouth, both online and offline. Branding vocabulary includes a range of constructs to apply to business contexts. These include, for example, brand identity, brand value, brand values, brand image, brand equity, brand loyalty, brand assets, brand personality, brand culture, brand community and brand heritage. These constructs are formed by pairing the noun 'brand' with words that are already in circulation. In other words, brand managers, consultants and scholars have simply adopted existing terminology from other fields, such as finance, psychology and sociology, and adapted it to their specific purposes in the business context.

Brand identity, for example, is the identity which an organization, such as a record label, concert hall or orchestra, seeks to present or project to its publics. Various scholars (Aaker, 2010; Keller *et al.*, 2010; Kapferer, 2012) have attempted to capture this notion of identity. In order to do so, it is necessary to include in definitions of brand identity things such as brand vision, brand values, the physique and psyche of the brand, and so on. Brand image, on the other hand, is the impression of the brand identity as received by the individual customer, consumer, or indeed any stakeholder. The challenge for the brand manager, whether this be a record label executive, a band's manager, the director of an opera house, or a PR person working for an orchestra, is to shape the brand identity in such a way that most stakeholders are able to broadly agree on what their brand images are – and these should preferably be positive.

There are several problems with brand discourse in general, and with its application to music in particular, which will be examined in Chapter 5.

Consumer studies

Very often in marketing studies, the majority of attention is paid to the issues of managing marketing. However, the marketing concept posits that for marketing to effectively achieve its goal of providing customer and stakeholder value, it must be based on a thorough and detailed understanding of consumers' thoughts, feelings and actions. The early efforts in consumer studies were undertaken in the service of marketing managers, helping them understand their current and prospective consumers so that they could efficiently facilitate exchange – or, put more simply, make sales. Thus, the focus was solely on buyers and purchasing; how people consumed a product once they had acquired it was of little interest. Consumer studies were dominated by a view of the consumer as a rational, utility-maximizing problem-solver (Bhat and Reddy, 1998) and centred around models such as the 'consumer decision making model' and its various extensions (Bettman, 1979). This model explains that purchases are the outcome of a process of problem solving, and that consumers are information-seeking and -processing decision-making machines.

It does not take much effort to see that in this form, the field of consumer behaviour would not have been able to provide a full and thorough understanding of the consumption of such an experiential product as music. However, the broadening of marketing to the service sector, combined with the emergence of the 'experiential perspective' in consumer studies and the associated interest in 'aesthetic products' (Holbrook and Hirschman, 1982), led to an increased interest in the marketing and consumption of music. Initially, research focused primarily on the choice and purchase of music. Studies that have investigated the intention to purchase music include those by Holbrook (1982), Mizerski et al. (1988), Kellaris and Kent (1993), Kellaris and Rice (1993), and Lacher and Mizerski (1994). There has also been some interest in the development of musical preferences. In a well-known study by Holbrook and Schindler (1989), the authors found that an individual's music tastes are set at around the age of 24.

In the years since Holbrook and Schindler's (1989) study, there has been an opening up of the scope of consumer studies to the entire phenomenon of consumption. For example, Arnould et al. (2004: 9) define consumer behaviour as 'individuals or groups acquiring, using and disposing of products, services, ideas or experiences'. The experiential, cultural, symbolic and political aspects of consumption have been acknowledged (Arnould and Thompson, 2005), and it is also widely recognized that people consume music for a range of reasons and in a variety of ways (e.g. Lonsdale and North 2011, North and Hargreaves 1997). However, as highlighted in this book, there is still much to be understood about how, when, where, who and why people consume music. For example, it is clear from everyday observation that music is one product around which people develop great passions and allegiances. People define themselves through their 'fandom' and engage in certain consumption practices as fans, as will be discussed in Chapter 8. Music is a fundamentally social product, and therefore communities of 'fans' form around music products (artists, venues, genres) in various forms, such as subcultures, scenes and tribes (see Chapter 9).

Structure of the book

There are four parts to this book. The different parts engage with the developing conceptual and empirical literature within marketing, consumer, media, music and cultural studies, and seek to apply the insights gleaned there to the marketing and consumption of music. Part I provides an introduction to classical marketing, branding and consumer issues (Chapter 1), and deals also with forces including technology, law, economics and policy (Chapter 2), and how they shape music markets and market behaviours. This is important for an understanding of the environment within which the music business and its consumers operate. An understanding of the macro- and micro-environments is regarded as an important precursor to any strategizing process by a marketer.

Part II is entitled *Production Perspectives*, and contains four chapters. The marketer of any product, including music, is seen as being on the supply or production side of the exchange relationship. Here, the design of the market offering by those who promote it is important. The first chapter in Part II considers how music can be construed as a 'product' offered for sale in a marketplace (Chapter 3). This requires a consideration of different understandings of the nature and value of music, and of music's relationship with other products. The second factor to be considered in this part is the musician. The important questions of who is a musician, what kinds of musicians there are, and how people become, and work as, musicians are addressed (Chapter 4). This chapter also includes a consideration of musical hierarchies and the notion of authenticity, as well as musical identities and musical groups. The third chapter in this part (Chapter 5) further draws out the idea of identities and deals with the notion of music brands, and the final chapter (Chapter 6) presents a socio-cultural approach to branding.

Part III, *Consumption Perspectives*, moves the focus to the other side of the exchange relationship, namely the demand or consumer side. This part has three chapters. The first considers how consumer studies and consumer behaviour theory relate to the consumption of music (Chapter 7). This brings together a range of insights in order to illustrate constructs that are more commonly used to analyse non-music offerings, and examines how they might be applied to music. This chapter also deals with the implications of different ways of framing the people who engage with music, be it as consumers, fans or audience members. Chapter 8 explores music fans and fandom in detail, highlighting the extent to which fan behaviour is creative and productive in nature, thus blurring the boundaries between the producing artist and consuming audience. In the third and final chapter (Chapter 9), the focus switches to collective consumption and discusses the implications of ideas such as brand community and consumer tribes for music consumption.

Part IV contains a single chapter (Chapter 10), which deals with live music and festivals. Venues are important for the production and consumption of live music, which has become more significant as a source of revenue for musical acts in recent years. Festivals have enjoyed considerable growth and cultural prominence in recent years, partly because of the attraction of live music, but also because of the particular consumption experiences and marketing opportunities they offer to fans and bands, respectively.

The concluding chapter briefly retraces the journey travelled and summarizes the reasons why marketing management in the music business differs from other kinds of marketing. Music is different, and, if it is to be useful, any conceptualization of music marketing and consumption needs to think through the notions of music as product, the role of musicians in the marketplace, the concept of music brands, the framing of people as consumers, fans and audience members, ideas about collectivity in music consumption, and the specific issue of live music. This has implications for any future formulation of music marketing theory.

References

Aaker, D. (2010) *Building Strong Brands*, New York: Pocket Books.

American Marketing Association. *Definition of Marketing*. http://www.marketingpower.com/aboutama/pages/definitionofmarketing.aspx. Accessed 5th May 2013.

Arnould, E. and Thompson, C. (2005) 'Consumer Culture Theory (CCT): twenty years of research', *Journal of Consumer Research*, **31** (4), 868-882.

Arnould, E., Price, L. and Zinkhan, G. (2002) *Consumers*, New York: McGraw Hill.

Attali, J. (1977/1985) *Noise: The Political Economy of Music*, Minneapolis: University of Minnesota Press.

Bagozzi, R. (1975) 'Marketing as exchange', *Journal of Marketing*, **39** (4), 32-39.

Baker, B (2012) *Guerilla Music Marketing Online*, St. Lois, MO: Spotlight Publications.

Bettman, J.R (1979) *An Information Processing Theory of Consumer Choice*, Reading: Addison Wesley.

Bhat, S. and Reddy, S.K. (1998) 'Symbolic and functional positioning of brands', *Journal of Consumer Marketing*, **15** (1), 32-43.

Borden, N. (1984) 'The concept of the marketing mix', *Journal of Advertising Research*, **24** (4), 7-12.

Constantinides, E. (2006) 'The marketing mix revisited towards the 21st century marketing', *Journal of Marketing Management*, **22**, 407-438.

Frith, S. (2007) 'Why music matters', *Critical Quarterly*, **50** (1-2), 165-179.

Frith, S. (1998) *Performing Rites: Evaluating Popular Music*, Oxford: Oxford paperbacks.

Gorn, G.J. (1982) 'The effects of music in advertising on choice behaviour: a classical conditioning approach', *Journal of Marketing*, **46** (Winter), 94-101.

Grönroos, C. (1994) 'Quo vadis, marketing? toward a relationship marketing paradigm', *Journal of Marketing Management*, **10** (5), 347-360.

Hargreaves, D. J. and North, A. C. (ed.) (1997). *The Social Psychology of Music*. Oxford: Oxford University Press.

Holbrook, M. (1982) 'Mapping the retail market for esthetic products: the case of jazz records', *The Journal of Retailing*, **58** (Spring), 115-129.

Holbrook, M, and Hirschman, E.C. (1982) 'The experiential aspects of consumption: consumer fantasies, feelings and fun', *Journal of Consumer Research*, **9** (September), 132-140.

Holbrook, M. and Schindler, R. (1989) 'Some exploratory findings on the development of musical tastes', *Journal of Consumer Research*, **16** (June), 119-124.

Jobber, D and Ellis-Chadwick (2012) *Principles and Practice of Marketing.* London. McGraw-Hill Higher Education.

Kapferer, J.-N. (2012) *The New Strategic Brand Management: Advanced insights and Strategic Thinking,* London: Kogan Page.

Kellaris, J.J. and Kent, R.J. (1993) 'An exploratory investigation of responses elicited by music varying in tempo, tonality and texture', *Journal of Consumer Psychology,* **2** (4), 381-401.

Kellaris, J.J. and Rice, R. (1993) 'The influence of tempo, loudness and gender of listener on response to music', *Psychology and Marketing,* **10** (Jan/Feb), 15-29.

Keller, K.L., Aperia, T. and Georgson, M. (2011) *Strategic Brand Management: A European Perspective,* 2nd edition, London: Financial Times/ Prentice Hall.

Kusek and Leonhard (2005) *The Future of Music: A Manifesto for the Digital Music Revolution,* Boston, MA: Berklee Press.

Lacher, K.T. and Mizerski, R. (1994) 'An exploratory study of the responses and relationships involved in the evaluation of, and in the intention to purchase new rock music', *Journal of Consumer Research,* **21** (September), 366-380.

Lonsdale, A.J. and North, A.C. (2011) 'Why do we listen to music? A uses and gratifications analysis', *British Journal of Psychology,* **102**, 108-134.

Marion, G. (2006) 'Research note: marketing ideology and criticism: legitimacy and legitimization', *Marketing Theory,* **6** (2), 245-262.

Mizerski, R., Pucely, M., Perrewe, P. and Baldwin, L. (1988) 'An experimental evaluation of music involvement measures and their relationship with consumer purchasing behaviour', *Popular Music and Society,* **12** (Fall) 79-96.

North, A.C. and Hargreaves, D.J. (1997) 'Music and consumer behaviour', in Hargreaves, D.J. and North, A.C. (ed.) *Social Psychology of Music,* Oxford: Oxford University Press, 268-289.

Park, C.W. and Young, S.M. (1986) 'consumer response to television commercials: the impact of involvement and background music on brand attitude formation', *Journal of Marketing Research,* **23**, 11-24.

Ries, A. and Trout, J. (1981) *Positioning: The battle for your mind*. Riverview, MI: Motor City Books.

Smith, P.C. and Curnow, R. (1996) 'Arousal hypothesis and the effects of music on purchasing behaviour', *Journal of Applied Psychology*, **50**, 255-256.

Van Waterschoot, W. and Van den Bulte, C. (1992) 'The 4P classification of the marketing mix revisited', *Journal of Marketing*, **56**, 83-93.

Wallin, N., Merker, B. and Brown, S. (ed.) (2000) *The Origins of Music*, Cambridge, MA: Massachusetts Institute of Technology Press.

Wikstrom, P (2009) *The Music Industry: Music in the Cloud*, Cambridge, UK: Polity Press.

Wilke, W.L. and Moore, E.S. (2003) 'Scholarly research in marketing: '4 eras' of thought development', *Journal of Public Policy and Marketing*, **22**, 116-146.

Zeithaml, V.A., Parasuraman, A. and Berry, L.L. (1985) Problems and Strategies in Services Marketing, *Journal of Marketing*, **49**, 33-46.

2 Shaping Forces

Introduction

As an 'industry', the music business can be analysed in terms of its micro-economic structure, conduct and performance (Anand and Peterson, 2000; Power and Hallencreutz, 2007; Asai, 2008), infrastructure (Burkart and McCourt, 2004) and restructuring process (Hardy, 1999). This kind of approach tends to lead us to focus fairly narrowly on the dominant players in the production side of the industry, such as the 'big three' record labels in the commercial music market (Universal Music Group, Sony Music Entertainment and Warner Music Group). However, it does not deal so clearly with non-mainstream and publicly funded music (Hesmondhalgh, 1997; Fonarow, 2006), and therefore blinkers our view of the many and various actors and actions that comprise the music market. In addition to the record labels and the management they provide, other actors include regulators, copyright owners, publishers, policy makers, sponsors, promoters, musicians, media, critics, audiences, social activists and researchers. A multitude of different and important relationships exist between these actors, most of which are not yet well understood in the marketing literature. The purpose of this chapter is to briefly introduce the key shaping forces behind the contemporary music industry. It first outlines the economic system of music activities, and then explores the role of cultural policy in the music business. It concludes with a review of technology as a significant driving force behind the change in the music industry.

Economics of music

At the beginning of the 21st century, Payne (2000) optimistically maintained that the whole music industry would continue to grow, along with the significance of music in human life. While her prediction remains as valid as it was 13 years ago, the digital revolution and declining album sales have fuelled drastic changes in the business and economic structures of the music industry, influencing the ways music is being produced and consumed today. The dominant trend has been driven by technological developments, the most visible aspect of which is the rise of digital music formats and the relocation of music distribution, storage and consumption to online sources.

Yet despite the rapid growth in digital downloads, their value has not been able to compensate for the loss of revenue from sales of CDs. According to the latest estimates, 2011 was the first year in which the sales of digital music topped the sales of physical music (Segall, 2012). The emerging music consumer is less interested in owning a physical product like a CD, than in having access to music everywhere through a portable music player, smartphone, tablet, or laptop, thereby fuelling the proliferation of new types of music businesses, such as online stores offering a-la-carte downloads (e.g. iTunes, Amazon.com), online streaming, downloading or file-sharing services (e.g. Napster, AOL Music, Yahoo! Music, Spotify), and online videos (e.g. YouTube). The changes have also impacted on the traditional bricks-and-mortar music retailers, with many closing their doors or, like Tower Records in the US or Virgin Megastores in the UK and several other countries, moving online. Furthermore, traditional record deals which so many musicians used to aspire to, are also disappearing. They are frequently being replaced by so-called '360 deals', where artists, in return for financial support, and especially at the beginning of their careers, offer a share of their future earnings. It is important to observe this major trend in the music industry; such contracts recognize that musicians' revenue streams have diversified. Musicians nowadays have to engage in a wide range of musical activities in order to be profitable, including recording albums, performing live and licensing their music to be used in marketing, film and broadcasting. This is why the contemporary music industry shares many of its products with other members of the broad entertainment family. For example, music is used in the gaming industry, film industry, services industry, marketing, retailing, broadcast entertainment and as mobile phone ringtones. Music has therefore become a much more important part of wider national and global economies.

The economic system of music activities is influenced by its funding model – with popular music relying primarily on market sales, and other genres, such as classical music and jazz, often having to rely on public funding. Music economics depends on a number of factors, including the nature and extent of economic rewards resulting from music activity, the extent to which professional music activity is possible (with varying degrees of professionalization in different genres), the control of any necessary technologies for recording and performing music (given the oligopolistic nature of the recording industry), and last but not least, the marketing and sale of music activity and products (Booth and Kuhn, 1990). All of these economic activities are performed by the many members of the music industry, including composers, musicians and other artists, producers, managers, music publishers, record companies, live music promoters, music entrepreneurs, media organizations, other creative industries, music education, music retailers, music industry organizations, manufacturers and distributors (Williamson et al., 2003; Williamson and Cloonan, 2007).

History of the music industry

Looking back at the history of music production and consumption in western Europe, Hull et al. (2010) identify three ages of the music industry.

First, in the agricultural age, music was only available in live form; it was created and consumed at the same time, and performed mostly by folk musicians and amateurs. The only professional musicians were employed by the church and wealthy aristocrats. The early medieval musicians, for example troubadours and trouvères in France and minnesingers in Germany, often travelled extensively from place to place and from patron to patron, entertaining wealthy aristocratic families and their courts. Some of these decided to settle at one court, and those who were fortunate enough to find permanent employment were rewarded in two ways: through financial support, or through other benefits, which usually included the opportunity to live in the patron's household (Wegman, 2005). This form of court patronage dominated the professional production of music until the middle of the 18th century. Towards the end of that era, socio-economic changes led to a decrease in the importance of the old system of feudal rule, and diminishing employment opportunities for musicians, forcing them to look for opportunities in the marketplace and the newly emerging music publishing industry. The end of the old era and a lack of fully developed free market structures supporting music activities meant that many musicians at that time could not find permanent employment and found it difficult to transition to a new market economy. Some of the first musicians who attempted to rely on the music market rather than the support of the court were Wolfgang Amadeus Mozart in late 18th century Vienna, and Josef Haydn (Tschmuck, 2012). The economic model of an independent musician relying on income from the music market was further developed by Ludwig van Beethoven, who lived from selling his music to a growing market consisting of a middle-class audience (Tschmuck, 2012).

The industrial revolution and the development of music technology brought music into the industrial age in the 19th century, when the music industry emerged, dominated by publishing houses and a new class of professional musicians. The new music industry of the 20th century was first dominated by sheet music, and then by audio recording in various formats. The invention of the gramophone by Thomas Edison in 1877, and the first commercial recordings 20 years later, marked the beginning of the modern music industry, which would flourish throughout the 20th century through sales of LPs, 45s, cassettes, CDs and finally music in various digital formats. The technological developments and mass marketisation of musical products led to the growth of various sectors of the music industry, such as A&R (artist and repertoire) specialists, music promoters and agents, recording studios, large music retail stores, music media (e.g. *Rolling Stone* magazine and MTV), ticketing companies, venues, festivals, and − last but not least −

a class of professional music makers. Yet, again, the 21st century and the information age brought a new and dramatic change to the music industry. The dominance of music in digital formats shifted the main product of the music industry from a physical good (first sheet music, then records) to music as digital content. The digitization of music has affected all members of the music industry, from musicians, to international record labels, to consumers.

The music industry now

The economic environment of the music industry is constantly evolving, with changing ownership structures and fluctuations in the availability of public funding. The socio-cultural and political changes of the 20th century, and the diminishing public support for the arts in many developed countries, have resulted in a diversification of revenue streams within the music industry, and turned the traditional models of arts patronage upside down. The contemporary music industry is an economy that is divided between a commercial sector and organizations supported by public subsidies; thus, different members of the music industry operate under different economic circumstances. While most commercial record labels rely on market revenue to survive, many not-for-profit arts organizations, like symphony orchestras and opera companies, survive thanks only to generous public support.

Since the early 1990s, the music industry has also been undergoing a wave of dramatic changes in the production, consumption and distribution of music, influenced by the globalization tendencies in the entertainment industry, mergers, vertical and horizontal integrations, the growth of illegal downloading and digital distribution, and the increasing importance of live music in generating revenue. But the economic importance of the music industry remains unquestionable. According to the International Federation of the Phonographic Industry the global recording industry is worth over US$160 billion (IFPI, 2009), over two million people find employment in the music industry, and the annual investment made by record companies in artists worldwide has reached US$5 billion (IFPI, 2010). Yet the industry is not an easy one to break into. While many amateur and semi-professional musicians are involved in music making for the sheer satisfaction derived from playing music and participating in the cultural life of their communities, economic success remains much more rare than one might expect. The IFPI report (2012) *Investment in Music* claims that a record label needs to invest US$1 million to break a successful pop act into a major market, where the majority of this money is spent on advances so that the musicians can concentrate on their artistic work (US$200,000), recording an album (US$200,000), producing a music video (US$200,000), tour support (US$100,000) and marketing and promotion (US$300,000). The investment can only be recouped when the musicians reach certain sales levels, making it very high-risk.

Music is now more than ever interwoven with broadcasting. National and local television and radio stations, both private and public, act as outlets for music. Television is changing the way in which acts are launched, shifting the emphasis from traditional long-term talent identification and development towards talent shows such as *Making the Band*, *Pop Idol* and *X-Factor*, giving birth to a number of artists and bands who often experience only short-lived fame (Amegashie, 2009). In the era of mergers and acquisitions, when pressure is focused on reducing the costs of music production and the risks associated with launching new artists, televised music talent contests provide an excellent 'opportunity for their producers to turn the often expensive and unpredictable process of finding and cultivating new talent into a profitable promotional spectacle' (Fairchild, 2007: 98). While in the 20th century 'most [music industry] successes relied on not only quality repertoire and artistry, but also on patient artist development' (Goldstuck, 2001: 50), increasingly, it has been argued, musicians are being promoted as commoditized products in a race in which the media focus on image rather than music (Sanjek and Sanjek, 1991). The convergence between music and other industries provides musicians with new opportunities to make money and deliver their work to much wider audiences. Yet many musicians, who are influenced by multinational record labels and the entertainment industry, torn between their artistic integrity and commercial necessity, and threatened by the danger of decreasing fan bases and diminishing sales, are often reluctant to take any artistic risk as a consequence (Miles, 2000).

Structure of the music industry

The music industry established itself firmly at the beginning of 20th century, and particularly began to flourish after the Second World War (Gronrow, 1983). However, it wasn't the record labels that dominated the industry in the first half of the century, but rather the publishing companies and their primary product: sheet music. It wasn't until the early 1950s in the US that records began to form a more important revenue stream than sheet music, and at this point record companies started to have more influence in the music industry than publishers (Garofalo, 1987). Further acceleration of technological development in music production and consumption has fuelled constant changes in the music business environment (Peterson and Berger, 1971), and one of the first by-products of those technological and economic changes was the emergence of independent music makers in the 1960s. Further, 1967 marked the beginning of a new era, as this is the first year in which the music industry reached billion-dollar profits (Denisoff, 1975).

The consolidation that has been driving the industry since its birth just over a century ago has reached the point where the overwhelming majority of entertainment reaching wider audiences – music as well as films, radio and television, newspapers and books – is dominated by a few international corporations (Bishop, 2005). In the past 15 years, the music industry has been undergoing a significant horizontal integration, from six 'majors' prior to 1999, five in 2004, four in 2008 and three in 2012 (the UK-based Association of Independent Music defines a major as a multinational company with a music market share greater than 5%). Currently, the music industry is highly concentrated, and is dominated by Universal Music Group (France), Sony Music Entertainment (Japan) and Warner Music Group (USA). According to the IFPI, the 'big three' together control nearly three-quarters of the global music market, while still increasing their share by taking over small independent labels (Hull *et al.*, 2010). The main three international music markets are the USA, Japan and the UK. Alongside these, and differing in terms of their corporate culture, are many small independent record companies ('indies', although the term 'independent' is often debated) whose activities focus on niche markets, less popular genres, and up-and-coming musicians. They are often used as testing grounds for the development of new sounds and artists, and it is not uncommon for them to be owned by one of the majors.

Apart from ownership concentration, evidence suggests that the music industry is also becoming more geographically concentrated. Throughout the 18th and 19th centuries, cities like Vienna, Paris, Berlin, London and Milan were the centres of musical creativity. More recently, Florida and Jackson's (2010) research points towards three main locations for musicians and musical establishments in the US: New York, Los Angeles and Nashville. In most countries, large metropolitan areas provide the social and institutional infrastructure required to commercialize musical products, attracting many young and aspiring musicians. Similar to what happens in other industries, musicians cluster around metropolitan locations that offer rich musical traditions and the biggest opportunities to perform, earn money and network with other members of the music industry. Those opportunities are most visible around vibrant music scenes in large cities.

Making music, making money

The reality of the music industry is that only very few musicians can make a living from their music. The never-ending global supply of new talent makes it a very competitive industry. Many musicians are forced to take up other jobs, remain amateurs or even give up their dreams of a musical career entirely. For those who can achieve economic success, the contemporary music industry offers three main revenue streams (Hull et al., 2010): songwriting, live music performance, and music recordings.

In the first stream, musicians compose music which can then be licensed to be used in the music and other entertainment industries, such as film and broadcasting, and the musicians receive royalties specified in the license agreement. Songwriting, from an economic point of view, is closely related to the concept of copyright, which provides legal protection to the author of an original work and is a form of ownership of their intellectual property. The length of the copyright term varies across the world, but in most countries it is somewhere between 50 and 70 years from the death of the last author of any particular song in question. Cabott (2009) identifies six main types of music royalties: mechanical license royalties, public performance royalties, synchronization license fees, copy license fees, compulsory license royalties and new-media royalties. A mechanical licence gives the owner the right to manufacture and sell copies of music in different formats, while public performance royalties are paid to the creator each time their music is performed in public (including on radio or television). Synchronization licence fees relate to music being used in advertising, film, video games or any form of broadcasting, and, in the case of the most popular music, can be a very lucrative revenue stream. Sales of sheet music attract payment in the form of a copy licence fee, and every time a 'cover' version of original music is released a compulsory licence fee is paid to the creator. New media licenses cover, for example, the use of original music online and as ringtones. When a piece of music becomes popular, all of these types of royalties can generate significant revenue, which is shared between all copyright owners, usually including the authors. Another important aspect of songwriting is the concept of moral rights, which are distinctive from the economically focused copyrights and protect the connection between creators and their work. Rushton (1998), for example, distinguished between four main moral rights: attribution (the right to be identified as an author), disclosure (the author's decision when and whether to publish the work), withdrawal (the right to withdraw a work from circulation) and integrity (to protect the integrity of work). In many European countries moral rights cannot be waived.

In the live music performance stream, musicians perform their own music or covers in front of a live audience in a particular venue. This has been the most important source of income for the majority of musicians in recent years, and is discussed in greater detail in Chapter 10. Some commercially successful musicians might also be signed by a record label to record an album, while other musicians may decide to do this on their own, using their own money or raising funds through initiatives such as Bandstock (which gives fans the opportunity to invest money in bands in return for a percentage of their future profits, a copy of their albums, or priority tickets to live concerts), or using digital distribution agencies – so-called aggregators (Walmsley, 2011). On the other hand, already successful musicians such as Radiohead, Prince and Nine Inch Nails, who all have well-established, large and vibrant communities of fans, have released their albums on the Internet for free, by-passing traditional music industry channels and giving their fans an option to donate money voluntarily – though this is not a business strategy that offers long-term success for the average musical act.

Most musicians attempt to pursue all three streams; some are more successful in songwriting (e.g. Burt Bacharach), others become recording artists, while most perform live to earn a living. Each revenue-generating stream can therefore be looked at as a set of economic activities contributing to the existence and well-being of the music industry. Hull et al. (2010) identified the participants in each of the streams, as outlined in Table 1.

Table 1: Main revenue streams of participants in the music industry (Hull et al., 2010)

Songwriting	Live music	Recorded music
Songwriters (musicians and lyricists)	Musicians and performers	Musicians
Publishers	Managers	Record labels
Performing rights organisations	Agents	Producers
Broadcasters (TV, radio and the Internet)	Promoters	Technicians
Entertainment industry (e.g. film)	Venues	Studios
Audiences	Audiences	Record manufacturers
		Distributors
		Retailers
		Performing rights organizations
		Audiences

Music policy

Music policy is generally incorporated within what is variously known as cultural or creative industries policy. Cultural/creative industries policy both structures and is structured by the political economy, wider culture, the nature of the industry and the technological ecology of the sector. Such policies formalize and regulate the actions of, and relationships between, actors in the cultural sector, identifying which are to be governed by policy and which by market forces.

Historically, the decision as to which cultural activities were subject to policy has been based on the Western distinction between high/elite art and low/popular art. The argument is that the cultural value of high/elite art can only be appreciated by those with the appropriate education and cultural capital (i.e. the elite classes). Due to its lack of popular appeal, high art would not survive in a free market economy; thus, its continued cultural, social and aesthetic contribution can only be assured through public governance. The high/elite art = market failure argument has long provided the basis by which states decide which arts they should support (Drummond et al., 2008: 11).

The relationship between the twin pillars of cultural policy – access and excellence – has also created tension that is resolved within policies. Investing in excellence would usually imply providing support through education and resources, to a select few talented artists. On the other hand, a focus on access seeks to educate the largest possible number of people in the arts so that they are then able to engage with them. However, Frith (2007) argues that in the case of popular music, these are neither mutually exclusive nor contradictory, because musical appreciation does not depend on musical education. Many people have engaging, moving and even transformative music experiences despite having little knowledge of music itself. Thus, access would be better understood as being about availability.

Exactly how cultural policy is articulated is determined locally, and depends on different ideologies of governance. However, general trends can be observed. Frith and Cloonan (2008: 189) provide a succinct summary of these global policy trends:

> From cultural policy to cultural industries policy, from treating
> popular music as a matter of social or cultural concern to treating
> popular music as a matter of economic concern, from devising
> policies to counter the local effects of international commerce
> to devising policies to embed local practices within the world
> marketplace.

The shift from cultural to creative industries policy is notable.
The high/low culture distinction between state-governed and
commercial art was deemed as too simplistic, as it did not account for
the great creative and innovative value that exists in the commercial
art sector (Drummond et al., 2008). Recognition of this led to the
birth of the 'creative industries' in the UK in the 1990s. This involved
a general shift from valuing the arts for their cultural and social value
to valuing them for their economic value and their role in growth and
development. It also meant that commercial art forms, such as popular
music, began to be brought under the aegis of creative industries policy.
Various consequences of this can be observed. For example, Frith (2007)
argues that creative industries policy shifts the attention away from
the conditions of music making to focus on the conditions of music
exploitation. In addition, as the value of music is increasingly seen to lie
outside of itself, such as in its economic value or its ability to facilitate
social inclusion or improve health and well-being, it is often subsumed
under other social and health policies.

One issue that has become pertinent is that of intellectual property,
including copyright, trademarks and patents. The notion of the 'creative
industries' privileges the market aspects of arts and culture, such as
notions of the commodity and ownership, and thus the shift from
cultural to creative industries drew attention to intellectual property
rights at a time when advances in technology were bringing traditional
notions of intellectual property into question (Drummond et al., 2008).
Intellectual property is one of the mechanisms by which a cultural text
(such as a piece of music) can be transformed into and managed as a
product, as it requires that a financial transaction take place in order for
one to be granted access to that property. Thus, intellectual property
elevates the economic value of art above other types of value.

In the case of music, copyright is the main form of intellectual property governing ownership and enabling harnessing of the economic value of popular music. It has become an increasingly significant, visible and contentious practice, in response to technological changes that have challenged the dominant structures of commodity product ownership (and thus power) in the music sector. Copyright has provoked much interesting debate – see, for example, the special issue on 'Cultural consumers and copyright' in *Arts Marketing: An International Journal* (2012, 2(2)). In the case of music, the way that copyright is constructed can be critiqued as it expresses certain interests over and above others. For example, Brabazan (2012) notes that copyright emphasizes melody and lyrics over rhythm or bassline. This is a very Eurocentric approach, providing little protection to world music, which is characterized by an emphasis on rhythm.

The goal of copyright should be to encourage production and public access. However, Boyle (2008: 224) argues that 'it has done its job in encouraging production. Now it operates as a fence to discourage access'. So the focus of copyright is actually on controlling, rather than enabling access. Rather than looking for ways to develop new music and musicians for audiences to access, the focus of copyright holders is thus turned to controlling the availability of existing copyrighted material. This contradicts what Frith (2007) argues should be the purpose of music policy: the development and sustainability of a vital music culture. Key resources are needed for this: (1) music resources (lesson, teachers, affordable instruments), (2) music spaces (rehearsal rooms, promoters and venues, art schools, universities, conservatoires, record shops), (3) time (being a student or unemployed), (4) people (mentors, models, other musicians to play with, networks, friendships), and (5) mobility (movement of new faces, ideas and sound). Developing a vibrant music culture provides fertile ground for, and therefore precedes, a successful music industry. Similarly, Lewis (2008) notes that the political economy of popular music relies on more than marketplace mechanisms. For example, 'independents' (even where they are no longer that independent from the major record labels) are vital to sustain a healthy music industry, but their existence should not be left to market forces alone. Support must come from local authorities and public funding agencies through initiatives such as subsidies of performance venues, rehearsal spaces, recording facilities, free performances and festivals, and even the provision of welfare support.

By highlighting some of the general issues and trends in cultural/creative industries and music policy, it becomes abundantly obvious that music policy is a complex shaping force within all aspects of music making and engagement. The intersection of music, markets and consumption is framed by music policy regardless of whether the particular musical activity in focus falls under the auspices of public governance, market forces or, in all likelihood, a combination of both.

Music and technology

On marketing planning or strategy modules, marketing students are schooled, generally speaking, to see technology as a force that is 'out there' in the macro-environment, along with other forces such as social and cultural trends, politics, law and the economy. Certainly, managers working for record labels or representing artists need to be aware of changing technological trends and how these affect competition and create threats or opportunities for their business. However, technology plays a far greater role in music than this rather simplified perspective recognizes; technology is in fact pervasive in music.

According to Jones (1992: 7), in the realm of music, technology basically takes two forms: music and instruments/equipment. First, music entails many terms which point to technologies of practice that have been developed over many years; for example, accompaniment, score, Gregorian chant, solo, tenor, woodwind, barcarolle, opera, octave, hornpipe, etude, chorus, bridge, key, orchestra, anthem, and so on. The marketing of music, whether popular or classical, ideally needs to be informed by a sound knowledge of music. Music consumers, fans and audiences can be extremely knowledgeable, and can expect, beyond the musical performance itself, a detailed account of its composition and production as part of the musical offering.

Second, the origination, production, recording, distribution, storage, playback, performance and consumption of music are all heavily dependent on technology. Indeed, Jones (1992: 1) argues that in popular music, it is the technology of music production – specifically the technology of sound recording – that organizes our experience of music. The practice of music origination or composition frequently makes use of technology, when, for example, a computer or computerized equipment is involved in making the sounds, or when a musician is playing their guitar or piano with the aim of identifying a musical phrase or riff on which to build a piece. The electrification of musical instruments such as the guitar and keyboard enabled significant changes in the production, amplification and consumption of music. The recording of sound goes back to the 1870s with the invention of the phonograph cylinder, and, since then, there has been a regular succession of other inventions, such as the gramophone disc, the magnetic wire recorder, magnetic tape, cassettes, CDs, DVDs, and Blu-ray discs. The actual production and recording of music has for a long time routinely made use of technology, most notably in recording studios, which contain all kinds of technology that can create, modify, and combine an enormous range of sounds. The ideas of the record producer as a quasi band member, and of the studio as a musical instrument, are well known. Instrument technology, for example that of drums, keyboards and guitars, is continually developing, creating new possibilities for musicians.

The distribution of recorded music is one of the areas in which businesses have undergone very major changes in recent decades. The emergence of the Internet has opened the door for 'bedroom producers', as well as peer-to-peer downloading services that allows music to be exchanged for free. The problems caused for record labels by the arrival of the Internet have been well documented (see, for example, Knopper 2009). The music industry is still struggling to find ways to stop losing money to 'piracy', and shares with other industries the challenge of making money from Internet-based offerings. This has led to music streaming services such as Spotify, which, at the time of writing, has been profitable for its owner, but less so for musicians. Artists and record labels have websites on which they can display, to anyone who has Internet access, a range of material, including sound recordings, music videos, blog entries, touring information, positioning statements, and artwork. They can also use these websites to transact business in music, merchandise and other products. In addition, websites can act as a home to fan forums and bulletin board systems, where fans can discuss the object of their adulation, build a sense of community, exchange information and develop their own identities in relation to music. Older technologies, such as television and radio, still have a very significant role to play in music circulation. Televised talent shows like *American Idol* and *The X-Factor* attract large audiences. What is interesting from the point of view of marketing is the way in which consumers are 'allowed into' the production process in television and film documentaries or programmes about the production process, which thus serve a brand-building function for the artists involved.

Live performance (see Chapter 10) is also heavily dependent on technology, either in terms of a festival stage, a band going on a full production tour, a venue investing in the latest lighting and sound equipment, or spectacular stages (such as on U2's 360° tour), which complement the musical performance, and often include giant screens projecting images of the performers or other material. Of course, the consumption of music is greatly facilitated by technological developments such as radio, television, video, and the Internet, as well as equipment such as the Apple iPod, or, much earlier, the Sony Walkman (Du Gay *et al.*, 1997). Contemporary consumers can easily download, store, collect, play and share large collections of music.

These two aspects of music technology – namely, music itself and the instruments and equipment by means of which it is produced, distributed and consumed – have significant implications for how we think about music marketing. While it is unlikely that music marketers, in a narrowly defined sense, would ever need to understand the finer points of technology, it is important that they grasp the ways in which it can be used to link production and consumption, as well as to build music brands (see Chapters 5 and 6).

Summary

This chapter has focused on a range of economic, policy, legal and technological issues which shape the business environment in which the music business operates. This is not intended as a comprehensive treatment of all the business-environmental issues which a music marketer will ever face. Instead, it has focused on a number of issues which are particularly salient or important in the music industry. In the next part of the book, the focus turns to production perspectives – in particular the idea of music as a product, the role of musicians, and the issue of brands.

References

Amegashie, A. (2009) 'American Idol: should it be a singing contest or a popularity contest?', *Journal of Cultural Economics*, **33** (4), 265-277.

Anand, N. and Peterson, R. (2000) 'When market information constitutes fields: sensemaking of markets in the commercial music industry', *Organization Science*, **11** (3), 270-284.

Asai, S. (2008) 'Firm organisation and marketing strategy in the Japanese music industry', *Popular Music*, **27** (3), 473-485.

Bishop, J. (2005) 'Building international empires of sound: concentrations of power and property in the "global" music market', *Popular Music and Society*, **28** (4), 443-471.

Booth, G.D. and Kuhn, T.L. (1990) 'Economic and transmission factors as essential elements in the definition of folk, art, and pop music', *The Musical Quarterly*, **74** (3), 411-438.

Boyle, J. (2008) *The Public Domain*. New Haven, CT: Yale University Press.

Brabazan, T. (2012) *Popular Music: Topics, Trends and Trajectories*, London: SAGE.

Burkart, P. and McCourt, T. (2004) 'Infrastructure for the celestial jukebox', *Popular Music*, **23** (3), 349-362.

Cabott, Ch.J. (2009) 'Understanding the music Industry's Changing Economy and Wall Street's Interest in song catalogs', *The Philadelphia Lawyer*, Winter, 50-54.

Denisoff, R.S. (1975) *Solid Gold: The Popular Record Industry*, New Brunswick, NJ: Transaction Books.

Drummond, J., Kearsley, G. and Lawson R. (2008) 'Culture Matters: A Report for the Ministry of Research, Science and Technology', Dunedin, New Zealand: University of Otago.

Du Gay, P., Hall, S., Janes, L., Mackay, H. and Negus, K. (1997) *Doing Cultural Studies: The story of the Sony Walkman*, London: Sage Publications.

Fairchild, C. (2007) 'Building the authentic celebrity: the "Idol" phenomenon in the attention economy', *Popular Music and Society*, **30** (3), 355-375.

Florida, R. and Jackson, S. (2010) 'Sonic City: the evolving economic geography of the music industry', *Journal of Planning Education and Research*, **2** (3), 310-321.

Fonarow, W. (2006) *Empire of Dirt: The Aesthetics and Rituals of British Indie Music*. Middletown, CT: Wesleyan University Press.

Frith, S. (2007) 'Why music matters', *Critical Quarterly*, **50** (1-2), 165-179.

Frith, S. and Cloonan, M. (2008) 'Introduction: special issue on popular music policy', *Popular Music*, 27(2), 189-191.

Garofalo, R. (1987) 'How autonomous is relative: popular music, the social formation and cultural struggle', *Popular Music*, **6** (1), 77-92.

Goldstuck, C. (2001) 'Industry must act now to prosper', *Music Business International*, **11** (6), 50.

Gronrow, P. (1983) 'The record industry: the growth of a mass medium', *Popular Music*, **3**, 53-75.

Hardy, P. (1999) 'The European **Music** Business: a **market** undergoing the process of restructuring', *Cultural Trends*, **9** (34), 57-60.

Hesmondhalgh, D. (1997) 'Post-punk's attempt to democratise the music industry: the success and failure of Rough Trade', *Popular Music*, **16** (3), 255-274.

Hull, G.P., Hutchison, T. and Strasser, R. (2010) *The Music Business and Recording Industry: Delivering Music in the 21st Century*, New York, NY: Routledge.

IFPI (2009) *Recording Industry in Numbers 2009: The Definitive Source of Global Music Market Information*, Report, May, [Accessed: 30 April 2013].

IFPI (2012) *Investing in Music*, report, 12 November [accessed 21 May 2013]

Jones, S. (1992) *Rock Formation: Music, Technology and Mass Communication. Foundations of Popular Culture*, Volume 3. London: Sage.

Knopper, S. (2009) *Appetite for Self-Destruction: The spectacular crash of the record industry in the digital age*, London: Simon & Schuster.

Lewis, J. (2008) 'Introduction to Part VII', in Lewis, J. and Miller, T. (ed.) *Critical Cultural Policy Studies: A Reader*, Malden, MA: Wiley-Blackwell 227-229.

Miles, S. (2000) *Consumerism as a Way of Life*, London: Sage.

Payne, J. (2000) 'Music industry futures: likely developments over the next 10 years', *Cultural Trends*, **38**, 41-42.

Peterson, R.D. and Berger, D.G. (1971) 'Entrepreneurship in organizations: evidence from the popular music Industry', *Administrative Science Quarterly*, **16** (1), 97-106.

Power, D. and Hallencreutz, D. (2007) 'Competitiveness, local production systems and global commodity chains in the **music** industry: entering the US **market'**, *Regional Studies*, **41** (3), 377-389.

Rushton, M. (1998) 'The moral rights of artists: droit moral ou droit pécuniaire', *Journal of Cultural Economics*, **22** (1), 15-32.

Sanjek, R. and Sanjek, D. (1991) *American Popular Music Business in the 20th Century*, Oxford: Oxford University Press.

Segall, L. (2012) 'Digital music sales top physical sales', *CNNMoney*, 5 January 2012, available online: http://money.cnn.com/2012/01/05/technology/digital_music_sales/index.htm, [Accessed: 30 April 2013].

Tschmuck, P. (2012) *Creativity and Innovation in the Music Industry*, Berlin Heidelberg: Springer.

Walmsley, B. (2011) 'The funding agenda: social relations and the politics of cultural production', in Walmsley, B. (ed.) *Key Issues in the Arts and Entertainment Industry*, Oxford: Goodfellow Publishers.

Wegman, R.C. (2005) 'Musical offering in the Renaissance', *Early Music*, **XXXIII** (3), 425-437.

Williamson, J. and Cloonan, M. (2007) 'Rethinking the music industry', *Popular Music*, **26** (2), 305-322

Williamson, J., Cloonan, M. and Frith, S. (2003) *Mapping the Music Industry in Scotland: a Report*, Glasgow Scottish Enterprise.

MUSIC, MARKETS AND CONSUMPTION

Part II
Production Perspectives

3 Music as Product

Introduction

In order to develop a more holistic and integrated understanding of the relationship between music and the market, and consequently of music production and consumption, it is necessary to examine the notion of music as a product. The very act of exploring the relationship between music, markets and consumption immediately frames music as a 'product'. In the marketplace, music is 'produced' and 'consumed' rather than made and heard. But the language and practices of the market and of marketing go far beyond the labelling of music making and listening in this way. They are pervasive and, as such, mediate our everyday engagement with music, regardless of the role we play in the market. The way the quality of music is evaluated is dominated by measures of sales success: songs 'top the charts', artists 'sell out' stadiums and tours, and recording companies sign 'the next big thing' to contracts in the expectation of future sales. Even a particular market can be held up as measure of success: in popular music, many bands, such as the Beatles, have been deemed to be successful only after they have 'broken America' by reaching high positions on the US music charts.

Marketing practices have long been utilized in music. For example, P.T. Barnum adopted a variety of promotional campaigns and innovative pricing tactics to ensure the success of Jenny Lind's 1850 debut in America (Waksman, 2011). Tickets for the best seats in the house were sold at auction. This served multiple purposes, such as increasing revenues by forcing up the price of the ticket through competitive bidding, generating further publicity for the concert through additional advertising of the auction itself, and ensuring that ticket dealers would not profit without adding value, by purchasing large blocks of tickets and selling them on at inflated prices. These are all practices, and problems, which have contemporary resonance. Many artists, managers and music-based organizations have expertly exploited branding and public relations, and in some cases the field of music has even been at the forefront of practice. The Rolling Stones lip and tongue logo, painted by John Pasche and first used on their *Sticky Fingers* album in 1971, is 'one of the most visually dynamic and innovative logos ever created' (Barrie, 2012) and, as such, is held in the collection of the Victoria and Albert Museum in London.

The notion of 'music as product' in contemporary life is not unproblematic. The framing of music as a product, like any framing, is neither value-free nor neutral. It highlights certain ways of seeing and masks others, and it can therefore influence the way people think and behave. Talking about music 'producers' and 'consumers' privileges a particular kind of musical engagement, and ignores the vast array of experiences people have when making and listening to music. 'Gone are the days when viewers went to galleries, audiences attended concerts or the theatre; they are all consumers', notes John Tusa, Director of the Barbican Centre in London (1997, cited in Chong 2003). This raises the potentially contentious nature of framing music as a product, making it all the more surprising that this perspective on music has not yet been examined in any great depth. After considering what the music product is, this chapter explores the different perspectives on the nature and value of music. This provides a basis for an emergent conceptualization of music as a product.

The music product

There is an implicit assumption that people know and agree on what is meant by the term 'product' in the context of music. There are, however, a range of possible answers to the question: 'What is the music product?' The most seemingly obvious answer is that it is the music itself. But complexity arises when one tries to specify exactly what that is. Music comes in many forms, some of which are recordings such as digital files, CDs, vinyl records (LPs or 45s), gramophone records, audio cassettes, eight-track tapes, video tapes and DVDs. These may contain single pieces or albums, symphonies, soundtracks and all manner of sound formats. But music can also be made and listened to live, so the product might then be a concert, or music one performs for one's own immediate listening pleasure.

Even this initial attempt to answer the question highlights a number of issues. Firstly, music is intangible by nature, as emphasized in *The Collins Beta Online Dictionary* (2011) definition of music as: '(1) an art form consisting of sequences of sounds in time, especially tones of definite pitch organized melodically, harmonically, rhythmically and according to tone colour; (2) such an art form characteristic of a particular people, culture, or tradition e.g. Indian music, rock music, baroque music; (3) the sounds so produced, especially by singing or musical instruments; (4) written or printed music, such as a score or set of parts; (5) any sequence of sounds perceived as pleasing or harmonious; and (6) (rare) a group of musicians'. However, music products all appear to manifest the desire to transform it into something tangible by capturing or recording music so that it can be more easily brought to market. Even in the case of live music, audiences often expect to hear live performances, or reproductions, of recorded music. Secondly, the separation and separability of music's sounds and visuals can be seen in the 'music product' frame.

Prior to the development of the recording industry, music was almost always experienced both aurally and visually as music could only be made and listened to in an immediate, live context. It is only recently, through the treatment of music as a tangible, recorded product, that musical experience has become primarily aural. The evolution of the music video challenged the dominance of music recordings, but in doing so attracted much resistance, and consequently the visual was subordinated and used primarily as a promotional tool for the sound recording (Laing, 1985).

There are more systematic ways one can approach the question of what comprises the music product. Turning to marketing theory, one could conceptualize the music product using the core-periphery and augmented product models found in many marketing textbooks (e.g. Keller, 2003). A simple version of this model is presented in Figure 1.

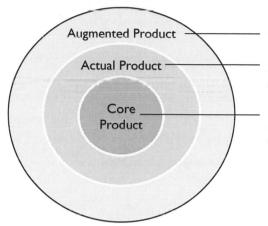

Augmented Product — Lyrics and cover art, hidden tracks, paraphernalia, concert recordings, introductory talks

Actual Product — Quality (aesthetic/aural), genre, artist, venue, producer

Core Product — Entertainment, emotional/aesthetic pleasure, symbolic representation, social cohesiveness

Figure 1: The music product

At the core of the music product is the music, the artists (musicians, conductors, sound engineers, DJs and so on), and the venues in which music is made and heard. However, closer examination of the artists indicates that there is a social hierarchy that organizes the relationships between those producing music. Cook (1998) identifies this 'hierarchy of value' within classical music, arguing that it is based on the authority one has over the music. Thus, a composer, as the author or originator of the music, has the greatest authority over it. This then leads to the subordination of the performer, as their role is to reproduce what the composer has created, rather than to produce something original. However, this is 'totally at odds with the adulation of charismatic performers in the marketplace' (Cook, 1998: 25), which indicates that the source of hierarchy is likely to differ across genres of music. In the popular music industry, the hierarchy is organized around a set of dichotomies:

> in which rock artists were favoured over pop and soul performers; albums were favoured over singles, and self-contained bands or 'solo artists' who were judged from a position derived from Romanticism, to 'express' themselves through writing their own songs were favoured over the more collaborative ways in which singers or groups of performers have, for many years,

worked with arrangers, session musicians and songwriters in putting together a 'package'. (Negus, 2002: 512)

According to the model in Figure 1, the music 'package' also extends to the augmented product. Many attributes can be included, such as lyrics sheets and album cover art, hidden tracks on the recording, the paraphernalia available at live concerts, the ability to purchase recordings of the concert immediately following the performance, pre-concert talks from conductors and soloists, artist signings, and so on. It is almost impossible, and certainly misleading, to consider any of the attributes at the different levels in isolation, as they all, in combination, make up the product offering (Kubacki and Croft, 2004).

Another approach is to compare the music product to other kinds of products. The differences do not lie in the tangible aspects of the music itself, but in the way that it is consumed, and it is the combination of factors which distinguish music from other products (Lacher, 1989; Lacher and Mizerski, 1994; North and Hargreaves, 1997).

First, music is not destroyed by consumption, and neither is its form altered. Due to advances in technology, a piece of music can be recorded and then experienced without the form of the music being altered in any way, particularly in the case of digital recordings. That being said, there are some exceptions. Other kinds of recordings, such as tape and vinyl, can be damaged or worn out (Lacher and Mizerski, 1994), although the actual form of the music is not altered. In a live performance context, the music itself is not destroyed, but the form may alter drastically as a result of the interaction between the musicians, audiences, the environment and so on.

Second, the same 'music' can be consumed many times and, due to the mobile quality of recorded music, in many places. Consumers acquire music in order to be able to experience it more than once, and also to have temporal control over the listening experience (Lacher, 1989). Ownership of the music affords the listener control over where, and in what situation, the music is consumed. Through technological advances in playback equipment, music has become entirely mobile.

'It can follow us around the house, from living-room to kitchen and bathroom; on journeys, as "in-car entertainment" and "the

Walkman effect"; across notional and political boundaries; in and out of love and work and sickness' (Frith, 1996: 236).

Although repeat purchase of the same piece of music is rare, repeat consumption occurs frequently (Lacher and Mizerski, 1994).

On a similar note, the third characteristic is that music can be consumed without purchase, and, when purchased, is often consumed prior to purchase. Music is often initially consumed through media such as radio, television and the Internet before it is purchased (Lacher, 1989). It can also be consumed without purchase, as it can repeatedly be heard on various media, downloaded free (legally or illegally), or received as a gift. However, some less mainstream genres of music may have to be purchased in order to be consumed, as they receive little airtime on commercial mass media (Lacher and Mizerski, 1994) and do not conduct extensive tours – although access to a huge variety of music has been greatly improved through the Internet. In general, purchase of music is not necessary unless the consumer wants to gain control of the consumption experience.

Fourth, the consumption of music may be active (choosing to listen to music) or passive (hearing music while performing day-to-day activities such as shopping, commuting and working). Music is pervasive in our everyday lives; therefore, people often consume music passively (Bradshaw and Holbrook, 2008). However, many consumers are in situations where they can select the music they wish to hear either by choosing something from their collection, or by creating their own mix of music on recordable or streaming media. The availability of a wide range of music on the Internet has further facilitated the self-selection of music. Finally, music can be consumed both privately (e.g. in consumers' own homes or via MP3 players) or publicly, in the presence of others.

Even this brief exploration of music as a product highlights its inherent complexity. However, rather than thinking about the core and periphery attributes of music or how music as a product differs from other kinds of products, perhaps the most fruitful and encompassing approach is to compare how 'music as a product' differs from other perspectives on the nature and value of music.

The nature and value of music

Philosophers have puzzled over the uniquely human behaviour associated with music for thousands of years, with the aim of understanding just what music is, and why it is so significant to humans – in other words, what its nature and value are. The answers that have been offered bring to light an impressive diversity of perspectives on music. Although they often obfuscate as much as they enlighten, certain themes are evident. Bowman (1998) provides a detailed account of the different philosophical perspectives on music, ranging from 'music as imitation' to 'contemporary pluralism', as outlined in Table 2.

A number of different dimensions can be identified in Table 2 which further assist our understanding of the nature and value of music. First, perspectives differ on whether or not music is viewed as a bridge to something else. The 'music as idea' perspective holds that music provides insights into the mind, and is therefore valuable as it relates to other human cognitive activity. In the 'music as imitation' perspective, music is a bridge to understanding the true nature of reality, as music is, and can only ever be, an imitation of the universal or archetype. This resonates with the postmodern view that there is no original art, and thus all art is reproduction. The underlying assumption is that no profound truths remain to be discovered, and therefore 'nothing genuine exists. Art objects are seen as mere copies, imitations, collages or bricolages of one other' (Bjorkegren, 1995: 12). Both are powerful ideas that contrast dramatically with the position taken by the 'music as autonomous form' perspective, which rejects claims that music is a bridge to anything beyond itself. Musicology is closely aligned with the 'music as autonomous form' perspective. As one of only a few academic disciplines dedicated to studying music, musicology has been influential in determining general perceptions of its nature and value. This has not always been to the advantage of music, as noted by Cook (1998: vii):

> there has been an academic tradition of thinking of music as 'purely musical', as being about nothing but itself, which has created a general impression among everyone except musicologists that in that case music can't matter very much.

Table 2: Philosophical perspectives on music

Nature of Music	Value of Music	Key Philosophers
Music as imitation		
Music is an imitative art.	Significance lies in music's resemblances	Plato (427–347 BC): doctrine of
Doctrine of mimesis: music is an imitation of	to other things (e.g. harmonious balance	mimesis.
the ideal.	and unity). Concern with potentially	Aristotle (384–322 BC): excellence of
Musical, social, political and moral concerns	adverse effects (e.g. capacity to deceive).	imitation vs. the goodness of what it
are intimately connected.		imitated.
Music as idea		
Music is a product of human minds.	Significance lies in music's relation to	Kant (1724–1804): account of aesthetic
Dualistic foundation: relationships between	other human mental activity. Music entails	experience.
music's ephemeral felt nature and the realm	some kind of knowing and awareness of	Hegel (1770–1831): artistic vs. natural
of ideas.	aesthetic value.	beauty.
Music as autonomous form		
Music is intrinsic and located wholly within a	The course of musical beauty is none	Hanslick (1825–1904): defence of
purely musical realm.	other than tonally moving forms. The	music's purely musical value.
Formalist foundations: focusing on the	meaning of music is wholly intra-musical	Gurney (1847–1888): musical
sonorous event.	and contained within music's own	experience mediated by a special
	materials, events and patterns.	mental faculty.

Music as symbol

Music is a symbol that mediates cognition and interpretations of the world. Semiotic theory: music is a distinctive kind of symbol situation with its own musically unique, semantic devices.	Music is an important vehicle by which humans construct their conceptions of 'reality'. Musical meanings do not have assigned reference and are multiple, fluid and dynamic.	Langer (1895–1985): music is a logical symbolic expression of the inner, felt life. Nattiez (b.1945): music is plural and dynamic, its meaning relative to interpretive variables.

Music as experience

Music is a lived, bodily experience. Phenomenological basis: resists efforts to explain what music is about, preferring to richly describe what music itself says and how music is experienced.	The world of music is vital, replete with its own meanings and values. The value of music can only be determined through close attention to how it is experienced.	Dufrenne (1910-1995): aesthetic experience deploys imagination. Clifton (1935–1978): music is what I am when I hear it.

Music as social and political force

Music is a human construction intimately connected to power. Cultural perspective: music is cultural and thus is constantly being created, recreated, modified, contested and negotiated.	Importance of music is the way it shapes and defines human society. Musical value is not absolute, but is culturally and historically relative. Human and social orders are, in turn, constructed and sustained by musical practices.	Adorno (1903–1969): normative, hierarchical account of musical value. Attali (b.1943): music indicates changes in socio-political and socio-economic relations.

Contemporary pluralism

Musical practices are plural, diverse and divergent. Pluralist perspective: shift away from grand theory to accounts that refer to plurality and difference e.g. feminism and postmodernism.	Musical value is not fixed, singular or uniform. What is important is how value and meaning has been constructed.	Göltner-Abendroth (b. 1941): articulation of a matriarchal alternative to the dominant patriarchal aesthetic. McClary (b.1946): link between music and matters of gender, sex and the erotic.

Music as product

Music is a form of capital. It can be recorded, stored and reproduced in a standardized manner by those who own the rights to it, for sale to others.	Music value centres around its economic value in exchange, and is market driven and extrinsic. Its value primarily lies in the ability to capitalize on all types of value which it may have for those involved in its production and consumption

(Adapted from Bowman, 1998)

Perspectives also differ in terms of the relationship between music and society – i.e. whether music functions separately from society, or as part of it. Many of the philosophical perspectives hold that music is inextricably tied to the social world in some way (e.g. music as imitation, music as symbol, music as experienced, music as social and political force and music as contemporary). For example, from the 'music as symbol' perspective, the meaning of music is expressive, heteronomous and extramusical. It emerges from the way one engages with music, and is fluid and dynamic. On the other side of the coin, from the 'music as autonomous form' perspective, musical meaning is formal, autonomous and intra-musical – it is entirely located within the music itself. In a similar vein, the 'music as idea' perspective views music as a product of the human mind, which functions apart from society; 'music deals not so much with the world "out there" as "in here"' (Bowman, 1998: 71). Kant's philosophy and his account of aesthetic experience and judgement of beauty, which is central to the 'music as idea' perspective, has had a significant impact on some beliefs about the nature and value of music. Aesthetic criteria are invariably promoted above all others as the primary means by which music should be evaluated and valued. The dominance of aesthetics has meant that the term has become interchangeable with 'art', and is thus the perspective favoured by many 'artists' involved in the making of music. Privileging the aesthetic view of music over all other perspectives is not without problems, however, as it subordinates all other kinds of musical value. For example, this is the cause of much conflict for musicians when they are subjected to the forces of the market while trying to make a living from their art (e.g. Kubacki and Croft, 2004).

Following on from this idea, the final dimension, and that which is most pertinent to this chapter, is whether music is located outside or within the market. The only perspective to explicitly acknowledge the presence and role of the market is that of 'music as social and political force', and it does so through a consideration of music in a commodity form. In part, this perspective reflects the creative and cultural industries view of music (and art products in general) as cultural texts or artefacts which engage in some form of industrial reproduction (Hesmondhalgh and Negus, 2002). However, the more critical considerations of how the commoditization of music is connected to issues of power and political influence dominate this perspective. Music is 'socially constructed, socially embedded, and its nature and value are inherently social' (Bowman, 1998: 304). Therefore, as such, it cannot be innocent, value-free or neutral. The work of both Adorno and Attali examine how music as a commodity is a powerful shaper of human consciousness, identity and social order. Adorno's (1903-1969) body of work has been greatly influential, and his view that music shapes social consciousness is well known. His argument was that as an industrial commodity created for mass consumption, popular music perpetuates and reinforces mindless, uncritical thought, facilitating a passive and unconscious conformity with the forces of monopoly capitalism. 'Good' music, on the other hand, challenges awareness, thus undermining 'false consciousness', and confronts the laws of the capitalist marketplace. In a similar vein, Attali's (1985) thesis is that sound or noise is fundamentally threatening and violent. The control and order of noise in a way that transforms it into musical practice illustrates how societies structure political power and economic relations. Thus, the control of noise (i.e. music) is a clear manifestation of power. These are necessary oversimplifications of this rich body of work, but the position is clear:

> Fetishized as a commodity, music is illustrative of the evolution of our entire society: deritualize a social form, repress an activity of the body, specialize its practice, sell it as a spectacle, generalize its consumption, then see to it that it is stockpiled until it loses its meaning. (Attali, 1984: 5)

However, Attali is not entirely committed to such a bleak view of the future. In a prophetic manifestation of his thesis that music is a mirror of society, he foresaw the changing dynamics of the music industry and a new mode of socio-musical relations that has the potential to transcend the oppression of repetitive and reproduced music, which he termed 'composing' (p.133). It entails, amongst other things, the breaking down of distinctions between the musician and the listener in making music for joy and other benefits it brings, all of which are new modes of musical engagement emerging in contemporary, everyday life.

It can be argued that although framing music as a 'commodity' provides certain insights into the relationship between music, markets and consumption, these will be quite different to those gained by framing music as a 'product'. A commodity is a good for which there is demand, but which is supplied without qualitative differentiation across the market. From Adorno's and Attali's perspective, the commoditization of music raises many issues which underpin their critiques. Although it is often said to be characterized by 'mass production', Laing (1985: 79) points out that the music industry would be more accurately described as engaging in 'multiple serial production'. This leans more towards the notion of a product which is differentiated within the market, and takes us into the realm of marketing theory and practice. The raison d'être of marketing is to turn objects, services and experiences into products and, ultimately, brands, by differentiating them so that they can then be positioned within the minds of the target customer in order to facilitate exchange. The dominant marketing management discourse positions this process and related practices as neutral, unproblematic, and rational. However the literature raises a number of political, functional, ethical and intellectual critiques of marketing (Hackley, 2009), which, when applied to music, echo a range of views including those expressed by Adorno and Attali. Thus, is it clear that these two positions are not mutually exclusive, especially given that as the interests of cultural institutions and businesses become intertwined, culture becomes less able to play a critical role (Chong, 2003). The space between the two positions of music as a commodity and music as a product is not clear or empty, but rather is filled with interesting tensions, issues and critiques. For example, can popular music really be considered to be differentiated? Does music really express creativity and artistic vision, or is it moulded into a standardized form that 'sells'? Does avant-garde music sit outside the reaches of the marketplace?

An emergent perspective on 'music as product'

This notwithstanding, the 'music as product' perspective does claim a particular position regarding the nature and value of music which should be identified and acknowledged. The nature of music can be seen as centring around several interrelated issues. Primarily, music is something that can be owned and replicated. Thus, music can be captured, recorded, stored and reproduced in a standardized manner for sale to others by those who own the rights to it. Live music is not excluded from this, as the artist generally attempts to capture a certain performance of a musical repertoire which is reproduced across various locations on tour. Invariably, differentiation in performance does occur, and it is arguably this differentiation which helps to make the live music experience so exciting. The recorded and live production process is increasingly technologically driven, and results in a growing array of types of music products. For example, American rapper Tupac Shakur, who died in 1996, was 'resurrected' via hologram and 'performed' alongside Snoop Dogg and Dr Dre at the Coachella Valley Music and Arts Festival in 2012. Finally, the relationship between production and consumption varies across different music products. At one extreme, and in the case of recordings, production and consumption are separated, and once the original recording is made, those involved in performing the music have little to do with the consumption of it. At the other end of the scale, production and consumption happen simultaneously and symbiotically in a live music context. However, Mauws (2000) cautions against taking what he describes as a 'materialist approach' which focuses on the cultural object of the music itself. Instead, music should be thought of as 'a process or, perhaps more accurately, a series of actions' (Bennett et al., 1993: 4). Music is not brought into being as a finished product. 'On the contrary, the production and consumption of these products entail the involvement of countless other "market makers" and, as a result, a wide range of practices beyond creating and consuming art' (Mauws, 2000: 232).

Following on from this view of the nature of music, the value of 'music as product' centres on its economic value in exchange. For the owners of the rights to the music, its value primarily lies in its ability to create capital surplus. But artistic value is often of equal, if not greater, importance to those involved in the production and consumption of music, and these two types of value do not always sit easily alongside one another in the marketplace. From the music consumer's point of view, the value of music is better captured by Vargo and Lusch's

(2004) notion of value in use, which is actualized at the moment of consumption and co-created through the interaction of all those involved in the process of bringing the music to market. 'Consumers' seek a range of different kinds of value from music, ranging from aesthetic pleasure to self-symbolic representation (e.g. Hargreaves and North, 1999; Larsen et al., 2010). Music consumption experiences will be examined in detail in Chapter 7. The value of 'music as product' is therefore market driven and extrinsic. It is also multiple; it is 'joy for the creator, use-value for the consumers, and exchange value for the seller' (Attali 1985: 9).

The conceptualization of 'music as product', and its associated nature and value, raise important issues regarding the relationship between music, markets and consumption. Two key issues are discussed below.

Exchange

The notion of exchange is central to both markets and marketing (e.g. Bagozzi, 1975). At a very basic level, the function of marketing is to aid in the creation of value which can be exchanged in the marketplace. In the music industry, the marketing task is performed by cultural intermediaries who 'shape both use values and exchange values, and seek to manage how these values are connected with people's lives through the various techniques of persuasion and marketing and through the construction of markets' (Negus, 2002: 504). One of the most contentious issues facing cultural intermediaries, and also the producers and consumers of music, is the relationship between the artistic and exchange value of music. Negus (1995) identifies four broad positions taken by those interested in the art-versus-commerce debate in relation to music:

1   *Commerce corrupts art*: based on classical Marxism, and Adorno's critique of the culture industry, this approach suggests that commercialization results in the co-optation of artists into the entertainment industry. Any radical efforts by musicians to overthrow the oppressive commercial system will simply be co-opted by the system, and thus commercial imperatives and

constraints will always determine the way in which music is produced – and consumed.

2   *Creativity in consumption*: this approach circumvents the co-optation of music and the capitalist organization of the production of music by relocating creativity to the act of consumption. In line with ideas on the co-creation of value (e.g. Vargo and Lusch, 2004), artistic value is only realized at the moment of consumption, which is uncontrollable by music producers and the commercial system. Consuming is reframed as an empowering and subversive act of production, rather than of reception (e.g. Fiske, 1992).

3   *Continual tension between commerce and creativity*: this approach holds that the current form of the recording industry creates a continual tension which can never be resolved. This is the defining characteristic of the music (and other cultural) industries, and one which all those involved must confront, experience and somehow attempt to resolve by either opposing or adopting a commercial attitude (e.g. Cohen, 1991).

4   *Simultaneous production of creativity and commerce*: this draws on the position taken by Simon Frith in much of his work, which argues that commerce and creativity are closely connected, complementary and possibly even indistinguishable. In popular music, particularly the rock genre, the popularity of a record indicates both its commercial and artistic success.

There are limitations and complexities in each and every one of these positions – hence the continuing debate. In practice, musicians express a multiplicity of views on how exchange value and artistic value interact within market spaces (Kubacki and Croft, 2004). Consequently, they use various strategies to ensure that they can retain artistic integrity while still participating in the marketplace, in order to make a living from the exchange value of their music (Bradshaw *et al.*, 2006). These views and strategies are discussed in greater detail in Chapter 4 ('Musicians'), but it is important to note that this is an area of continuing debate.

Inherent in the exchange value of music is the idea of ownership, which is at the core of many of the recent technology-driven challenges faced by the music industry. The illegal downloading of digital music flouts the market-mediated process of ownership exchange by effectively taking possession, and drawing out the use value, of music without paying the predetermined economic value. Research on downloading and file sharing has primarily focused on who (Fox and Wrenn, 2001), what, where (Moore and McMullan, 2004) and how (Langdenderfer and Cook, 2001), but there remains little understanding of why. There has been some suggestion that music consumers have embraced illegal downloading not only as a way of experiencing music for free, but as a means to voice their own frustrations at the structure and control of the music industry (e.g. Khiaban and Larsen, 2011). Music consumers have also shown great support for musicians who have challenged conventional forms of exchange. For example, Radiohead independently released their album *In Rainbows* (2007) as a digital download through their own website, and asked consumers only to pay what they wanted for it. Although they reportedly sold fewer albums than if they had distributed it through traditional channels (Randall, 2011), Radiohead made more money and gained much acclaim – from music consumers and critics alike – for both the album and their unconventional and provocative approach to marketing.

Relationship with other products

Within the field of marketing music has often been used as a sales tool, as it has been shown to increase the effect of marketing practices. It seems that when used in marketing-related contexts, music is 'capable of evoking non-random affective and behaviour responses in consumers' (Bruner, 1990: 99). Consequently, music has been used in advertising to condition preferences for the product being advertised (e.g. Gorn, 1982, Brierly *et al.*, 1985; MacInnis and Park, 1991; Morris and Boone, 1998; Stewart and Punj, 1998) and to influence consumption behaviour in retail environments through atmospherics (e.g. Smith and Curnow, 1966; Milliman 1982) and musical fit (e.g. Areni and Kim 1993; North *et al.*, 1999; Mattila and Wirtz 2001). However, in this context music is treated not so much as a product in itself, but as a sales or marketing tool.

As a product, the use and value of music is often defined in relation to other products. Music is frequently included in product constellations which are clusters of 'complementary products, specific brands, and/ or consumption activities associated with a social role' (Solomon and Assael 1987: 191) and which can be used to define certain lifestyles. A good example is the constellation of 'sex, drugs and rock 'n' roll' which is a rhetorical device used to capture the heady days of the 1970s lifestyle. The value and meaning of music therefore determines, and is determined by, the value and meanings of the other products, services, ideas and experiences with which it is associated. Constructed in the social world, these meanings and values are fluid and constantly changing, although at certain times they can be captured by a social group and can therefore play an integral role in particular subcultures, such as indie (e.g. Fonarow, 2006) and hipster (Arsel and Thompson, 2011). Music is often also described as an adjunct to other activities, such as feasting and celebration (Kubacki and Croft, 2004), and sometimes plays the role of 'sonic wallpaper' in social interactions (Larsen et al., 2010). But much remains to be understood about how music relates to other products. For example, how does music influence our experience of other cultural products, such as movies or fine art? Can and should music be used in political campaigns? How is music used in relation to other consumer actions to critique the market and marketing?

Summary

The treatment of music as a product is ubiquitous in contemporary consumer society. Much engagement with music, either as music maker or as listener/audience member/fan/passer-by, is mediated by the market and by marketing practices. However, framing music as a product raises important questions, possibilities and tensions around the concept of the nature and value of music. Our reactions and responses to those questions are likely to be influenced by both the context in which music is made and experienced, and by our own personal philosophical positions. This chapter examined the wide range of perspectives that inform and frame our existing understanding of the nature and value of music, noting that some perspectives, such as 'music as social and political force', provides insight into the relationship between music, markets and consumption. However, the notion of a 'commodity', upon which that perspective is based, is slightly different to that of a 'product', and therefore the 'social and political force' perspective is not sufficient to provide a full account of 'music as product'. An emergent conceptualization of 'music as product' claims that a variety of market makers are able to own, capture, record, store and reproduce music in a standardized manner for sale to others. Thus, the value of music as a product lies in its economic value in exchange and use.

References

Areni, C.S. and Kim, D. (1993) 'The influence of background music on shopping behaviour: classical versus top-forty music in a wine store', *Advances in Consumer Research*, **20**, 336-340.

Arsel, Z. and Thompson, C. (2011) 'Demythologizing consumption practices: how consumers protect their field-dependent identity investments from devaluing marketplace myths', *Journal of Consumer Research*, **37** (5), 791-806.

Attali, J. (1985) *Noise: The Political Economy of Music*, Minneapolis: University of Minnesota Press.

Bagozzi, R. (1975) 'Marketing as exchange', *Journal of Marketing*, **39** (4), 32-39.

Barrie, D. (2012) 'Rolling Stones lips and tongue logo by Jon Pasche' http://www. vam.ac.uk/content/articles/r/rolling-stones-lips-and-tongue-logo/ Accessed: 13 May 2012

Bennett, T., Frith, S., Grossberg, L., Shepherd, J. and Turner, G. (ed.) (1993) *Rock and Popular Music: Politics, Policies and Institutions*, London: Routledge.

Björkegren, D. (1995) *Culture Business: Management Strategies for the Arts-Related Business* Andover, UK: Cengage Learning EMEA.

Bowman, W.D. (1998) *Philosophical Perspectives on Music*, Oxford: Oxford University Press.

Bradshaw, A. and Holbrook, M. (2008) 'Must we have muzak wherever we go? A critical consideration of the consumer culture', *Consumption, Markets and Culture*, **11** (1), 5-44.

Bradshaw, A., McDonagh, P. and Marshall, D (2006) 'The alienated artist and the political economy of organized art', *Consumption, Markets and Culture*, **9** (2), 111-118.

Brierley, C., McSweeney, F.K. and Vannieuwkerk, R. (1985) 'Classical conditioning of preferences for stimuli', *Journal of Consumer Research,* **12** (December), 316-323.

Bruner II, G.C. (1990) 'Music, Mood, and Marketing', *Journal of Marketing,* **54**(4), 94-104.

Chong, D. (2003) 'Revisiting Business and the Arts', *Journal of Nonprofit & Public Sector Marketing* **11** (1), 151-165.

Cohen, S. (1991) *Rock Culture in Liverpool. Popular Music in the Making,* Oxford: Clarendon Press.

Collins Beta Online Dictionary (2011) http://www.collinsdictionary.com Accessed: 17 May 2011

Cook, N. (1998) *Music: A Very Short Introduction,* Oxford: Oxford University Press.

Fiske, J. (1992) 'The cultural economy of fandom' in Lewis, L. (ed.) *The Adoring Audience. Fan Culture and Popular Media,* London: Routledge, 30-49.

Fonarow, W. (2006) *Empire of Dirt: The Aesthetics and Rituals of British Indie Music.* Middletown, CT: Wesleyan University Press.

Fox, M. and Wrenn, B. (2001) 'A Broadcasting Model for the Music Industry' *Journal of Media Management,* **3** (2), 112-119.

Frith, S. (1996) *Performing Rites: Evaluating Popular Music,* Oxford: Oxford University Press.

Gorn, G.J. (1982) 'The effects of music in advertising on choice behaviour: a classical conditioning approach', *Journal of Marketing,* **46** (Winter), 94-101.

Hackley, C. (2009) *Marketing: A Critical Introduction,* London: SAGE.

Hargreaves, D.J. and North, A.C. (1999) 'The functions of music in everyday life: redefining the social in music psychology', *Psychology of Music,* **27**, 71-83.

Hesmondhalgh, D. and Negus, K. (2002) *Popular Music Studies,* London: Arnold.

Keller, K. (2003) *Strategic Brand Management: Building, Measuring and Managing Brand Equity,* 2nd Edition, Upper Saddle River, NJ: Pearson Education.

Khiaban, P. and Larsen, G. (2011) 'Exploring illegal music acquisition strategies', Paper presented at the 10th International Colloquium of the Academy of Marketing SIG on Arts, Heritage, Nonprofit and Social Marketing, 7 September 2011, Leeds.

Kubacki, K. and Croft, R. (2004) 'Mass marketing, music and morality', *Journal of Marketing Management,* **20**, 577-590.

Lacher, K.T. (1989) 'Hedonic consumption: music as a product', *Advances in Consumer Research*, **16**, 367-373.

Lacher, K.T. and Mizerski, R. (1994) 'An exploratory study of the responses and relationships involved in the evaluation of, and in the intention to purchase new rock music', *Journal of Consumer Research*, **21** (September), 366-380.

Laing, D. (1985) 'Music video: industrial product, cultural form', *Screen*, **26** (2), 78-83.

Langenderfer, J. and Cook, D.L. (2001) 'Copyright policies and issues raised by A&M Records v. Napster: "The shot heard 'round the world" or "Not with a bang but a whimper?"' *Journal of Public Policy & Marketing*, **20** (2), 280-288.

Larsen, G., Lawson, R. and Todd, G. (2010) 'The symbolic consumption of music', *Journal of Marketing Management* **26** (7/8), 671-685.

MacInnis, D.J. and Park, C.W. (1991) 'The differential role of characteristics of music on high- and low-involvement consumers' processing of ads', *Journal of Consumer Research*, **18** (September), 161-173.

Matilla, A.S. and Wirtz, J. (2001) 'Congruency of scent and music as a driver of in-store evaluations of behaviour', *Journal of Retailing*, **77**, 273-289.

Mauws, M. (2000) 'But Is It art? Decision making and discursive resources in the field of cultural production', *Journal of Applied Behavioural Science*, **36** (2), 229-244.

Milliman, R.E. (1982) 'Using background music to affect the behaviour of supermarket shoppers', *Journal of Marketing*, **46** (Summer), 86-91.

Moore, R.M. and McMullan, E.C. (2004) 'Perceptions of peer-to-peer file-sharing among university students', *Journal of Criminal Justice and Popular Culture*, **11** (1), 1-19.

Morris, J.D. and Boone, M.A. (1998) 'The effects of music on emotional response, brand attitude and purchase intent in an emotional advertising condition', *Advances in Consumer Research*, 25, 518-526.

Negus, K. (1995) 'Where the mystical meets the market: creativity and commerce in the production of popular music', *The Sociological Review*, **43** (2), 316-341.

Negus, K. (2002) 'The work of cultural intermediaries and the enduring distance between production and consumption', *Cultural Studies*, **16** (4), 501-515.

North, A.C. and Hargreaves, D.J. (1997) 'Music and consumer behaviour', in Hargreaves, D.J. and North, A.C. (ed.) *Social Psychology of Music*, Oxford: Oxford University Press, 268-289.

North, A.C., Hargreaves, D.J and McKendrick, J. (1999) 'The influence of in-store music on wine selections', *Journal of Applied Psychology,* **84** (2), 271-276.

Randall, M. (2011) *Exit Music: The Radiohead Story,* London: Omnibus Press.

Smith, P.C. and Curnow, R. (1966) 'Arousal hypothesis and the effects of music on purchasing behaviour', *Journal of Applied Psychology,* **50**, 255-256.

Solomon, M. and Assael, H. (1987) 'The forest or the trees? A Gestalt approach to symbolic consumption', in Umiker-Sebeok, J (ed.) *Marketing and Semiotics: New Directions in the Study of Signs for Sale,* Berlin: Mouton de Gruyter, pp. 189-217.

Stewart, D.W. and Punj, G.N. (1998) 'Effects of using a nonverbal (musical) cue on recall and playback of television advertising: implications for advertising tracking', *Journal of Business Research,* **42**, 39-51.

Vargo, S. and Lusch, R. (2004) 'Evolving to a new dominant logic for marketing', *Journal of Marketing,* **68** (January), 1–17.

Waksman, S. (2011) 'Selling the nightingale: P.T. Barnum, Lenny Lind, and the management of the American crowd', *Arts Marketing: An International Journal,* **1** (2), 108-120.

4 Musicians

Introduction

Being a musician can be like playing the Lottery – many try it, almost all enjoy the thrill, but very few win the jackpot. The reasons why someone decides to become a musician can be puzzling: it offers irregular and, on average, rather low income, is a competitive job market with low barriers to entry, entails a need to rely on financial support from others and the necessity to subsidise artistic work by taking jobs outside the music industry, and relies on self-proclaimed music experts who vote with their money and can make or break the musician's career. And although practically everyone, at some point in their lives, has known at least one person who has claimed to be a musician, still only one out of thousands achieve any financial stability. Of those lucky ones who sign up with a record company, only about 5% break even (Seifert and Hadiba, 2006), and those who manage their own careers often end up spending more time on non-musical activities then they do actually playing music. Most musicians find it impossible to support themselves from their creative work alone. The old economic models tell us that no rationally thinking individual should decide to become a musician (Nagel, 1988).

Yet despite the financial worries troubling so many musicians, especially those who are at the early stages of their career, the industry is not facing a shortage of new talent. So why do these aspiring artists 'behave[e] in an irrational manner' (Gray, 1986: 231)? The opportunity to realize their dreams motivates young and emerging musicians to pursue their ambitions in search of internal satisfaction, artistic fulfilment, and potential financial rewards and fame. As discussed in Chapter 2, the

Noughties have witnessed some of the most important technological developments in the music industry, creating many opportunities for musicians to market themselves using social networking websites and the Internet in general to find their audiences in the online space. Such changes have turned many musicians into online entrepreneurs, who are recording, producing and distributing their music independently of the traditional music industry. And as many successful examples show us, perseverance and a little bit of luck are often the only determinants of success (Csikszentmihalyi, 1996; Ferguson, 2002). Last but not least, there is also an image and lifestyle associated with musicians: as Wassall and Alper argue, 'the public stereotype of the artist is of a person who is in many ways different from the "rest of us"' (1984: 213). Musicians are surrounded by a magical aura of mysterious creative processes, bizarreness, fans and fandom, not to mention wealth associated with commercial success. The purpose of this chapter is to explore the many dimensions of being a musician in the contemporary music industry. It therefore begins with an attempt to provide an understanding of who a musician is, and the main types of musicians. The chapter then outlines the role of formal and informal learning in becoming a musician, and the main challenges of being a musician. It is followed by an overview of musical hierarchies and identities. The chapter concludes with some observations on music groups.

Who is a musician?

The occupational label 'musician' is nowadays applied in many contexts quite freely to describe a wide range of people and their activities. One may talk about people composing their own music, and people performing music written for them and others; there are composers who never perform, and there are DJs and music producers who never compose *sensu stricto*; there are also professional and amateur musicians, recording musicians and sessional artists. Although requiring different musical skills, they are all engaged in the same activity – creating music. Making music is undoubtedly a form of artistic engagement, yet even such a commonly used concept as art provokes vivid discussions among theoreticians who cannot agree on a single understanding of it (O'Reilly and Kubacki, 2009). It is beyond the scope of this book to engage in this kind of discussion, and therefore our assumption is that all musicians are artists, and all music is an art form. The *Oxford English Dictionary*'s (2012) definition of a musician seems somewhat narrow to adequately capture all types of music-making activities mentioned earlier, as it refers to 'a person who plays a musical instrument, especially as a profession, or is musically talented'. If one takes a closer look at the definition of an artist proposed by UNESCO's International Art Association, and considers music as an organized use of sound and silence, it is possible to obtain an understanding of who a musician is and what they do (Burgoyne, 1990: 29):

▷ 'any person who creates, or gives creative expression to, or re-creates works of art' – to be a musician one needs to create using sound and silence;

▷ 'who considers his/her artistic creation to be an essential part of his/her life' – to be a musician one needs to consider music an essential part of their life;

▷ 'who contributes to the development of art culture' – to be a musician one needs to be actively engaged in the musical life of society, the music industry, and art culture;

▷ 'and who asks to be recognised as an artist, whether he/she is bound by any relations of employment or association' – to be a musician one needs to represent onself as a musician.

Musicians are also both producers and consumers of their work; they are created through a continuous process of production and consumption of art. Using their creative artistic labour, artistic codes, their life experience and social context they infuse their music with meaning, contributing to the discourse of art which in turn reciprocates by providing their own lives with a sense of artistic identity and purpose (Meamber, 2000). Musicians can be products of a very strong artistic culture, as in the case of classical musicians, or products of the manufactured pop industry. Musicians can be shrewd commentators on the social world and harsh critics of the market, yet their engagement with it creates many opportunities to articulate their views. Many musicians are infused with social and political ideology and use their status and attention from the media to propagate the causes they consider important and worthy of public attention (e.g. Bob Geldof and Live Aid). On the other hand, within music as a primary social frame, contemporary society expects artists to rebel against established norms, and confront and challenge them, providing critique which questions authority and threatens the status quo (Bain, 2005). By shocking their audiences, artists stimulate them to see more and to perceive the world around them through the artists' own ideological lenses. By broadening people's vision they often cause upset, but are also able to inspire.

Musicians draw inspiration in their work from a variety of different sources, from other musicians and political ideologies, to drugs and alcohol. For example, disenchantment with the welfare state, the crisis facing the record industry, critique of the traditional social order, and rebellion against the parental world and religious traditions and the native rock tradition were all important factors that inspired the new wave of Dutch rock groups in the 1980s (van Elderem, 1984). Musicians are also often admired for being innovators, breaking stylistic boundaries and creating new art forms, as in the case of progressive rock groups such as Pink Floyd, King Crimson or Genesis, who introduced elements of classical music and jazz into rock in the 1970s (Keister and Smith, 2008) to establish their artistic credibility. But musicians are often treated as gods, from the Argentine Carlos Gardel, – who is recognized as the greatest tango singer of all time, and who, through personifying the values and Argentinian identity of the early 20th century, is idealized for his commitment to tango (Taylor, 1987) – through to the quintessentially American icon Elvis Presley, and contemporary pop stars like Lady Gaga and Madonna.

Musicians: types and roles

At the beginning of this chapter the question was asked: Why would anyone want to become a musician? In a climate where parental support for music has been observed to have decreased rapidly, fuelled by worries about insecurities and the lifestyle associated with a career in music (Nagel, 1988), a young person's engagement in music is affected by several different factors. Although an initial interest in music can develop independently of external influences, when it comes to motivations to engage in musical activities at a very young age, support received not only from parents, but also teachers and peers, seems to be crucial (Sichivitsa, 2007). All of these factors enhance young musicians' self-concepts of ability, learning environment, interest in music and persistence, which play an increasing role. Later on, the role of the learning community cannot be ignored, as many young musicians develop their skills and understanding of musical cultures by practising and rehearsing with their bands.

Over time, differences grow between those engaged in making music and those engaged as listeners and fans. As development as a musician involves prolonged training to perform complex physical and mental operations, studies have shown that differences occur in the brains of musicians compared to non-musicians when performing motor, auditory or somatosensory tasks (Gaser and Schlaug, 2003). There are also further differences among musicians themselves. Despite engaging in the same basic activity – making music from sound and silence – musicians are a very diverse social group. One important distinction from the music market point of view is between professional and amateur musicians, who often appear to be two subsystems of a larger system (Stebbins, 1997). For example, a study of German rock musicians revealed that nearly half of them did not make any money from playing music; on average they managed to play between five and six gigs in 12 months, and only 6% of groups classified themselves as professional and working only as musicians (Niketta, 1998). Although the main difference is that 'an amateur musician is one who makes music but doesn't get paid for it' (Brandfonbrener, 1994: 61) and 'one whose interest and participation in music is prompted primarily by his love for music and by no ulterior consideration' (Drinker, 1967: 75), research tells us that the differences run deeper than financial rewards. For example, Lotze *et al.* (2003), who studied string players, suggested that there are differences between the brain processes of professional and amateur musicians.

The next question, then, might be what kind of people musicians are. There is a large body of research on the personalities of musicians.

Several different characteristics typical for creative people have been associated with the personalities of classical musicians, such as introversion, independence, sensitivity, anxiety, emotional detachment, exhilaration, dominance, androgyneity, adventurousness, imaginativeness and a propensity to taking risk (Kemp, 1996; Lund and Kranz, 1994). The study of rock and popular musicians, on the other hand, has revealed high levels of neuroticism and openness to experience, which is associated with creativity, imagination, unconventionality, a willingness to embrace new ideas, and below-average agreeableness and conscientiousness (Gillespie and Myors, 2000).

When it comes to musicians being a very diverse social group, Groce (1989) gives us a glimpse of several potential problems. In researching local artists, he observed a clear divide between musicians. Those writing their own music primarily perceived themselves as artists whose creative work was more important than its financial rewards; on the other hand, musicians playing covers were inclined to see musical performance as 'an economic enterprise' and themselves as 'audience-oriented technicians'. Cover musicians were more likely to present themselves as entertainers capable of providing their customers with the music they want to hear, and for those musicians the financial rewards were the primary objective. Original music performers, on the other hand, were found to value the creative process above technical abilities. In other words, Groce's classification differentiates between self-oriented artists focused on composition, and audience-oriented entertainers focused on the repetition of musical texts (Attali, 1985; Mullen, 1987). These two groups are not mutually exclusive, and many musicians would define themselves as both artists and entertainers.

Becoming a musician

People are not born musicians, but rather acquire the skills necessary to become musicians. With the decreasing role of religion and politics, as well as parents as role models, young people reach for music to inform and influence their formation of the self. Nowadays, virtually all young people listen to some kind of music, and some also decide to get involved in playing it. Music becomes an important ingredient in their individual and social identities, and the process of learning music informs and shapes their musical identities. There are two main types of music education, which can be broadly divided into formal and informal education.

Formal music education takes place in regular schools, non-compulsory music schools, and conservatories, and via structured private lessons. The time and effort it takes to train as a competent musician means that achieving success in music entails a life-long commitment to practice and education, which often means that young artists' non-musical opportunities narrow the more they commit themselves to music. This, in turn, impacts on their ability to pursue other employment opportunities in life. Undoubtedly, music requires talent. But even the most talented musicians will not succeed without investing time and effort into developing their skills through practice and rehearsals. Researchers are telling us that there is a strong correlation between the amount of formal practice and musical achievements (Sloboda et al., 1996). It is not only fame and fortune, but, hidden from the eyes of ordinary fans, many years of practice, that are often necessary to achieve a high level of musical competency. For example, top violinists in a conservatory can accumulate up to 10,000 hours of practice by the age of 21 (Ericsson et al., 1993). But hours spent in rehearsals won't guarantee success – practice needs to be highly targeted and focused on relevant skills and elements of performance that require improvement (Williamson and Valentine, 2000). In classical music and jazz, formal education serves as a cultural production and reproduction system, where younger musicians join established bodies such as music schools (e.g. The Juilliard School or The Royal Academy of Music in London) and orchestras, and where working with more accomplished artists allows them to acquire skills and social status among peers. Formal education also provides young artists with self-awareness and an identity as musicians. There is also a large group of successful musicians who can be referred to as 'stage-school' musicians – such people are trained in the music industry, and develop their musical abilities by performing on stage. The BRIT School for Performing Arts & Technology, which is a product of collaboration between the British Government and the British Record Industry Trust, is one of the better-known schools providing young artists with education and vocational training. Some of its former pupils include Adele, Leona Lewis, Jessie J, Amy Winehouse, Katie Melua and The Kooks.

While this kind of formal music education is a pre-requisite for classical musicians, it is often considered too restrictive in other genres. Lack of formal education leads many young musicians to pursue an informal musical education, which is often perceived as a rebellion against parental supervision, society and its institutions. For example, informal musical learning has been observed in hip-hop, where the focus is on intertextuality and the collective nature of the creative process (Fornäs et al., 1995). In addition, rock musicians, as much as young hip-hop artists, tend to follow a more informal learning experience that is focused on groups rather than individual musicians, music and organizational and practical skills such as linguistic training and the development of a personal and social identity (Clawson, 1999; Fornäs et al., 1995). They are often self-taught and acquire skills outside of any formal institutions. For many young people, joining a rock band is a self-defining act In the same way that joining a gang is for others: it provides an outlet for self-expression, gives a sense of belonging and respect, and acts as a substitute for family. A rock band represents a distinctive musical world (Campbell, 1995); young musicians develop their skills by working as a group in which socializing is as important as music, by observing more accomplished artists, and by participating in a community of like-minded individuals. Rock bands are often formed through early social networks, and they tend to be dominated by male musicians (Campbell, 1995). Although informally trained, musicians often try to distance themselves from the ethos and culture associated with formal education; it has been claimed that even rock music has been infected with the Romantic idea of autonomous art, so prevalent in classical and jazz music, for example when young artists educated at British art schools began to emerge through the rock scene (Wicke, 1990).

Following the introduction into professional and semi-professional music, the phrase 'successful career' may have many meanings in the music world, ranging from artists being able to create music to express themselves, through having devoted and loyal fans and followers, signing recording contracts, and earning respect from critics and journalists, to generating large commercial income opportunities. Success can also be subjective (as seen by the musicians themselves), and objective (as perceived by others), often using verifiable measures such as the value of recording contracts, charts and numbers of albums sold). Whether they learn their trade formally or informally, however, musicians' careers often follow similar patterns. Yet individual career trajectories can vary significantly. For some, early stardom leads to quick disappearance from the music scene, while others painstakingly build their careers over decades. Social support, professional attitude, and professional network have been shown to lead to successful music careers (Zwaan et al., 2010). A longitudinal study of pop musicians in the Netherlands showed that all three of these factors were important for stable, successful careers, while musicians with careers that were on the way up were able to achieve more success if their professional attitudes were stronger, and for musicians with careers that were waning, better professional networks guaranteed more success. When it comes to classical composers and film composers, various studies have shown that they tend to achieve their first important success in their late 20s and early 30s, are most productive and make their most important contribution between their late 30s and early 40s, and achieve their last major success in their early 50s (Simonton, 2007). Biographies of successful jazz musicians also reveal several typical career stages from introduction to a national band, through climbing the hierarchical ladder within the band, becoming a bandleader, having their innovations accepted, to a decline due to new artists emerging with their own new styles and innovations (Kirschbaum, 2007).

Being a musician

Throughout history, musicians have been involved in music making in an endless variety of roles, from town musicians, cantors, troubadours, minnesingers, jongleurs and spielleute, to contemporary pop stars and buskers. In the current music industry, the role of the musician is a complex one. Intertwined in a close network of the industry's executives, marketers, A&R people, technicians, journalists and other media professionals, critics and audiences, and, last but not least, other musicians, music makers often assume many of those roles. Beyond being artists and creators, they often have to be entrepreneurs (as most musicians are self-employed), marketers and brand managers, stars, celebrities, composers, producers and performers. It is beyond the scope of this chapter to discuss all of these roles in detail. Musicians operate within a wider production system comprising the main actors, such as artists themselves, their agents and promoters, record labels and studios, and other intermediaries responsible for facilitating the production, distribution and consumption of music.

The literature on being a musician remains very limited. One of the key works exploring the social conditions of musicians in Germany from the Middle Ages up until the 19th century was a socio-historical collection of studies edited by Salmen (1983). This appears to be the only available study focusing solely on the working lives of early professional musicians within the field of the sociology of music. From the 19th century, the self-perception of artists was dominated by the romantic 'art-for-art's-sake' philosophy and a Bohemian ideology (Bradshaw *et al.* 2005; Fillis, 2006). Still highly influential in studies of musicians, the art-for-art's-sake approach saw the existence of art as independent from utilitarian, religious and political contexts (Fillis, 2006), revealing the first signs of tension between musicians and the market. This philosophy gave rise to the belief that artists, and particularly musicians, were creative geniuses existing for their art and above the mundane needs of ordinary human beings, creating the Bohemian 'stereotype of the artist as starving, deviant, alcoholic, suicidal undiscovered genius' (Bradshaw *et al.*, 2005: 221) and the romantic association between poverty and artistic achievement (Baumol and Bowen, 1965). Both the art-for-art's-sake philosophy and the Bohemian ideology proved to be influential in theorizing about musicians throughout the 20th century. In the 20th century, published work about musicians can be broadly classified as representing two major schools of thought: the Frankfurt School of Critical Theory and the Chicago School.

The work of the highly influential Frankfurt School, in particular researchers such as Theodor Adorno, Max Horkheimer and Walter Benjamin, dominated the field from the early 1920s. Within their study of culture, they were primarily concerned with the criticism of the mass media, its role in contemporary society, and their debilitating effect on people's ability to think individually and critically. In their *Dialectic of Enlightenment* (1973), Adorno and Horkheimer portrayed the culture industry as reflecting wider society and the capitalist culture. Mass culture, their argument ran, driven by financial profit and the repetition of well-established canons, led to the replacement of art by mass-consumed entertainment. Adorno argued that culture was just one more industry manufacturing standardized products, for example songs, which had to match the expectations of the mass market and generate profits (Negus, 1995). Adorno's work was often seen as a defence of high culture, although he himself argued that the origins of classical music and jazz arose out of the culture industry and were for him 'coopted, standardised and adapted for distribution on the commercial market' (Negus, 1995: 319). The main limitation of theorists such as Adorno, Horkheimer or Benjamin is that although they provided a very critical discussion of the industrialization of the arts, their work did not stretch to actually include a consideration of the working lives of artists.

The work of the Frankfurt School's researchers appears to be still relevant to today's discussion on the art-versus-money dichotomy, with some authors arguing that 'entertainment culture now occupies the centre ground of society, while classic middle-class culture is in a peripheral position together with avant-garde culture and folk culture' (Smart, 1999: 140). Similar to the Frankfurt School researchers, music theorist Jacques Attali (1985) saw music as a kind of mirror held up to a society, which encouraged repetitive mass production of increasingly uniform cultural products, eroding any differences between them. However, he questioned the Frankfurt School approach, arguing that music may also be a form of 'prophecy', with musicians venturing into the unknown to challenge the existing boundaries of society and its rules.

Another significant contribution to the discussion on musicians in the 20th century was made by one of the key representatives of the Chicago School – Howard Becker. From his seminal work exploring jazz musicians as a deviant group (Becker, [1963] 1997) emerged a picture of artists influenced in their thinking by the above-mentioned romantic discourses and the art-versus-money dilemma. The isolation of musicians from a larger society led to them describing themselves as 'cats', and non-musicians and the conventional society making commercial demands on them as 'squares'.

Today, the inherent conflict that many musicians face – the conflict between artistic ambitions and financial rewards, the conflict between arts and the market – still appears to be as relevant as before. Although most professional musicians are trained (formally or informally, as mentioned earlier) in their trade, and possess the skills to compose, produce and perform music, the music market requires them to become entrepreneurs, marketers and brand managers, stars and celebrities. The majority of musicians nowadays are self-employed, and although they may not always like it they are entrepreneurs running a music business under their own name, and have to manage their health insurance and taxes, create their (musical) product, promote themselves and deal with their customers. Their everyday life as a musical entrepreneur (or a 'musicpreneur' (Kubacki and Croft, 2011)) also makes them marketers and brand managers, as in order to survive as professional musicians they need to identify their unique artistic values and products which will appeal to the market (regardless of whether they are in search of commercial opportunities or public patronage), and clearly communicate these to the target audience (e.g. fans, concert-goers, booking agents and promoters). Most commercially successful musicians employ music managers (sometimes called artist managers, band managers or talent managers) or music management companies to manage their affairs for them. Some examples of well-known managers include Brian Epstein, often called the 'Fifth Beatle'; Albert Grossman, who managed Bob Dylan, Janis Joplin and John Lee Hooker; and, more recently, Louis Walsh, who has managed groups like Westlife, Boyzone and Girls Aloud. Managing their careers themselves or with help from others, successful musicians become stars and celebrities, who are worshipped by their fans (see Chapter 8 on fans and fandom), attracting media attention and recording and commercial contracts worth millions of dollars, and becoming tempting targets for other brands trying to use musicians to reach out to their consumers and get a slice of their credibility for their products.

There is a growing body of knowledge that attempts to understand the relationship between contemporary musicians and the music market in the context of the long-standing debate regarding the art-versus-money dichotomy (Holbrook, 2005). This work reflects an attempt to come to terms with the problem of being an artistically and financially successful artist in a world where 'having' defines 'being', and the music market is driven by charts and initiatives such as *X-Factor*, rather than long-term talent identification and development. Increasingly, it has been argued, musicians are promoted as commoditized products in a race in which the media focuses on image rather than music (Sanjek and Sanjek, 1991). Musicians, who are influenced by multinational record labels, torn between their artistic integrity and commercial necessity, and threatened by the danger of decreasing fan bases and diminishing sales, are often reluctant to take any artistic risk as a consequence (Miles, 2000). This is an important and timely problem, as in the 20th century 'most [… music industry] successes relied on not only quality repertoire and artistry, but also on patient artist development' (Goldstuck, 2001: 50). Artistic identities can be a source of conflict in a less commercially driven environment, as in the example of the musicians' strike at the Atlanta Symphony Orchestra (Glynn, 2000), where artistic qualities clashed with economic reality. Nowadays, musicians are often faced with a choice between artistically fulfilling work and engaging in the creation of music that will be more commercially rewarding. There is, though, an ever-growing group of contemporary musicians who balance their career between the demands made by both camps using the financial and symbolic resources that come with the contemporary music industry.

Musical hierarchies and authenticity

From the early studies of musicians by Becker (1951) and Stebbins (1966), one can observe strong hierarchies among musicians, with, for example, jazz musicians looking down at more commercially driven musicians. More formally, such as in classical music, the conductor imposes an artistic vision on the orchestra, for example, and string quartets have their first violinist as the leader, whose part often dominates the performance, and leaves the remaining musicians to fulfil very specific roles (Murnigham and Conlon, 1991). Strong hierarchies among musicians also elevate those who create music above those who merely perform music composed by someone else (Groce, 1989). Original music performers express themselves through their music, earning artistic credibility and respect, while musicians who perform music composed by others and try to appeal to mass markets end up at the bottom of the musical hierarchy (Cook, 1998), as they are often seen as manufactured and inauthentic. The relationship between music creator and performer is one of the most complex in the music industry. In what Eckstein (2009) calls 'the art music world', which mostly includes classical music, the priority is given to the composer as the creative genius (who is even more important than the lyricist – while Mozart is a household brand, only the greatest classical music aficionados remember Lorenzo da Ponte, the librettist behind his three greatest operas). Authenticity of performance is judged based on the similarity with the written text, the composer's intentions, and what is recognized by experts and critics as stylistic correctness. In popular music, on the other hand, performers are prioritized over creators of music, and are marketed as the key ingredients in the popular music industry. Public recognition is mostly given to performers, and the creators of music are either known only to the biggest fans, or remain completely hidden in the background (for example, while Dionne Warwick and Dusty Springfield are household names, Burt Bacharach is less known to wider audiences). Hence, the interpretation dominates over the musical text.

Authenticity is one of the key issues in the music industry. It is often used to make value judgements about a particular musician or a piece of music, locate musicians in a musical hierarchy, and serve as a 'defence against commercialization' represented by manufactured bands such as, for example, the Monkees, the Backstreet Boys and the Spice Girls (Leach, 2001; Stahl, 2002; Jamieson, 2007). Although the overwhelming majority of contemporary music is an outcome of a complex process, with inputs from a variety of people identified at the beginning of this chapter, , artists and artistic integrity remain the main creative force of the music industry. So-called authentic and artistically valuable music is presented in opposition to fake, commercially driven and mass-produced music. Perceived authenticity is a desired property in music, by both artists and audiences, yet the universal markers of authenticity are hard to identify. Most commonly, the more commercially successful the artist is, the harder it is for them to make a claim to authenticity, as there is a belief that mass-produced music does not allow for authentic artistic expression. When it comes to contemporary music artists, Keightley (2001) distinguishes two main ways by which to claim authenticity and artistic credibility: romantic authenticity and modernist authenticity. Romantic authenticity evolved from folk music and involves disassociating oneself with the music industry through minimalistic use of technology and the creation of highly emotional, expressive and often confessional music, which is performed as an authentic representation of the artist's experience (e.g. Bulat Okudzhava, Bob Dylan). A recent example of romantic authenticity is Hirschman's (2010) ethnography of the Appalachian producers of bluegrass music, which explores the music's roots in the community from which it emerges and its uncommercialized purity and authenticity. Modernist authenticity, on the other hand, elevates technology and experimentation as the main forms of artistic expression, which can be alienating in its elitism and semantic complexity.

Musical identities

Musical identities develop through a complex process of interactions between musical adepts and other members of the music industry, including teachers, musical gurus and authorities, and audiences. Young musicians develop their artistic language by studying music, and interacting with the market through their commercial selves. Since the work of Adorno and Becker, relatively little empirical research has been conducted into musicians' relationship with the market, with only a handful of studies coming from outside of the USA. For example, in Groce's (1989) work, musicians writing their own music perceived themselves primarily as artists, whose creative work was more important than its financial rewards; these musicians looked down on more commercially driven musicians. They valued their artistic reputation much more highly than any monetary value of their work. On the other hand, artists playing covers were inclined to see musical performance as an economic enterprise, and themselves as audience-oriented technicians, who were forced to perform other people's music in order to move up the career ladder and become more commercially successful (Groce, 1989). Juniu et al.'s (1996) analysis of the views of professional and amateur musicians echoed some of Groce's findings, and revealed that while amateur musicians perceived both rehearsals and performances as leisure activities, professional musicians viewed them as work, and were 'motivated primarily by the pay-off' (1989: 44). In a study by Frith and Horne (1987), British pop musicians' self-identities were investigated; here, romantic discourses were identified in their anti-market attitudes. Finally, Cottrell's (2002) work with professional musicians in London explored the relationship between economic and music capitals, reminding us of the importance of the art-versus-money dilemma in musicians' working lives.

Recently, several studies have emerged that have investigated the identities of musicians in Britain (MacDonald and Wilson, 2005; Dennis and Macaulay, 2006), France (Madiot, 1996), and Poland (Kubacki and Croft, 2011). A lot of this new work appears to be a natural extension of the earlier work of the Frankfurt School and Becker into the contemporary music market. For example, Macdonald and Wilson (2005: 405) looked into the musical identities of jazz musicians and reported that their respondents often played unfulfilling gigs for money only because that was a 'part of being a musician'. In another recent study conducted by Bradshaw et al. (2005: 234), the experience of musicians performing live music in bars and cafés and for corporate entertainment was investigated and the respondents divided into two groups: musicians who 'succeed[ed] in gaining the attention of the audience', and those who did not. The latter group perceived their gigs as rehearsals and opportunities to earn money. Bradshaw and Holbrook (2007), in a recent study examining the life and work of Chet Baker, showed how audience demands, influenced by Romantic ideas and the art-versus-money dichotomy, may lead to the self-destruction of artists. However, arguments for studying jazz's great men were rejected by Hollerbach (2004: 156), who, in his study of local jazz musicians, accused researchers who focused exclusively on jazz stars of reductionism and thereby of misrepresenting the jazz world:

> 'they ignore – and therefore dismiss – the many musicians who labour in relative obscurity on jazz scenes worldwide and thus maintain the music's viability through a multidimensional act of commitment no less intense than that of those documented, "real" jazz musicians of jazz historiography'.

And although jazz seems to be the most fertile ground for studying musical identities, there is also research looking into other genres. Keyes (2000), for example, distinguishes four categories of female rappers, and considers them as representatives of African American women in contemporary urban culture: *Queen Mother* emphasizes African heritage and demands respect for African women, *Fly Girl* and its construction centres on being chic and fashionable, *Sista with Attitude* perceives attitude as a way to empowerment, and *Lesbian* includes artists who write about lesbian lifestyle.

Music groups

So far, the discussion has largely focused on musicians as individuals. However, performing music is a social activity, which may also be studied in the context of the interaction between either musicians and their audience, or musicians themselves. In the final section of this chapter the attention turns to the complexities involved in groups of musicians working together. Musical groups, like any other social groups, have their own identities, structures, hierarchies, ideologies, processes, artefacts and rituals. There are many types of musical groups, from manufactured pop groups and boy- and girl-bands put together by a record company to deliberately fill a gap in the market and achieve financial success (e.g. the Spice Girls, Girls Aloud), through garage rock groups put together by young and aspiring musicians (e.g. Arctic Monkeys, The Libertines), to supergroups formed by already successful rock musicians (e.g. SuperHeavy with Mick Jagger, Velvet Revolver). Some groups of musicians, for example many rock bands, often stay together throughout their career. Others, like jazz musicians, tend to perform with different groups, under different names, and in different configurations – even on the same evening. Playing jazz music has often been compared to a conversation in which musical ideas are exchanged, and which do not require stable membership as each musician is an individual artist in their own right (Wilson and MacDonald, 2005). Musical groups are also an organizational microcosm, with all their internal strengths and weaknesses, and external opportunities and threats. In the face of conflict between one's artistic individuality and a sense of belonging to a group, their success depends on their ability to work together off-stage and interact musically on-stage.

Musicians working as a group are crucial in the socio-cultural construction of rock music, where a band is recognized as a main creative unit (Clawson, 1999). Yet the abilities of often very individualistic, ego-driven and extravagant musicians to work together throw many challenges at musical groups. Musicians stay loyal to a band for many reasons, from commercial success to difficulties with solo careers. Conflicts between characters may be one reason behind breakups, but more technical issues can also present themselves as a challenge. One of the key skills in musical groups is the ability to work together, the so-called 'listening ability' (Adorno, 1962). Sicca (2000), for example, talks about the ability that musicians must have to listen to themselves and adjust their playing, but also about musicians' ability to listen to other musicians. A lack of any of these abilities can impede the work of any artistic group. The history of music is full of breakups caused by difficult personalities (Oasis), solo ambitions (Diana Ross and The Supremes), illness and addiction (Blondie), lawsuits (Boston), disputes over royalties (N.W.A), interference from third persons (Yoko Ono, who is often criticized for her role in the breakup of the Beatles), the death of a frontman (Jim Morrison and The Doors), and the manager's suicide (Husker Du). The glue that holds a group together, beyond commercial success, might come from a sense of togetherness, collective consciousness, or shared culture and values. Therefore, one may argue, regardless of genre, ideological cohesiveness and a similar level of musical ability facilitates bands' survival. Although this is usually associated with rock, similar aspects (though expressed somewhat differently) have been identified in the field of classically trained and formally educated musicians in Brodsky's (2006) study of an English orchestra: opportunities to socialize with like-minded people, camaraderie, teamwork, solidarity and friendship. It is important to note, however, that the life of a professional orchestra also brings many bitter moments, including long periods spent away from home touring, which can lead to romantic and sexual liaisons that may result in many tensions, as well as late working hours (e.g. performances), which make it difficult to have a private life, a family, or a social life. Low pay, few permanent positions, a reliance on public funding and uncertainty regarding the future in many professional orchestras means that musicians often have to take additional jobs playing in different bands, teaching or working outside the music industry.

Conflicts between musicians can also lead to frequent changes in band membership. In Lankford's (1997: 40) words, 'Nothing is as unstable as a band ... The slightest unresolved argument can wreck months of work'. One of the problems facing each group is the paradox of identity (Smith and Berg, 1987), with each group member and the group itself trying to create a unique identity that is shared and co-constructed by all. An individual musician must become a part of the group, but the group must also be an integral element of each musician's individual identity. Conflicting identities within a group, and creative, artistic and commercial differences, can easily cause a break-up, and need to be managed carefully (Ferguson, 2002). Although band break-ups are complex issues, each is unique and different, and there is usually a wide range of factors that contributes to them; for example, in jazz and classical music conflicts are more likely to occur at the creative level, while in rock they tend to have a more ideological character. In reality, both types of disagreements, creative and ideological, are, at least in part, likely to cause trouble in musical groups, and frequently spark the processes that lead to breakups. The same pressures identified at the beginning of this chapter, such as financial troubles, limited work opportunities, artistic and commercial pressure, stress associated with performance, and a culture of intoxication and drug abuse (Brodsky, 1995; Raeburn, 1987), impact musicians' abilities to stay and work together. While in classical music, according to Murningham and Conlon's (1991) research, successful string quartets were able to resolve their conflicts by simply exercising compromise or playing more and talking less, this is not always sufficient in genres such as rock. In chamber music, on the other hand, which represents an early form of counter-culture created outside any traditional institutional attachments, all musicians, working without a conductor, equally share the responsibility for their work (Sicca, 2000). Therefore, musicians become a creative task group responsible for managing their artistic productions.

Summary

This chapter has illustrated the many dimensions and aspects of becoming and remaining a musician in contemporary society and the music industry. At the beginning of the chapter some of the difficulties in defining musicians were noted, along with the many different ways they engage in the production of music. The discussion then explored how formal and informal learning shape the worldviews and careers of musicians, and also considered the conflict between the arts and the market, and the role of this in our understanding of musicians and their hierarchies, identities and work. Finally, consideration was also given to some of the issues surrounding musicians in groups, from rock groups, through jazz ensembles, to orchestras.

References

Adorno, T.W. (1962) *Einleitung in die Musiksoziologie. Zwölf Theoretische Vorlesungen*, Frankfurt am Main: Suhrkamp Verlag.

Adorno, T.W. and Horkheimer, M. (1973) *Dialectic of Enlightenment*, trans. John Cumming, London: Allen Lane.

Attali, J. (1985) *Noise: The Political Economy of Music*, trans. Brian Massumi, Minneapolis: University of Minnesota Press.

Bain, A. (2005) 'Constructing an artistic identity', *Work, Employment and Society*, 19 (1), 25-46.

Baumol, W.J. and Bowen, W.G. (1965) 'On the performing arts: the anatomy of their economic problems', *The American Economic Review*, 55 (1/2), 495-502.

Becker, H. (1951) 'The professional dance musician and his audience', *American Journal of Sociology*, **57** (2), 136-144.

Becker, H. (1997) *Outsiders: Studies in Sociology of Deviance*, new ed., New York, NY: Simon & Schuster Ltd.

Bradshaw, A., and Holbrook, M.B. (2007) 'Remembering Chet: theorising the mythology of the self-destructive bohemian artist as self-producer and self-consumer in the market for romanticism', *Marketing Theory*, **7** (2), 115-136.

Bradshaw, A., McDonagh, P., Marshall, D. and Bradshaw, H. (2005) '"Exiled music herself, pushed to the edge of existence": the experience of musicians who perform background music', *Consumption, Markets and Culture*, **8** (3), 219-239. Brandfonbrener, A.G. (1994) 'Just what is an "amateur" musician?', *Medical Problems of Performing Artists*, **9** (3), 61-62.

Brodsky, M. (1995) 'Blues musicians' access to health care', *Medical Problems of Performing Artists*, **10** (1), 18-23.

Brodsky, W. (2006) 'In the wings of British orchestras: A multi-episode interview study among symphony players', *Journal of Occupational and Organizational Psychology*, **79**, 673-690.

Burgoyne, N. (1990) 'Status of the artist information session', *Art Bulletin*, **14**, 28-30.

Campbell, P.S. (1995) 'Of garage bands and song-getting: the musical development of young rock-musicians', *Research Studies in Music Education*, **4**, 12-20.

Clawson, M.A. (1999) 'Masculinity and skill acquisition in adolescent rock band', *Popular Music*, **18** (1), 99-114.

Cook, N. (1998) *Music: A Very Short Introduction*, Oxford: Oxford University Press.

Cottrell, S. (2002) 'Music as capital: deputising among London's freelance musicians', *British Journal of Ethnomusicology*, **11** (ii), 61-80.

Csikszentmihalyi, M. (1996) *Creativity*, New York: HarperCollins.

Dennis, N. and Macaulay, M. (2006) 'Marketing and jazz – the views of leading jazz musicians', *Proceedings of the Academy of Marketing Conference*, Middlesex University Business School, London, 3-6 July.

Drinker, H.S. (1967) 'Amateurs and music', *Music Education Journal*, **9**, 75-78.

Eckstein, L. (2009) 'Torpedoing the authorship of popular music: a reading of Gorillaz' "Feel Good Inc."', *Popular Music*, **28** (2), 239-255.

Ericsson, K.A., Tesch-Romer, C. and Krampe, R.T. (1993) 'The role of practice and motivation in the acquisition of expert-level performance in real life: an empirical evaluation of a theoretical framework', in Howe, M.J.A. (ed.), *Encouraging the Development of Exceptional Abilities and Talents*, Leicester: The British Psychological Society.

Ferguson, H. (2002) 'In search of bandhood: consultation with original music groups', *Group*, **26**, 4, 267 282.

Fillis, I. (2006) 'Art for art's sake or art for business sake: An exploration of artistic product orientation', *The Marketing Review*, **6** (1), 29-40.

Fornäs, J., Lindberg, U. and Sernhede, O. (1995) *In Garageland: Rock, Youth and Modernity*, London: Routledge.

Frith, S. and Horne, H. (1987) *Art into Pop*, London: Methuen & Co.

Gaser, Ch. and Schlaug, G. (2003) 'Brain structures differ between musicians and non-musicians', *The Journal of Neuroscience*, **23** (27), 9240-9245.

Gillespie, W. and Myors, B. (2000) 'Personality of rock musicians', *Psychology of Music*, **28**, 154-165.

Glynn, M.A. (2000) 'When cymbals become symbols: conflict over organizational identity within a symphony orchestra', *Organization Science*, **11** (3), 285-298.

Goldstuck, C. (2001) 'Industry must act now to prosper', *Music Business International*, **11** (6), 50.

Gray, C.M. (1986) 'The economics of arts labor markets: an overview', *Artists and Cultural Consumers*, in Shaw, D.V., Hendon, W.S. and Waits, C.R. (ed.), *Proceedings of the Fourth International Conference on Cultural Economics*, Avignon, France: Association for Cultural Economics, **III**, 66-76.

Groce, S.B. (1989) 'Occupational rhetoric and ideology: a comparison of copy and original music performers', *Qualitative Sociology*, **12** (4), 391-410.

Hirschman, E.C. (2010) 'Bluegrass revival. Marketing and authenticity in the hill of Appalachia', in O'Reilly, D. and Kerrigan, F. (ed.) *Marketing the Arts: a Fresh Approach*, London: Routledge, 171-189.

Holbrook, M.B. (2005) 'Art versus commerce as a macromarketing theme in three films from the young-man-with-a-horn genre', *Journal of Macromarketing*, **25** (1), 22-31.

Hollerbach, P. (2004) '(Re)voicing tradition: improvising aesthetics and identity on local jazz scenes', *Popular Music*, **23** (2), 155-171.

Jamieson, D. (2007) 'Marketing androgyny: the evolution of the Backstreet Boys', *Popular Music*, **26** (2), 245-258.

Juniu, S., Tedrick, T. and Boyd, R. (1996) 'Leisure or work?: amateur and professional musicians' perception of rehearsal and performance', *Journal of Leisure Research*, **28** (1), 44-56.

Keightley, K. (2001) 'Reconsidering rock', in Frith, S. and Straw, W. and Street, J. (ed.), *The Cambridge Companion to Pop and Rock,* Cambridge: Cambridge University Press, 109-142.

Keister, J. and Smith, J.L. (2008) 'Musical ambition, cultural accreditation and the nasty side of progressive rock', *Popular Music*, **27** (3), 433-455.

Kemp, A.E. (1996) *The Musical Temperament: Psychology and Personality of Musicians*, Oxford: Oxford University Press.

Keyes, C.J. (2000) 'Empowering self, making choices, creating spaces: black female identity via rap music performance', *The Journal of American Folklore*, **113** (449), 255-269.

Kirschbaum, C. (2007) 'Careers in the right beat: US jazz musicians' typical and non-typical trajectories', *Career Development International*, **12** (2), 187-201.

Kubacki, K. and Croft, R. (2011) 'Markets, music and all that jazz', *European Journal of Marketing,* **45** (5), 805-821.

Lankford, M. (1997) *Life in Double Time: Confessions of an American Drummer*, San Francisco: Chronicle Books.

Leach, E.E. (2001) 'Vicars of 'Wannabe': authenticity and the Spice Girls', *Popular Music*, **20** (2), 143-167.

Lotze M., Scheler G., Tan H.R., Braun C. and Birbaumer N. (2003) 'The musician's brain: functional imaging of amateurs and professionals during performance and imagery', *Neuroimage*, **20**, 1817-1829.

Lund, N.L. and Kranz, P.L. (1994) 'Notes on emotional components of musical creativity and performance', *Journal of Psychology,* **128**, 635-640. MacDonald, R.A.R. and Wilson, G.B. (2005) 'Musical identities of professional jazz musicians: a focus group investigation', *Psychology of Music*, **33** (4), 395-417.

Madiot, B. (1996) 'Identité sociale et positionnement dans le champ professionel: le cas des musiciens de jazz', *Les Cahiers Internationaux de Psychologie Sociale*, **32**, 33-53.

Meamber, L.A. (2000) 'Artist becomes/becoming artistic: the artist as producer-consumer', *Advances in Consumer Research*, **27**, 44-49.

Miles, S. (2000) *Consumerism as a Way of Life*, London: Sage Publications.

Mullen, K. (1987) 'Audience orientation and the occupational rhetoric of public house performers', *Popular Music and Society*, **11**, 15-29.

Murnighan, J.K. and Conlon, D.E. (1991) 'The dynamics of intense work groups: A study of British string quartets', *Administrative Science Quarterly*, **36**, 165-186.

Nagel, J.J. (1988) 'Identity and career choice in music', *Journal of Cultural Economics*, **12** (2), 67-76.

Negus, K. (1995) 'Where the mystical meets the market: creativity and commerce in the production of popular music', *Sociological Review*, **43** (2), 316-341.

Niketta, R. (1998) 'Rock musicians in Germany and ideas for their promotion', *Popular Music*, **17** (3), 311-325.

O'Reilly, D. and Kubacki, K. (2009) 'Arts marketing is what you can get away with', *Zeszyty Naukowe Politechniki Rzeszowskiej (Folia Scientiarum Universitatis Technicae Resoviensis): Zarządzanie i Marketing*, **260** (16), 125-131.

Oxford English Dictionary (2012) 'Musician', Available online: http://oxforddictionaries.com/definition/musician?q=musician, [Accessed: 10 May 2012].

Raeburn, S.D. (1987) 'Occupational stress and coping in a sample of rock musicians', *Medical Problems of Performing Artists*, **2** (2), 41-48.

Salmen, W. (ed.) (1983) *The Social Status of the Professional Musicians for the Middle Ages to the 19th Century*, New York: Paragon Press.

Sanjek, R. and Sanjek, D. (1991) *American Popular Music Business in the 20th Century*, Oxford: Oxford University Press.

Seifert, M. and Hadiba, A.L. (2006) 'Facilitating talent selection decisions in the music industry', *Management Decision*, **44** (6), 790-808.

Sicca, L.M. (2000) 'Chamber music and organisation theory: Some typical organisational phenomena seen under the microscope', *Studies in Cultures, Organizations and Societies*, **6**, 145-168.

Sichivitsa, V.O. (2007) 'The influences of parents, teachers, peers and other factors on students' motivation in music', *Research Studies in Music Education*, **29**, 55-68.

Simonton, D.K. (2007) 'Cinema composers: career trajectories for creative productivity in film music', *Psychology of Aesthetics, Creativity, and the Arts*, **1** (3), 160-169.

Sloboda, J.A., Davidson, J.W., Howe, M.J.A. and Moore, D.G. (1996) 'The role of practice in the development of professional musicians', *British Journal of Psychology*, **87**, 287-309.

Smart, B. (ed.) (1999) *Resisting McDonaldization*, London: Sage Publications.

Smith, K. and Berg, D. (1987), *Paradoxes of Group Life*, San Francisco: Jossey-Bass.

Söderman, J. and Folkestad, G. (2004) 'How hip-hop musicians learn: strategies in informal creative music making', *Music Education Research*, **6** (3), 313-326.

Stahl, M. (2002) 'Authentic boy bands on TV? Performers and impresarios in The Monkees and Making the Band', *Popular Music*, 21 (3), 307-329.

Stebbins, R. (1966) 'Class, status and power among commercial jazz musicians, *Sociological Quarterly*, **7**, 197-213.

Stebbins, R.A. (1977) 'The amateur: two sociological definitions', *Pacific Sociological Review*, **20**, 582-606.

Taylor, J. (1987) 'Tango', *Cultural Anthropology*, **2** (4), 481-493.

Wassall, G.H. and Alper, N. (1984) 'Determinants of artists' earnings', in Hendon, W.S., Grant, N.K. and Shaw, D.V. (ed.), *The Economics of Cultural Industries*, Proceedings of the Third International Conference on Cultural Economics, 1, 213-230.

Wicke, P. (1990) *Rock Music: Culture, Aesthetics and Sociology*, Cambridge: Cambridge University Press.

Wilson, G.B. and MacDonald, R.A.R. (2005) 'The meaning of the blues: musical identities in talk about jazz', *Qualitative Research in Psychology*, **2**, pp. 341-363.

Williamson, A. and Valentine, E. (2000) 'Quantity and quality of musical practice as predictors of performance quality', *British Journal of Psychology*, **91**, 353-376.

van Elderem, P.L. (1984) 'Music and meaning behind the Dykes: the new wave of Dutch rock groups and their audiences', *Popular Music*, **4**, 97-116.

Zwaan, K., ter Bogt, T. F. M. and Raaijmakers, Q.A.W. (2010) 'Career trajectories of Dutch pop musicians: A longitudinal study', *Journal of Vocational Behaviour*, **77**, 10-20.

5 Music Brands

Introduction

Fender Stratocasters, Steinway grand pianos, Marshall amplifiers, the iPod – these are all brands associated with the music business in one way or another. However, in addition to these product brands, there is regular talk within the music industry of pop idols, rock icons, pop stars, jazz greats, rock gods, legendary opera singers, cult bands, guitar heroes, stellar performances, trademark sounds, signature tunes, classic albums, breakthrough singles, rock 'n' roll myths, anthemic songs, breakout/breakthrough recordings, and – of course – hype. These terms have in common the signification of some kind of, or some claim to, cultural distinction. From a marketing point of view, this kind of talk fits very easily into the strategic notion of positioning, as well as the discourse of branding.

Branding is a discourse which (primarily) marketing practitioners and scholars have developed to talk about the symbolic or cultural aspects of business. Commentators in other disciplines have also contributed to the discussion about branding (Lury, 2004; Arvidsson, 2005). However, in this book, the initial focus is on the marketing perspective, with the discussion broadening out in Chapter 6 to take in a perspective which is closer to cultural studies. There are several reasons for an extended treatment of branding in this book.

First, a discussion of branding is important in the context of the book's intended purpose, because branding is closely associated with the strategic marketing notion of 'positioning' (see Chapter 1). Positioning is about winning the battle for the consumer's mind (Ries and Trout, 1981), i.e. developing a brand image that works for musicians, their managers or agents, and their record labels, a practice on which a lot of time and money are spent in the music business.

Second, branding terminology is regularly used, particularly within the more commercially oriented areas of music, and it is important to gain a clear understanding of what is intended by such use. Scholarly research around brands and branding has developed an extensive range of terms, and an understanding of these and their referential scope can help non-marketing scholars and practitioners to understand where branding proponents obtain their ideas, and what purpose these ideas serve.

However, this chapter reflects also on a number of challenges which complicate the application of branding to music. These include issues around important characteristics of music itself (aural, social, cultural), the number of different stakeholders involved in musical projects, the complexity and continually changing nature of music production, marketing and consumption practices, and problems with brand discourse (including its commercial tone, its multi-strandedness, the indiscriminate application of the term 'brand' to everything, and branding proponents' lack of linguistic reflexivity – the fact that those who speak about 'branding' are not always clear on what they mean).

Cultural branding

The notion of 'cultural brands' is gaining currency in marketing. However, the phrase is at risk of appearing tautological, because all brands or signs are cultural by definition. Nevertheless, the idea of cultural branding has taken root, and it is worthwhile to set down a number of specific ways in which one may construe it. In his book on cultural branding, Holt (2004) develops the idea of 'how brands become icons'. He uses a number of case studies to argue that certain products acquire an identity value which makes them iconic (Apple, Coke, Harley, Bud). According to Holt's line of thinking, iconic brands address acute contradictions in society and perform identity myths that address these desires and anxieties. These identity myths reside in the brand, which consumers experience and share via ritual action, and are set in populist worlds. The brands serve as activists, leading culture by relying on breakthrough performances rather than consistent communications, and enjoy a cultural halo effect. Setting aside the commercial associations of the above brands, within the area of music several iconic artists can be identified who fit the profile that Holt has outlined to different degrees and in different contexts; for example, Bob Dylan, Green Day, or Edith Piaf.

More generally, one may take cultural branding as:

1   the idea that in order to understand branding one needs to understand brands as cultural signs;

2   the idea that corporations 'brand' (shape, form, mark) people through the creation of organizational 'cultures' and so on;

3   the idea that corporations create cultural artefacts when they make products (iPod), or promotional cultures when they carry out marketing communications campaigns;

4   the practices of appropriating, co-opting or commodifying culture by means of capitalistic interventions such as music sponsorship (e.g. Tommy Hilfiger and the Rolling Stones, or Blackberry and U2), celebrity endorsement (Madonna and GAP), or product placement (e.g. rappers' lyrics); and

5   the practices whereby arts/heritage organizations use cultural strategies to promote their offerings.

Art brands and music brands

Within marketing, there is a sub-field known as arts marketing (O'Reilly and Kerrigan, 2010; O'Reilly, 2012; O'Reilly et al. (forthcoming)). This strand of work has to do with the application of marketing theory to the arts, but also – far more broadly – with the relationship between the arts and commerce. There is still relatively little work on arts branding, a couple of exceptions being Schroeder (2006), who discusses branding in the context of the production and consumption of artistic images and offers an artist case study to explore the relationship between branding, consumption and art, and O'Reilly and Kerrigan (2013), who offer a conceptual framework for the analysis of the film brandscape, which can be adapted to music.

Although this work has been conducted within the broader area of arts branding, very little scholarly work has gone into presenting specific theories on the notion of music brands. There are a number of possible reasons for this. These include antipathy to commercial ideology within some areas of the music industry, the broad referential scope of the term 'brand', the complexity of music production, communication and consumption practices, and the muddled nature, and indeed often the linguistic redundancy, of branding discourse. In other words, there are two challenges to the development of a branding theory for music; namely, the complex set of players, offerings and practices within the music domain, and the rather clunky discourse which promoters of branding have developed. In fact, one of the major problems with branding is its marketing proponents' lack of reflexivity about the language and politics of branding practices. These points are considered in due course below. Firstly, however, consideration is given to a managerial view of branding and how it might be applied to the domain of music.

Mainstream ideas of music branding

Over the past half-century or so, brand managers, consultants and scholars have outlined an extensive range of constructs in the domain of branding. Apart from the notion of 'brand' itself, an extensive range of nouns have been paired with the word 'brand', including advocate, asset, awareness, community, culture, equity, essence, experience, heritage, icon, identity, image, leverage, loyalty, magic, passion, personality, power, recall, recognition, relationship, spirit, story/narrative, symbol, value, values, and so on.

In addition, the idea is commonly voiced in the media that everything is a brand, and indeed that everyone is a brand. When considering the idea, beloved of advertising agencies and branding consultants, that everything is a brand, leaving aside ideological issues around neo-liberal ideology, commercialism, and consumerism, and using conventional brand-speak, several different types of brands might be identified within music, as indicated in Table 3:

Table 3: Different kinds of music brands

Type of brands	Example
Performer/artist	Lady Gaga, Kurt Cobain, Kiss, Mozart
Content provider/ media	Record labels, radio and TV stations, websites – e.g. MTV, YouTube, Classic FM
Cultural intermediary	Record producers
Manager	Managers, such as Led Zeppelin's Peter Grant
Distributor	Rough Trade
Promoter	Live Nation
Event	Music festivals, e.g. Glastonbury, SXSW, Roskilde, Glyndeborne
Award	Hall of Fame, Grammy
Venue	Brixton Academy, Rock City, The O2, The Fillmore, CBGBs, Shea Stadium
Character/personae	Artists' personae, e.g.: Bowie's 'Aladdin Sane'; Madonna's 'Material Girl'
Instrument	Marshall, Yamaha, Les Paul
Component	Riffs, hooks in particular musical texts

At a simplistic level, it is possible to regard anything in music as if it were a brand and then apply brand terminology to it. For example, brand managers can talk about Beethoven's brand legacy, Live Nation's brand image, Lady Gaga's brand equity, Pink's brand leverage, the Bruce Springsteen brand's authenticity, Kraftwerk's brand relationship with its fans, Glyndeborne's brand personality, Rolling Stones fans' brand loyalty, Slash's brand profile, Oasis' brand DNA, the Hacienda brand experience, Sony Music Entertainment's brand reputation, Schoenberg's brand resonance, Mussorgsky's brand awareness rating, Santana's brand identity, and so on. However, if one removed the word 'brand' from the above passage, arguably the sense of the phrases would change little. This redundancy is a feature of branding discourse, which has grown by associating itself with, or piggybacking on, extant discourses.

The following question then arises: why bother with branding discourse if it is not really adding to the conversation? The answer lies in the ubiquity of managerially driven branding ideas and talk – 'brandthink' and 'brandspeak'. Brandthink is being used to contest or win everyday business and cultural arguments. A theory of music marketing – or indeed the marketing of any offering within the creative and cultural industries – needs to get to grips with branding and find a way of dealing with or challenging it in both practice and theory.

Before moving further, it is necessary to consider a few basic points about brands and branding. 'Brand' can be read as a narrow, commercially toned word for what should more broadly be understood as a sign. In the cultural and creative industries, and in the arts and entertainment sector, it is the culture, the art, the entertainment practices and their signs (meanings) which must be respected and analysed in cultural terms. This is not to say that the commercial meanings and implications of music marketing are unimportant. An analytical stance which acknowledges both the commercial and cultural/ artistic/musical dimensions of musical phenomena is important.

To say that a brand is a sign singularizes the issue and makes it static. For most people, the word 'sign', in general speech, refers to for example, a sign on a wall, a neon sign, a sign on a van, a road direction sign, and so on. It refers therefore to a mark on a physical surface, a mark which conveys information of some kind. Within marketing, examples of signs in this sense are, therefore, logos, as displayed on products, in advertisements, on websites, on delivery vehicles, on employee uniforms, on retail fascias. However, this is conventionally seen now as limiting the significance of the brand. A brand is more than the logo.

What the brand stands for or represents – its referent – can be vast and complex. If one says that the city of Los Angeles is a brand, one is faced with the challenge of mastering the complexity of how it is a brand, and what this adds to our understanding of the city (if anything).

There is also a general tendency to equate a sign with something visual. However, in the broader sense, a sign can be multi-sensory. That is to say, when one speaks, sings or plays guitar, one makes a sound, and this is an aural signifier. If one touches somebody, this can also be read as a signifier, as signifying or meaning something. A gesture, mark, physical movement, or anything which is visible is also a signifier. Smells and tastes are also signifiers. This book uses this broader sense of what a sign is, and therefore takes a wide view of the ways in which brands can mean or signify.

In the following sections, consideration is given to some of the issues which arise if one is seeking to apply branding ideas in a 'mainstream' way to specific categories of musical artists. It is a much different matter to brand-manage a musical artist(s), compared to the average FMCG, and the next few sections aim to give some insight into why this is so. Firstly, we consider briefly why music is different from some other products, e.g. the average FMCG product (see also Chapter 1, as well as the extended discussion of music as a product in Chapter 3).

Music is different

Music is a cultural, oral/aural and social offering. Music production and consumption is not just visual, but aural, haptic, visual, olfactory, and gustatory. Music may, in this sense, be considered an aural sign. It is a way of exchanging meaning in social interaction. The plucking of a string, the blowing of a wind instrument, the striking of a key, the singing of a note, the banging of a drum, any musical sound – or indeed the absence of sound – may be heard as a sign, as signifying something to someone from someone else. Sounds are the aural equivalent of visual marks on a surface. Reading these aural marks or, rather, listening to them, people make interpretations according to musical codes and form an image of what is being sounded. Music brands are primarily sonic, but the circumstances in which they are heard may involve multi-sensory perception – consider, for example, the sights, sounds, smells and movements experienced at an open-air festival. If a branding perspective on music is to be viable, it must take account of these factors.

Stakeholders in music projects

Another aspect of music is that the number of stakeholders in any musical project can vary considerably. Since the social and musical interaction between these individuals is what constructs the brand, it is necessary to get a clearer understanding of who one is talking about.

Because a musical 'product' may be sold by a single artist, a record label, an orchestra, a rapidly morphing set of interconnected jazz group members, and so on, it may be helpful to think about music brands in terms of musical projects (see Kubacki and O'Reilly, 2009). In any music project, there may be a wide range of roles, including producer, artist, consumer/fan/audience member (see Chapter 7), critic, investor, regulator, sound technician, crew member, cultural intermediary, plugger, owner, manager, administrator, trustee, beneficiary, and promoter. Not all of these roles are explicitly concerned with marketing in a narrow sense, but any of these roles may be involved, to different degrees, in the marketing of a musical offering. For example, sending out e-flyers and selling merchandise at a concert stall might be considered marketing roles. In a broader sense, however, marketers would argue that an artist performing at a concert is also marketing herself. The relationships between these stakeholders may be clearly defined to the extent that there are agreed industry norms – ideas about good practice, rules of business or even laws which govern their relationships with one another. Since all of these people are involved in the production and consumption of branding, they may play a part in the constructing of a brand.

The brand is not just the logo; it is everything which the stakeholders do in interaction with one another. In other words, to understand a music brand, one needs to understand its positioning, pricing, promotional communications, product design, people, processes and organizational culture – i.e. the totality of what the brand stands for (see Chapter 1). The implications of this are that we cannot understand what a music brand is – what is stands for, what mark it wishes to make in the world – unless we analyse the meaning of all of those constituent parts and somehow calculate their supposed sum. This is not to say that brands have essences, i.e. true meanings, whatever their managers or supposed owners might wish to think. Their meanings are continually produced, negotiated and consumed through social and economic interaction. The totality of the meanings projected by a music brand makes up its brand identity. Every stakeholder has, potentially, a different viewpoint on, and image of, this brand identity. The analytical task of grasping the meanings of a music brand is, therefore, a complex one.

Musical artist brands

Musical artists are commonly referred to in media parlance as 'brands'. Artists such as Madonna, David Bowie and Lady Gaga have been frequently admired for their ability to manage their musical and artistic identities, as well as for their handling of changing cultural trends, and their continuing commercial success. Mainstream commercial brand managers tasked with selling commercial products would like to be able to manage and change brand identity flexibly, but are usually constrained by corporate fears – 'don't f*** with the brand'! Musical artists can afford to be more culturally transgressive and to take bigger risks with their identities, as scandalization strategies are, to some extent, more culturally acceptable or expected coming from artists. Key branding constructs here are the notions of brand identity and brand personality. Brands are often spoken and written about in an anthropomorphic sense. For example, in a kind of animistic way, branding scholars, consultants and managers talk about a brand's 'personality'. Brand personality traits have been identified, based on the possibility that organizations or products can be classified and differentiated along these traits (see for example, Aaker, 1997, who identified five dimensions of brand personality, namely Sincerity, Excitement, Competence, Sophistication, and Ruggedness). Such frameworks, when expressed as scales, hold out the possibility that brand personality can be measured and tracked over time and against competitors on these key traits. Thus, Live Nation Entertainment could, theoretically, score higher on competence and ruggedness than its competitors, but lower on other traits. However, this kind of brand-think, when it focuses on objects or large organizations, can seem rather far-fetched. Quite apart from the fact that ascriptions of personality traits are culturally variable rather than statistically generalizable, and depending on a particular view of human psychology, it is easier to understand the idea of personality when it is related to an actual human being, i.e. to an individual musical artist. Even here, it is necessary to be careful, because an artist's personality off-stage may be different from the one they project on-stage. It makes more sense, perhaps, to use the term 'brand persona' when speaking of an individual artist in their role on stage. Even then, whether trait-lists can do justice to the depth of a musical brand persona or personality is questionable. Other discourses are needed in order to give richer accounts.

Apart from an individual artist's persona and private personality, there are many other factors which can help to construct their brand identity, or need to be taken into account in doing so. First and foremost, an artist's ability as a songwriter, instrumentalist, vocalist, or show business personality, will help to define their brand identity. But other factors not normally explicitly considered in branding discourse are also relevant, such as their race, creed, colour, country of origin, gender, sexual orientation, ability/disability, language, political beliefs or religion, with some being more salient in certain cultural contexts than in others. It is also common in interviews for musical artists to talk about those who have influenced them, which provides a useful opportunity for them to associate or dissociate themselves with or from other kinds of musical expression and scenes, and thereby position and enrich their brand identities.

Musical group brands

One of the brands that a music marketer may have to manage is a group brand. A group may be mainly or purely vocalists (e.g. Westlife, Spice Girls), or may include musicians as well as vocalists (e.g. just about any rock band), or only instrumentalists (e.g. the Borodin Quartet). The management of these kinds of brands presents many issues, the primary one being the management of brand identity.

For popular music acts, external brand identity has a number of key dimensions. A popular music act's identity is above all a musical one, and is usually characterized by a genre, or mix of genres. Another important aspect of brand identity, certainly from a marketing point of view, is commercial identity. Issues of commercial identity are very important in fan and academic discourse. This may include the extent to which a band and/or its sound may be described as 'commercial', the degree to which the band and its members embrace commercial relationships, and their approaches to merchandising, celebrity, product placement, and sponsorship. Another important aspect of popular music brand identity is the subcultural aspect. In the past five decades, a significant number of sub-cultural identities have emerged, such as goth (Hodkinson, 2002), punk (Colegrave and Sullivan, 2001), crustie, mod, and so on. Some bands become closely associated with a particular subculture, which can be a threat to band longevity if the subculture becomes unfashionable. Geographic identity, another important aspect of popular music brand identity, is often associated with a particular sound, such as The Beatles with Liverpool. An act's national and political identity can be closely linked or widely differentiated. Coming from a particular country can authenticate the sound. Increasingly, as part of their political identity, it is common for bands to get involved with cause-related marketing, e.g. U2 and Amnesty.

There is also the issue of the balance between an act's collective and individual identities. Take, for example, Kiss, the '70s US rock band (Lendt, 1997), in which each of the four members had his own Kabuki-style makeup and was a character with a name and identity of its own. The band members' removal of this make-up and the revelation of their identities became a media event in itself. More recently, in the UK, the Spice Girls was a group of female artists who each had her own individual identity. These identities have now been spun off into their own celebrity orbits, with varying degrees of success. Perhaps more common in the rock scene are acts with one or two band members who are more prominent. Within each group act, there will be roles which people can make their own – for example drummer or bassist, in terms of either musicianship, songwriting or performing. There is also the question of the identity life cycle, wherein popular music acts may be said to be fads, fashions, slow burners or 'growers', or have real staying power. Some popular music brands have considerable talent at changing – and thereby prolonging – their brand identity. Key brand managers in this sense include Madonna (Taraborrelli, 2002), David Bowie (Sandford, 1997) or Kylie (Scatena, 1997). Other artists use shock to gain and maintain impact, such as Marilyn Manson (Baddeley, 2002) and Jim Morrison (Hopkins and Sugerman, 1991).

This issue of identity is important, because, psychologically speaking, it is consumers' perception of this identity that determines commercial success or failure. Yet a group's identity is a fragile thing, which depends on perceptions of the general behavioural practices of its members – not just its musical practices. There is also the issue of who 'owns' the brand and who speaks for it. Depending on the power structures within the group, the individual members may have varying amounts to say about its brand identity.

One fundamental issue is the group's membership or composition. A typical four-person rock band faces the problem of managing identities at different levels: its group identity, the individual identity of its members, and its members' relationships both to one another and to the group. There are different patterns in this; for example, a band may have just one dominant member, each member may have his/her own identity (Kiss, Queen, The Beatles, The Spice Girls), or there may be two players who dominate (e.g. a band with a strong songwriting partnership of two members). Managing the salience of certain personalities and the backgrounding of others requires careful work behind the scenes in the interests of group/brand coherence and continuity. Bands commonly generate stories about the formation of the band, how they got their name, and why they chose it. Line-up changes also have to be explained, be it through death, musical differences, or members being sacked. Recruitment of new band members also needs to be 'managed' or explained in a way that is credible to fans. This is, of course, more salient for pop and rock than for jazz, where groups form and reform and form again in an endless flow of network changes. When bands reform or have a reunion, this also needs to be accounted for. Cynical fans, misinformed as to the true artistic/musical purpose of a reunion, may think it is 'just for the money'. Efforts to allay fan suspicions and uncertainties about reunions may involve the investment of considerable amounts of money. For example, given the suddenness and unexpected nature of UK pop group Steps' break-up, the artist/brand management challenge was to remake the brand image of the group in the minds of the consumers, and provide a convincing account of the reasons for the break-up and an opportunity for the reconciliation of differences within the group. The prize would be a return to considerable revenue streams. In order to remake their identity, Steps' reunion was televised in four episodes and screened on a number of channels. Cameras were allowed 'behind the scenes' to see the group meeting for the first time in years, sorting out who was to blame for what and why certain group members behaved in the way they did at the time of the break-up.

The group's internal processes, or dynamic, its way of doing things in rehearsal, its musical, business and other practices, in the studio, on tour, and on stage are all parts of the group's organizational culture. When handled in the right way, this is gold dust for brand building. Selective disclosure of back-stage information, and other forms of moving back the boundary between the professional and personal or private, is a powerful brand management tool. For example, Cole and Trubo's (2004) stories of Led Zeppelin's tour behaviour helped to build a particular kind of identity. By way of contrast, Metallica's disclosure (2004) of its group therapy work opened a new frontier and helped to feed fans' curiosity or need for information about the object of their affections.

Group membership, composition, and therefore identity may need further explanation where there is another person that is heavily involved in the creation of a successful record. For example, it is clear from many of the Classic Albums documentaries how important the producer is to the output of a band. It is as if the producer becomes, for a time, a member of the band, and the studio becomes another instrument. But producers cannot actually become genuine members of the band, so they are positioned as being 'like a fifth member' of it. Yet they leave a significant mark on the creative labour of the band, for better or worse. Arguably, successful producers can also be read as brands in their own right.

Corporate brands in music

Commercial branding terminology has the most relevance in the branding of large, commercially oriented corporations, such as the major labels Warner Music Group, Universal Music Group and Sony Music Entertainment, or multinational promoters Live Nation Entertainment. These vast corporations, which earn billions of dollars in revenue, and have an extensive international reach, can be said to operate large 'brand portfolios'. At the time of writing, Warner Music Group is owned by Access Industries, and has a large number of subsidiaries organised in five groups, including Atlantic Records and Warner Bros. Each record label brand, for instance, faces a different market and gives the corporation access to a different talent roster, back catalogue, revenue/profit stream, investment history and set of market opportunities. A marketer analysing this brand portfolio would conventionally be expected to arrange the brands along two axes, namely global market opportunity and competitive strength. This would enable the analyst to see the respective strengths and weaknesses of the different brands within the portfolio, enabling him/her to consider which merited continued investment, and to what degree, and which should be scheduled for review or even divestment. A key issue here is whether the corporation is publicly quoted. Companies listed on the stock exchange are subject to intense pressure to generate quarterly earnings performances that are comparable to or better than other investment opportunities in the capitalist casino.

At the level of each record label subsidiary, a similar portfolio analysis will be undertaken of artists on the roster. This would involve the subsidiary brands reviewing the musical acts currently under contract against, for instance, units sold, perceived potential, musical talent, cultural trends and fashions, general manageability and other relevant criteria. In turn, this will lead to decisions about the management of the portfolio in the interests of the capital owners (the shareholders), including further investment, new projects to scout and sign other talent, and decisions to cull artists whose commercial performances do not meet the required rate of return on capital.

Celebrity and sponsorship

A very noticeable feature of the contemporary musical industry is the treatment of popular musicians and singers as celebrities. Celebrities gain cultural influence because they are perceived as having certain skills, or being attractive in some way to fans/consumers. By projecting identities and personalities which are seen as trustworthy and credible, they can be contracted to endorse products and act as a sales tool. Popular musicians who have become successful are often asked their opinion on non-musical issues by journalists. They thus acquire and develop the power to speak out on social and political issues, for example in the Rock Against Racism movement, as well as in charity concerts and recording projects such as Band Aid, Live Aid, and Live 8. U2's lead singer, Bono, along with fellow Irishman Bob Geldof, plus Midge Ure and other music celebrities, are closely associated with efforts to alleviate the difficult issues experienced by so-called less developed countries. Their campaigns have ranged across a number of issues, from debt relief to AIDS awareness. These events and campaigns often depend heavily on media exposure. At one point, MTV became an important tool in the World Health Organization's (WHO) efforts to raise global awareness of AIDS, and its related campaign offered an interesting example of the aestheticization of public health messages (Martens, 2010), as well as what marketers might call cause-related marketing. Bono's tie-in with American Express in the 'Red' campaign is an interesting example of social, or cause-related, marketing involving mainstream commercial corporations and popular music celebrities. Other musicians have endorsed commercial brands (e.g. Iggy Pop and Swiftcover insurance, Johnny Rotten and Country Life Butter, Madonna and GAP).

In addition to celebrity endorsement, the commercial sponsorship of band tours, music festivals and concerts has also grown. Sponsorship involves an alliance between a sponsor and sponsee, or property. Within this alliance, the sponsor pays a cash or in-kind fee in return for access to the exploitable commercial potential associated with the property. This can include the funding and/or support of performances, tours, seasons, projects and festivals. The motives of sponsees (e.g. orchestras, bands, artists, festivals) are to obtain investment funding to enable them to do more things commercially and artistically. Sponsors' objectives include the generation of increased brand awareness, adding personality or an emotional dimension to their brand, building goodwill, entertaining corporate clients, or changing brand identity or consumers' attitudes to and preferences for the brand, facilitating product trials, or driving sales, including those from the sponsees' fanbase.

Different approaches to branding

To be fair to management scholars, a considerable amount of empirical work has been done on branding. Heding et al. (2008) helpfully identify seven strands in the branding literature, each of which deals with a specific approach to branding, namely: identity, image, personality, economic, relationship, community, and culture. These are discussed below in that order. It is important to note the extensive scope of branding theory which these seven strands encompass. This might be read as an indicator of marketing's institutional hunger for an understanding of, and power over, the cultural/symbolic dimensions of business.

The **identity** approach to branding assumes that consumers attribute identity characteristics to organizations. Visual and behavioural signifiers of identity are important in constructing a sense of identity. The supporting themes identified by Heding et al. (2008) are reputation, image, organizational identity and corporate identity.

Image refers to creating a consistent image in the minds of all stakeholders, although consistency is problematic, as stakeholders' interest may sometimes conflict. Reputation has to do with the long-term positive or negative stakeholder image of the brand. Corporate identity relates to what is projected physically, visually, and behaviourally by the organization as a whole, and can relate to the organization's vision and mission. Organizational culture, finally, has to do with the basis on which employees of the organization build a mental and emotional attachment to the brand.

The **personality** approach builds on the idea that consumers attribute personality to brands. Of course, this is easier to accept when the brand is a person, such as a singer; however brand communications practices seek to imbue a range of products with 'personalities', e.g. by using celebrity endorsers, animals, or animated characters as proxies. The more complex the brand referent, e.g. a country, the more difficult the personality approach is to sustain – c.f. the personality of France, for example. If a personality is strong, attractive and relevant to a consumer, then it is more likely to work. It is supposed to drive the emotional bond between consumer and brand. The personality approach draws on work in psychology on personality traits, as well as on the idea of the consumer self-construct as an independent individual with an actual, ideal and desired self, or a dependent individual in social relationships with an in-group and out-groups. According to Aaker (1997), brand personality has five generic dimensions, namely sincerity, excitement, competence, ruggedness and sophistication.

The **economic** approach draws upon transaction cost theory and the marketing mix, and treats the consumer as a rational person working on cost-benefit trade-offs when making a brand purchase. This approach requires an understanding of the organization's cost base, the competitors' price points and the consumers' willingness and ability to pay.

In the **consumer** approach, understanding the consumer is of primary importance. This approach draws on strands of thinking about consumer choice and the consumer as exercising cognition. The consumer gets information about brands, processes it, and makes a choice. This approach most closely fits the price/quality positioning chart, and implies that understanding the consumers' perceptions is critical to successful brand management.

The **relational** approach makes use of an anthropomorphic view of the brand, in which the brand is seen as being in a relationship with the consumer. This brings notions of trust into the economic exchange, and places the emphasis on the perceived quality of the relationship.

The **community** approach to branding (Muñiz and O'Guinn, 2001) is also a social approach. It places the emphasis on consumer-to-consumer relations and decentres the brand-consumer relationship. This approach is dealt with in Chapter 9.

In the **cultural** approach to branding, the brand can be read as a cultural artefact. This is consistent with the AMA definition of a brand as a sign. Schroeder and Salzer-Mörling (2005: 1) posit the notion of brand culture as a context, a 'third leg' for branding theory to rank alongside brand identity and brand image. Aside from this macro-environmental view, a cultural approach also needs to take account of the internal culture of the organization, as part of the identity approach), as well as the culture within which the offering is consumed, and the cultural aspects of the offering itself.

But how does this relate to music? The identity approach lends itself to an analysis of any musical organization, whether this be one of the major record labels, a promoter, a symphony orchestra or even a smaller organization such as a rock band or a string quartet. Clearly, the scale of analysis differs hugely from a major conglomerate to an orchestra, a band or an individual musician or vocalist, but the principle remains. A musical organization has a short-term image and a long-term reputation. It projects a corporate identity by means of its physical assets, its behaviour, and its visual, aural and other signifiers. A musical organization or act can be analysed for its brand personality. Within a record label, the personality of the president or CEO may even be taken as a proxy for the corporation's brand personality. In the case of a band or group, there will be a number of personalities which go towards making up the brand. Whatever the type of music brand, the relationship with fans, the economics of the musical project, the image that fans have in their minds, the nature of the fan tribe or brand community, and the promotional culture are all relevant to an understanding of the brand.

Branding discourse and music

Having considered some of the issues raised by attempts to brand different players in the music business, the discussion now turns to brand discourse itself. In some music scenes, to talk about music using branding discourse is not appropriate. The application of this particular terminology to music, particularly music which is seen as somehow more artistic, carries risks. Where branding stands for the commercial, it risks being caught up in the ever-present tensions between the corporate world and the world of the musician, between 'suits' and creatives, between those who are interested in 'filthy lucre' and those who are pursuing their art. Branding is seen as a commercial discourse, and therefore tainted, and brand marketers are considered money-changers in the sacred temple of music. Branding discourse is therefore a matter of choice, and the choice a speaker makes in using branding discourse may be read by others as originating in a value system which is flawed, or ethically, morally, artistically or politically inferior, insofar as it reveals an interest in capital or money. However, there are plenty of examples in music where the musicians, and the managers and others who work with them, are deeply, piratically, interested in pursuing money, as well as music.

Independence and ideology

An example of the tensions between culture and commerce in music is the dichotomy between independent and mainstream music. There are major cultural distinctions made by fans between authentic acts and 'sell-outs'. This is often also a distinction made between rock and pop music. It is tied into anti-capitalist sentiment and rhetoric, as well as the separation between musical talent and corporate control. Being 'tainted' by commerciality can be a bad thing.

First, within some parts of musical culture there are strong strands of antipathy to the commercialism which is associated with brands. Within popular music, take, for example, the independent or indie ethos as dissected by Fonarow (2006). Within the music business (and indeed in other parts of the wider cultural industries), the term 'independent' is heavily loaded with connotations of a stance which is apart from, and, by implication, artistically uncompromised by, the commercial mainstream. Being seen as independent and 'authentic' matters to a band's perception amongst fans. The term 'independent' has become shortened to 'indie' in media and popular parlance, and has come to denote or connote quite a wide range of meanings. The result is that musicians (or indeed fans, for that matter) who might regard themselves as independent might not necessarily agree that they were 'indie'. The resonances of 'indie' may not always sit quite so easily with stricter notions of economic and artistic independence. However, it is important to consider the relevant literature. In her monograph on the aesthetics and rituals of British indie music, Fonarow (2006: 25ff.) discusses what is at stake in the label 'indie'. Fonarow points to the difficulty that 'indie' community members have in defining what 'indie' means. She considers 'indie' to be a discourse, specifically:

> The indie community's arguments over … the nature of the ownership of musical recordings and their mode of distribution to a larger public, the nature of musical production practices and their relationship to musical forms, and the relationship between audience members and the music.

Fonarow, an anthropologist, suggests that 'the common goal set forth for music listeners within indie cosmology is to have a communion with the sacred quintessence of music' (Fonarow, 2006: 28). She argues that 'indie's core values promote and replicate the core doctrine of a particular brand of Protestant religiosity: Puritanism'. She argues that within indie are two parallel strands. The first is the Puritan strand, which places an 'emphasis on distrust of authority … simplicity in musical form, production and style, a promotion of high moral standards regarding issues of sexuality and conduct … and an underlying theme of austerity and abstinence' (2006: 28). The second of the twin strands identified by Fonarow is 'Romanticism, with its characteristic cultivation of emotion, passion, and the spirit … its respect for local identities and the working class, and its distaste for middle-class society while being itself middle-class' (28). As far as indie as a genre is concerned, 'simplicity is a dominant motif permeating indie musical practices … much of indie has a raw, underproduced quality… while the guitar is the most highly valued instrument in indie, there is a pride in the avoidance of the guitar solo, or any solo, for that matter' (2006: 41-42).

Table 4 contrasts the key values of indie and mainstream popular music, as identified by Fonarow.

Table 4: Indie versus Mainstream Values

Indie	Mainstream
Independent labels	Major corporations
Gigs	Stadiums
Local	Global
Intimate	Distant
Personal	Impersonal
Simple production	Elaborate production
No guitar solos	Guitar solos
Modest	Self-indulgent
Live	Pre-fabricated
Self-made	Other-made
Authentic	Phony
Original	Generic
Specific	General
Lean	Fat
Transit vans	Tour buses
Unprofessional	Muso
Raw	Slick
Austere	Lavish
Intelligent	Insipid
Substantive	Empty
Art	Commerce

Source: Assembled from Fonarow, 2006

Fonarow argues for a view of indie fans as the 'Puritan reformers against the established Roman Catholic Church of the mainstream music industry' where the core values of indie are 'individualism and local identity' (2006: 67). She sees the indie artist as like the 'Romantic ... artist as a natural self-actuated genius born of emotional pathos, self-referential introspection, and internal longings – the eternal outsider' (2006: 73). Just as Puritans favoured an ideology which permitted unmediated and direct access to the numinous or divine (p. 77), indie ideology favours direct access to the spirit of music. Indie prides itself on a spirit of egalitarianism (2006: 186). Its language is the 'language of emotion, told in word and sound' (2006: 201).

This notion of ideology is important for a discussion of branding. Insofar as brands are systems of meaning, they may be read as always already ideological, but this is not a line of thinking which has received much attention within marketing (see O'Reilly, 2006).

Genre and commerciality

Musical genre is an important signifier, or element of brand identity, in music marketing, retailing and promotion. Within popular music, issues of genre are often debated. For example, Shuker sees 'rock' as 'the broad label for the huge range of styles that have evolved out of rock 'n' roll' (1998: 263). He adds that 'rock is often considered to carry more weight than pop, with connotations of greater integrity, sincerity and authenticity'. Grossberg urges caution in the use of 'authenticity' to characterize rock music. In opposition to co-opted, commercialized rock music. He sees 'three versions of this ideological distinction'. The first:

> Assumes that authentic rock depends on its ability to articulate private but common desires, feelings and experiences into a shared public language. The consumption of rock constructs or expresses a 'community'.

The second 'locates authenticity in the construction of a rhythmic and sexual body'. And the third 'is built on the explicit recognition ... that the difference that rock constructs ... is always artificially constructed' (1992:62). Fornäs, writing in the academic journal *Popular Music* (1995:111) states that:

> Like all other genre concepts, rock is very hard to define. A genre is a set of rules for generating musical works. Using such conventional sets of rules in producing or interpreting musical pieces can give rise to classificatory systems, but actual musics do not in themselves fall unambiguously into any simple classes. It all depends on which rules are used, and this choice is situationally bound. Genres are, however, more intersubjective than subjective phenomena. In each temporal and spatial context, there are certain genre definitions that are relevant and used by the

most important groups of actors in the musical field: musicians, producers, marketers and audiences.

He sees

rock/pop as one single, continuous genre field rather than as distinct categories. This field contains a wide and open range of subgenres, moving within certain similar economic and social frames and circuits', and adds that as long as the definitional struggle is going on within the business and fans it seems reasonable to 'treat rock as an open and unfinished category (112).

The genre(s) of music which a band plays is/are an important part of how it is perceived and of the account which it gives of itself, and can therefore be seen as one component of a band's identity. To the extent that genre needs to be considered here, the focus in this study is more about how a rock band or its fans might make use of genre discourse to signify or make sense of their band-fan relationships. In other words, a construct such as 'rock' can be read as a mobile signifier which is contextually and strategically invoked to achieve certain discursive outcomes or positionings. For example, an important aspect of the rock artiste's identity is the notion of rebel. Featherstone (2007: 25) notes that the idea of the artist 'as an expressive rebel and stylistic hero has been a strong theme' in popular music, and that various forms of music, including rock, were 'presented as direct forms of emotional expression ... [and] more pleasurable, involved and authentic by predominantly young audiences'.

These ideas of authenticity, legitimacy, expressiveness and rebelliousness are important in the production and consumption not just of music, but of other arts offerings (and indeed of mainstream commercial brands). Since branding may be regarded as a kind of ideology (O'Reilly, 2006), the next chapter develops an approach to branding which can help cultural and commercial analysts to understand the situatedness of music brands.

Summary

This chapter discussed various aspects of brands in relation to music, including the characteristics of music itself, the number of stakeholders in musical projects, the complexity of music production and identity management issues, celebrity endorsement and sponsorship, and the ideological issues around genre and perceptions of commerciality. All of these present challenges to the development of an approach to the marketing of music which takes account of cultural and symbolic issues. In order to overcome these challenges, marketing needs to engage more reflexively with the fact that branding is about signs. Cultural studies has a lot to say about signification, whether it be in the music business or any other. In Chapter 6, a framework is provided based on the circuit of culture (Du Gay et al., 1997) which, among other things, enables brands to be analysed as part of a series of cultural moments. The circuit of culture framework has been considered within the marketing literature (O'Reilly, 2005), but, as we shall see, needs to be adapted to the task of framing an approach to music branding.

References

Aaker, J.L. (1997) Dimensions of Brand Personality. *Journal of Marketing Research* (JMR). Aug1997, Vol. 34 Issue 3, p347-356.

Arvidsson, A. (2005) 'Brands: A critical perspective', *Journal of Consumer Culture*, 12 (2), 235-258.

Baddeley, G. (2002) *Dissecting Marilyn Manson*, Medford, NJ: Plexus Publishing.

Cole, R. and Trubo R. (2004) Stairway to Heaven, London: Pocket Books.

Colegrave, S. and Sullivan, C. (2005) *Punk: The Definitive Record of a Revolution.* New York: NY: Thunder's Mouth Press.

Du Gay, P., Hall, S., Janes, L., Mackay, H. and Negus, K. (1997) *Doing Cultural Studies: The Story of the Sony Walkman.* London: Sage Publications.

Fonarow, W. (2006) *Empire of Dirt: The Aesthetics and Rituals of British Indie Music.* Middletown, CT: Wesleyan University Press.

Fornäs, J. (1995) The Future of Rock: Discourses that struggle to define a genre. *Popular Music*, 14 (1), 111 – 125.

Grossberg, L. (1992) *We Gotta Get Out of This Place: Popular Conservatism and Postmodern Culture*. London: Routledge.

Heding, T., Knudtze, C. and Bjerre, M. (2008) *Brand Management: Research, Theory and Practice*, London: Routledge.

Hodkinson, P. (2002) *Goth: Identity, Style and Subculture*. Oxford: Berg.

Holt, D.B. (2004) *How Brands Become Icons: The Principles of Cultural Branding*, Harvard Business School Press.

Hopkins, J. and Sugerman, D. (1991) *No One Here Gets Out Alive: The Biography of Jim Morrison*, Medford, NJ: Plexus Publishing.

Kubacki, K. and O'Reilly, D. (2009) 'Arts marketing', in Maclaran, P. and Parsons, E. (ed.) *Contemporary Issues in Marketing and Consumer Behaviour*, Oxford, UK: Elsevier.

Lendt, C.K. (1997) *Kiss and Sell: The Making of a Supergroup*, New York, NY: Billboard Books.

Lury, C. (2004) *Brands: The Logos of the Global Economy*, London: Routledge.

Martens, C. (2010) 'Branding HIV/AIDS communication: The social marketing campaigns of MTV and Viacom', *International Journal of Nonprofit and Voluntary Sector Marketing*, 15 (1), 91-103.

Metallica (2004) *Some Kind of Monster. Film*. Directed by Joe Berlinger and Bruce Sinofsky. USA: Radical Media and Third Eye Motion Picture Company.

Muniz, A. M. and O'Guinn, T. (2001) Brand Community. *Journal of Consumer Research* 27 (4), 412-432.

O'Reilly, D. (2005) 'Cultural brands/branding cultures', *Journal of Marketing Management*, July, 21, (5/6), 573-588.

O'Reilly, D. (2006) 'Branding ideology', *Marketing Theory*, 6, (2), 263-271.

O'Reilly, D. (2012) 'Maffesoli and consumer tribes: developing the theoretical links', *Marketing Theory*, 12, (3), 341-347.

O'Reilly, D. and Kerrigan, F. (ed.) (2010) *Arts Marketing: A Fresh Approach*, London: Routledge.

O'Reilly, D., Rentschler, R. and Kirchner, T. (forthcoming) *Routledge Companion to Arts Marketing*. London: Routledge.

O'Reilly, D. and Kerrigan, F. (2013) 'A view to a brand: introducing the film brandscape', *European Journal of Marketing*, 47, (5/6).

Ries, A. and Trout, J. (1981) *Positioning: The Battle for your Mind*. Riverview, MI: Motor City Books.

Sandford, C. (1997) *Bowie: Loving the Alien*, London: Time Warner Paperbacks.

Scatena, D. (1998) *Kylie: An Unauthorised Biography*, London: Penguin Books.

Schroeder, J.E. (2006) 'Aesthetics awry: The Painter of Light™ and the commodification of artistic values', *Consumption Markets & Culture*, **9**, (2), 87-99.

Schroeder, J. and Salzer-Morling, M. (2005) *Brand Culture*. London: Routledge.

Shuker, Roy (1998) *Key Concepts in Popular Music*. London: Routledge.

Taraborrelli, R. (2002) *Madonna: An intimate biography*. London: Pan Books.

6 Socio-Cultural Music Branding

Introduction

All of the issues in the preceding chapter come under the heading of meaning. Although there is some acknowledgement within the marketing discipline of the notion of brand meanings, relatively little attention has been paid to an underlying theory of cultural meaning. In order to deal with this, it is helpful to turn to cultural studies and a socio-cultural approach to branding. In this chapter, a framework is proposed for how music brands are created.

Branding discourse is not good at understanding the meaning of arts and entertainment offerings. Because branding terminology has been largely developed by business academics, practitioners and intermediaries, it is a very blunt instrument in the cultural arena. By framing something or someone as a brand, the speaker invokes a particular way of speaking, a discursive repertoire, or a lens, which focuses on certain features of a phenomenon and pushes others out of focus. In fact, a serious failure of mainstream branding theory as applied by commercial marketers is its failure, relatively speaking, to handle the cultural dimensions of arts brands. It is unhelpful to apply commercial branding terminology to arts and entertainment brands without carefully considering the cultural context, the social interaction between all of the stakeholders, what meanings are generated and understood around the specific musical project or scene, what art-generic conventions apply, and what ideologies and values inform production and consumption practices in the project in question.

The purpose of this attempt is to get beyond the instrumental and unreflexive use of 'brandthink' and to ask the following questions: In whose interest is branding discourse or terminology being mobilized? On what terms is the branding discussion being held? What are the implications of branding discourse for ways of thinking and talking about music? While those on the more commercial side of music (e.g. marketers) may be comfortable talking about music brands, others (e.g. songwriters, musicians, composers) may feel a strong resistance to their work being treated as a 'brand', for example on grounds of artistic integrity or psychological congruence. No doubt this resistance can partly be traced to the long-running tensions between commerce and art which have been so frequently written about. By working out an analytical framework which enables both cultural and commercial meaning to be considered, it is hoped that these tensions can be seen and judged in a clearer light.

Branding is the principal cultural practice of the marketing imagination. Branding puts the 'mark' into 'mark-eting'. Arguably, branding discourse represents marketing's attempt to co-opt language and signification for capital, and is a key discursive resource in marketing ideology (O'Reilly, 2005). Commercial success relies significantly on consumers' extractions of cultural meanings from musical offerings, and those meanings of music are shaped and constrained by the conditions – including economic, commercial and political conditions – of its production and consumption. Understanding the cultural dimensions of music marketing practices can provide music marketers and brand managers with a better understanding of what they are marketing to whom. Branding is fundamentally about signification, i.e. meaning, and a discussion of branding can bring the cultural and commercial dimensions of music marketing into a common focus.

To talk of anything as 'a music brand' is a discursive move rather than an ontological statement. Branding is simply one of many lenses through which one may regard the phenomenon of music. Because of the symbolic nature of music as cultural text, it is particularly necessary to accommodate this cultural dimension into any theory of music marketing. Music is a vehicle for cultural meaning.

Cultural view of branding

Branding may also be seen as the cultural strand in marketing thought. The AMA's definition of 'brand' is a 'name, term, sign, symbol or design, or a combination of them, intended to identify the goods and services of one seller or group of sellers and to differentiate them from those of competition' (2007). This is a rather limited definition. The important point here is that, in characterizing a brand as a 'sign', the AMA is signalling that a brand is a cultural artefact, object, or entity.

Historically, the right to brand in a physical sense was derived from political or religious authority, or from social or commercial power. The practice of branding has been applied, for example, by governments to individuals to signify a change in their status as criminals or outlaws. Contemporary use of branding in a commercial context tends to ascribe the power to brand to corporations, as providers of commercial offerings. However, in its wider sense as a signifying practice, branding or marking is by no means restricted to enterprises. From a culturalist point of view, everyone is a sign-maker. The commercial practice of branding is simply a special case of a wider human signifying practice. Using the word 'sign' to define a brand moves the discussion into the domain of semiotics, or semiology (the study of signs or meaning). In that sense, branding, when considered as a sign-making practice, can be seen as only one example of human beings' many sign-making practices. In a narrow sense, branding, as commercially understood, is restricted to the practice whereby capitalist organizations invest heavily in coordinating their communications processes and outputs for profit. Although some marketing and branding commentators seem to believe that branding *is* the culture, there are strong grounds for inverting this assertion, and arguing instead that commerce, including commercial branding, is simply one part of the totality of human culture.

The symbolic dimension of brands is antecedent to their construction as, for instance, a sign of ownership. A brand may be read as the sum total of the meanings of a branded entity, be it a product, organization or artist. Brand meanings are constructed not just by managers, but also by artists, consumers, intermediaries and other stakeholders. Signification can be performed just as well by consumers as by producers and providers. The production and consumption of brand meanings are, culturally speaking, mutually constitutive. In a holistic account, it is important to always keep in mind this dialogic character of branded communications.

The more postmodern understanding of identity adopted in this book, and one which is consistent with a culturalist understanding of meaning production and consumption, rejects the underlying assumption in mainstream social science that identity is something that is stable, consistent and internally owned, or in some way unchanging and essential, and replaces it with a conceptualization of identity as dynamic. Identity is understood as a fluid accomplishment, the sense of which is actively renewed by self and others in the context of consumption activities, and offline and online social interaction. Identity is not something that you 'are' – i.e. something tangible; rather, it is a process, something that you 'do' (Sacks 1984). This orientation points to an analysis of the ways in which different identities are made visible within an interaction, and the consequences of categorizing self and others in one way rather than another. It sees identity as discursively, contextually and strategically constructed. A discursive approach to musical identity sees it not as something that is ideally fixed, with a permanent core and a changeable periphery, but as being regularly constructed and re-constructed in social interactions among record label executives, musicians, promoters, audiences, and other stakeholders. The identity (or, to put this more widely, the meaning) of a brand is negotiated and constructed in its interactions with its stakeholders. Brand identity is therefore potentially a very fragile signifier which is at risk in every interaction between, for instance, any music provider and its publics, with consequences for the business's durability.

Here, a socio-cultural branding 'lens' is employed to examine the music industry. The purpose of this is to see what branding discourse can 'buy' the analyst in terms of insight. The reason for taking this approach is because it is a better fit, compared to other perspectives, for the particular complexities and circumstances of the music industry.

This approach works from the assumption that everything is always already cultural. This examination is not without its challenges, because, quite apart from its ideological implications, branding discourse was not developed specifically to talk about music, and so needs to be adapted to the musical context. Also, from some of the 'purer', more independent domains within music, any talk of brands and branding may carry unwelcome commercial connotations and raise ideological issues – is Beethoven a brand, for example? There is, it seems, a potential underlying tension in discussions of branding in relation to certain art forms.

Music as a social and cultural phenomenon

In order to understand how branding may be of use in understanding the marketing and consumption of music, it is necessary to briefly revisit the social and cultural aspects of music. From the social point of view, music has a wide range of social functions (Gregory, 1997; Crozier, 1997; Rouget, 1985). The performance of music is essentially a social experience (Crozier, 1997; Frith, 1998; Hargreaves and North, 1997). From a social-psychological viewpoint, Hargreaves and North (1997) argue that, for the individual consumer, the social functions of music create a context in which three issues are key: the management of self-identity, the management of interpersonal relationships and the management of mood. They find that musical preference acts as a mark of identity, particularly during adolescence.

From the cultural point of view, Middleton (1990), identifies three different approaches to the study of popular music. The first of these is the structuralist approach, which examines how meaning is generated in musical texts, how the structure of the text produces meanings, how the audience member is constructed and positioned, as well as musicological and semiotic perspectives on the subject. The second approach, the culturalist one, is about constructing consumption of popular music as an active, rather than a passive process; oppositional politics in popular music; tensions and contradictions in popular music; music and youth subcultures; the individual as determiner of cultural meaning; creative consumption; and consumer autonomy. And the final approach, the politico-economical one, engages with issues such as the corporate power of the capitalistic music industry and its role in determining the tastes of the audience. Broadly speaking, then, the political-economic approach is about the power of the supply side, and the culturalist approach is about power on the consumer side.

The mutual constitutiveness of cultural production and consumption offers an alternative to managerial notions of brand development. The managerial perspective holds that brand managers play the more, or most, important role in brand development. The culturalist perspective suggests that the fans and other stakeholders have a considerable role as co-authors of the brand's meanings. The idea that popular music brands are co-constructed by bands and their fans (as one group of stakeholders) attributes greater agency and power to fans than the more managerially-driven versions of brand development by mainstream brand thinkers.

Brands as socially constructed

From a socio-cultural perspective, a brand is continually socially constructed by the ongoing production and circulation of texts amongst and between its stakeholders. In other words, the meaning of a musical brand is never fixed, as it is continually being experienced, negotiated, discussed and argued about by everyone involved. This formulation avoids the idea of a brand as a fixed, static entity which always has one specific meaning, or essence. It is important to avoid this limited notion of a brand, as it prevents us from seeing a much wider picture. One might say that you never hear the same band twice, in the sense that something will always be different, something will always be changing. However, this is not to say that fans do not share some degree of agreement about what a band means or stands for; that is a different issue, namely one of brand image and its commonality across the range of stakeholders.

Brand discourse

As we saw in Chapter 5, brand discourse is heavily metaphorical. In fact, marketing is full of metaphors masquerading as solid analytical constructs. Davies and Chun (2003), for example, identify three 'root metaphors' in branding discourse: brand as differentiating mark, as person and as asset. This line of thinking can be taken much further. Consider the number of compound nouns which are hybrid metaphors used by branding practitioners and scholars, such as brand heritage, brand asset, etc. Placing the word 'brand' before a noun results in little meaning being added to the compound term, but simply points to whatever the 'brand' referent is, be it a record label, a CD, an artist, a festival, or a venue.

There are several different sub-discourses within the branding literature. These include financial discourse about brand equity, assets and value; religious discourse about brand soul, essence, spirit and alchemy; cultural discourse about brand identity, culture, and values; literary discourse about story, character and text; social discourse about relationship and community; psychological discourse about image, choice, and loyalty; engineering discourse about brand leverage, brands as tools or devices; and so on. In this sense, rather like Barker's definition (2004) of cultural studies, branding is a language game. Many branding academics seek to connect these metaphors empirically through hypothetico-deductive methods and statistical investigation, as if these metaphors have an objective correlative which is measurable. This process of inquiry results in a range of constructs which serve to make up the mainstream branding lexicon. It can also result in discourse which can seem dense and impenetrable.

Circuit of culture

Given the polysemic character of 'culture' and the fact that the field of inquiry contains many of the different aspects of culture, it is important to identify an overarching idea that will help to weld many of the different meanings together and make symbolic production and consumption more salient. This follows a culturalist line of argument, which sees production and consumption as mutually constitutive. In their monograph case study of the Sony Walkman, Du Gay et al. (1997) introduced the idea of the circuit of culture as a framework for the circulation of cultural meaning.

Five processes of production, consumption, representation, regulation and identity form the circuit of culture. A full analysis of a cultural artefact requires attention to be paid to each of these processes. This goes beyond other attempts to illustrate cultural production, such as the cultural diamond (Alexander, 2003), by introducing representation, identity and regulation as key components of the framework. Du Gay et al. point out (1997) that meaning is not sent from one stage, e.g. production to consumption, as in a transmission model, but rather is 'more like the model of a dialogue'. Note that four of the five elements have to do with processes (production, representation, consumption and regulation), whereas the fifth (identity) denotes a category of cultural meaning rather than a dynamic process. In the following section, Du Gay et al.'s (1997) line of thinking about four of the five elements in the framework is discussed, and their relevance to the present book are explained. Regulation has been the least developed of these elements; at this stage, regulation can be seen either as a process imposed by a third party, such as a government, on the producers and consumers of signs, as a process which is a function of the power balance in the dyadic discourse, or a combination of both of these. Du Gay et al. (1997) see production and consumption not as separate spheres of existence, but rather as mutually constitutive.

During production, the encoding of meanings into products takes place, for instance through product design activities. Every site or organization engaged in the production of culture has, in turn, a culture of production which is 'an integral part of the company way of life that informs intra-organizational decisions and activities' (such as staff recruitment policies, departmental organizational arrangements and general management strategies). But it also informs the perceptions of outside observers. A rock band has its own production culture, and its own sense of musicianship and 'bandhood'. It is also engaged in the production of culture when it designs and produces sounds, images, lyrics and performances.

Consumption involves meanings being made in actual social usage. Du Gay et al. (op. cit.) trace different approaches to consumption. The Frankfurt School's 'production of consumption' approach sees consumption as being determined by production; there is no agency on the demand side; rather, mass consumption is the pursuit of cultural dupes. Baudrillard (1998: 91), on the other hand, argued that consumption has identity value, as well as use or exchange value. Consumption can be used as a marker of social and cultural difference. This goes back to Veblen's theory of the leisure class (1899). Finally, there are those who see consumption in terms of appropriation and resistance. Subcultural analysts like Hebdige (1979) saw consumers as using commodities to signify an identity for themselves which was in opposition to the perceived dominant culture. From this perspective, consumption is an active process, and consumers can put producers' signifiers to other uses as they are polysemic. De Certeau et al. (2002) argued that meaning is produced by consumers through the use to which they put objects in their everyday lives. Cultural studies gives us a theory of active consumers. One can relate this to Elliott and Wattanasuwan's idea (1998) that consumers use brands as resources to construct identities (see Chapter 7). This view sees social subjects as active agents who play a crucial role in creating their own identities through consumption.

Fans have a stake in their idols' durability, because part of their identities are wrapped up in their idols' image, reputation and continuity. This, however, does not address the question of where the sources of power lie in cultural exchanges, and who owns them. Arguably, for both musical acts and consumers/fans/audiences, there is a lot of cultural, personal and business risk involved in the musical project. Rock fans or consumers of rock music, as we shall see, engage in practices of interpretation, sense-making and symbolic consumption in these ways. A danger of misuse in the circuit of culture model is that the producers of goods risk always being seen as producers of symbols, while consumers of goods are seen as always being consumers of symbols. The roles of goods/service producers and signifier producers need to be separated, as do those of goods/service consumers and signifier consumers. In this sense, symbolic consumption, i.e. the signification involved in consumption practices, may be recast as symbolic production.

Representation is the practice of constructing meaning through the use of signs. Meaning is constantly being produced and exchanged in every personal and social interaction in which one takes part. There are two main approaches to signifying practice, namely the semiological and the discursive. The semiological approach is more concerned with how language produces meaning – its 'poetics' – and the discursive approach is more concerned with effects and consequences of representation – its 'politics'. Within cultural studies, Hall (1997) asserts that there are three 'approaches to explaining how representation of meaning through language works' (24): reflective, in which language is thought to 'reflect true meaning as it already exists in the world'; intentional, in which it is held that 'words mean what the author intends they should mean'; and, finally, constructionist/constructivist, in which it is held that things do not have an inherent meaning, nor do the authors or speakers fix meaning, but 'we construct meaning, using representational systems – concepts and signs … According to this approach, we must not confuse the *material* world, where things and people exist, and the *symbolic* practices and processes through which representation, meaning and language operate' (25). From this perspective, a musical act can be seen, through its sounds, images, lyrics, merchandise, performances and media interviews, as representing or constructing representations of the world around it – including politics, social issues, the music industry, everyday life, and of course images of the band itself, the fans and the band-fan relationship.

As far as identity is concerned, Du Gay et al. (1997) see marketers as people who articulate or connect production and consumption through signifying practices such as constructing ideal identities or subject positions for consumers. A band will, through its identity work, project its own identity for consumption by fans. For example, a rock band's songs may offer fans the opportunity to experience certain emotional subject positions through singing along at a performance.

Whilst remaining for a little longer within the exposition of t
of culture' construct, it is also helpful to retain an idea of subj
both in the sense of the subjectedness of the individual's psych
context of social and ideological forces, and of self-consciousne.. as
'I', the thinking, feeling, agent ... giving expression to its emotions and
fulfilment to its talents and energies (Mansfield, 2000: 171-2). These
constructions of identity may also imply constructions of agency. A band
may see itself – and therefore cause some of its fans to see it, as well
as themselves – as a free creative agent; it may also, equally, see itself
as being subjected to hegemonic forces which seek to discipline and
structure its sense of itself. Within cultural studies, 'Consumers are now
seen as active creators of meaning bringing previously acquired cultural
competence to bear on texts' (Barker and Galasinski, 2001: 7). Yet there
are others who will emphasize the fact that consumers – i.e. fans – may
also be read as being subjected to more powerful forces (Adorno, 2001).

There are a number of ways in which the circuit of culture model can
be adapted. Firstly, it places a heavy emphasis on identity, partly because
of the intense discussion of the politics of identity at the time it was
introduced. This is consistent with cultural studies' preoccupation with
this topic throughout the 1990s (Barker, 2004). Secondly, the term
'representation' carries the metaphorical notion of making something
present again. The notion of 'signification' does not carry this notion of
presence or absence. Thirdly, there is one important element missing
from the circuit, which is the stage of mobilization. This is when
the producer of a text makes a paradigmatic selection of discursive
resources prior to their syntagmatic combination during the production
phase. These discursive resources may be an image, a sound, a concept,
or a code by which these elements are encoded in the text. Adding
these further elements would make the roles of signification and
discursive resources more salient in cultural circuits.

Cultural circuit and cultural economy

The 'circuit of culture' metaphor constructs culture as something which moves in or on a circuit. This could invoke a range of associations in the mind of a reader. The category of 'things which move in/on a circuit' could include facets as diverse as electrical current, motor-racing cars, or professional tennis players. Du Gay et al. (1997) state that the metaphor suggests 'that, in fact, meanings are produced at several different sites and circulated through several different processes and practices (the cultural circuit)' (p.3). The notion of 'circuit' is helpful in the sense of creating a notion of movement along a pathway which involves some changes in direction, but is less helpful insofar as it also connotes ideas of circularity. Circuits are usually closed; they end back at the beginning. They may be interrupted by a switch, or a tap, or a start/finish line, but they are 'circles' of sorts, like closed systems. When talking about representational or language circuits, there is a considerable risk in the idea of closed symbolic systems, because of the idea of intertextuality, where 'all meanings depend on other meanings generated and/or deployed in alternative contexts' (Barker, 2004: 101). In that sense, any sign economy or cultural economy is a system that is open to an infinite range of other cultural resonances.

The cultural circuit must be capable of handling meaning-flow in multiple directions, and not just from producers to consumers. As mentioned above, the way in which Du Gay et al.'s (1997) Walkman case study is written assumes that the producer of culture is synonymous with the producer of the product. This tends to conceal the idea that consumers, or music fans, may also be producers. Everyone is a producer insofar as their speech and behaviour is communicative, or subject to reading and interpretation. Therefore, it is necessary to detach the processes of production from any relationship tied to cultural producers or consumers. A band plays a song and thereby produces cultural signifiers; a fan sings along and does something very similar. It is necessary to see the circuit of culture as reversible. To put this in marketing channel terms, the flow of signifiers may go 'upstream' (from the consumer of the offering to its producer) as well as 'downstream' (from producer to consumer).

A more important, and superordinate, metaphor, however, is contained in the idea that signifiers are 'produced' and 'consumed'. This clearly applies an economic metaphor to culture, so that one can speak of the 'cultural economy'. This term, in Du Gay et al. (1997) usage, has a number of different meanings.

First, the term is intended to signify that 'the economic is the crucial domain of existence in modern societies and it too is thoroughly saturated with culture' (1997: 4-5). '[E]conomic processes and practices' are 'cultural phenomena' and 'economics can be seen to be a cultural phenomenon because it works through language and representation'. He adds that the key point about 'cultural economy' as a term is 'the crucial importance it allots to language, representation and meaning – to "culture" – for understanding the conduct of economic life and the construction of economic identities'.

There is a second sense in which Du Gay et al. (1997) talk about 'cultural economy', which they suggest 'refers to the increasing importance of "culture" to doing business in the contemporary world'. They highlight growth in the importance of cultural industries, the 'aestheticisation of seemingly banal products'. They also point to the 'increased influence of what are often termed the cultural intermediary occupations of advertising, design and marketing' professionals who 'are concerned to create an identification between producers and consumers through their expertise in certain signifying practices' (Du Gay et al., 1997:5). Finally, the increase in the deliberate design of organizational culture is seen as evidence of this second sense of 'cultural economy'.

Arguably, there is a third sense of cultural economy: the circuit of culture offers another image, namely that of an economy of signs, which has its own manufacturers (producers), users (consumers) and symbolic order (regulation). This metaphor may be understood in a macro sense, as the totality of meanings in a particular culture, but it might also be applied in a micro sense, as a trope with which to signify the cultural aspects of a music brand's relationship with its fans. Of course, the cultural economy is closely tied to the materials and services economy, but, for analytical purposes, one may conceive of it as separate.

Representation and text

In this section, a connection is made between a key element of the circuit of culture framework, namely 'representation', and another key construct within cultural, popular music, and indeed interpretive marketing studies, namely 'text'. A key construct which enables us to analyse the representational moment of the circuit of culture is the notion of text. Barker (2004: 199) suggests that a text is 'anything that generates meaning through signifying practices' and 'a metaphor that invokes the constitution of meaning through the organization of signs into representation', while 'meaning is a product of textual arrangements' which is 'produced in the interplay between text and reader, that is, the hermeneutic circle'. Titon (2003: 80) cites Geertz as likening culture to 'an assemblage of texts' (1973: 448).

The idea that everything can be read as 'text' is found in cultural studies, communications studies, folklore studies, literature studies, popular music studies, performance studies and other disciplines, such as consumer studies. It is a key heuristic trope across a wide range of disciplines. Apart from the original, literary, meaning of the word 'text', there is also a more technical meaning within linguistics which suggests that a text is a system of signifiers. 'Text' is a metaphor which enables us to talk about the meaning-related aspects of phenomena.

Barker (2011:11), a leading culturalist, says:

> Since images, sounds, objects and practices are sign systems, which signify with the same mechanism as a language, we may refer to them as cultural texts.

Titon (2003:76), a folklorist, says:

> In this enlarged sense, a text is any humanly constructed object. It need not be words: it may be an artefact such as a painting or a building or a pot, or it may be an action or event such as a ritual, or it may even be a person or a group of people. Text in this view becomes a key metaphor for any humanly constructed sign system, and we inhabit a semiotic world of signifiers that are not limited to words but include the entire human universe ... if we overlook the relations between individual people and the

texts that they (we) generate, we will never understand texts – or people.

And Shuker (2001: 14) places the notion of text firmly into a social context:

> The 'meaning' of any engagement between a text and its consumers cannot be assumed, or 'read off' from textual characteristics alone. The text's historical conditions of production and consumption are important, as is the nature of its audience, and the various ways in which they mediate their encounter with the text.

Brands and texts

The definition set forth by the AMA enables a brand to be read as a sign, thereby placing it within the semantic domain of language and culture. Building on this, it may be said that a text is a set of signs which are organized in a certain way. Hesmondhalgh (2005) suggests that cultural offerings may be read as texts, because they are products which are primarily symbols. Producing a text involves the selection of (discursive) resources and their arrangement according to certain conventions or codes, depending on the kind of text and the social context. Each text has certain referents, or things which it wishes to speak about. The meanings of a text may be constrained by its features, and are read off from it by its readers. Texts are polysemic – that is, the same may be read in different ways by one or more readers. Readers are agentic and reflexive, making their own meanings from readings of texts. The utterance of a text is itself an act which may have a social meaning that is separate from the intended meaning ('content') of the text. The variety of popular music texts is considerable. One can regard band-fan relationships as being rich in textual generation and interpretation, as well, of course, as being located in a range of different discursive 'con-texts' – e.g. political, social, economic, cultural, global, local, etc.

Brand meanings can be read as cultural texts which function as symbolic articulators of production and consumption. This is a relatively new line of thinking in mainstream branding, though it has begun to enter branding discourse (O'Reilly, 2005; Hatch and Rubin, 2006). Hatch and

Rubin (2006) go so far as to say that they 'regard brands to be one of the most text-like artefacts of contemporary business culture and therefore appropriate for a demonstration of the potential contribution of hermeneutics'. These texts represent or construct identities for their referents, be these organizations, people, places, or cultural offerings. Brand meanings may be read as emerging from socially produced and consumed texts which mediate meanings between and amongst consumers and producers.

Musician-fan interactions, then, can be read as texts, i.e. structured and performed sets of signifiers, from which meanings may be read. The possible meanings of each text are understood to be limited by the shaping of the text by its author or originator, but open to variation depending on the pre-judgements of the reader, the musical and other cultural codes in operation, and the culture-historical context.

Writing and reading musical texts

Extending the textual metaphor, one may speak of the symbol producer as a writer of text, and the symbol consumer or interpreter as a reader of text. Authors have a key role in shaping texts. When producing their texts (e.g. lyrics, melodies), musical authors have intentions and motivations, conscious or unconscious, and a study of this aspect of textual production can be helpful to those interested in understanding where their texts are 'coming from'. Of course, 'intentions' are also constructed and occasioned.

Whilst the treatment of all communicative interaction between and amongst, for instance, rock group members and fans as textual 'buys' the researcher a 'common factor' which has to do with their readability and signification potential, it also raises a challenge. A live concert, though theoretically (on this reading) the same as a T-shirt insofar as it is a 'text', is clearly quite a different phenomenon. A T-shirt is a material artefact, whereas a live concert is a cultural ritual and a performance (Weinstein, 2000; Kruse, 2003; Fonarow, 2006). Within music, a musical score can be read as a text in which sounds, or notes, are organized in accordance with certain conventions, such as genre, rhythm, harmony, the tonic sol-fa, etc. A rock gig can be read as a text which is structured according to certain conventions about sign behaviour at live concerts, for example: call and response, the set list, the ritual encore, and the way a frontman or frontwoman 'should' move, use a mic, or relate to the audience. A song is a set of verbal and aural signs (lyrics and melody), which are blended together to create certain kinds of text, such as a power ballad, a rock anthem, a folk song, or an aria. The notion of text is useful, because it is used in popular music, as well as in marketing and consumer studies and in creative and cultural industries theory. Such a move – i.e. reading gigs, CD covers and songs as texts – privileges a certain view of the world, which is interested in meaning and is primarily cultural. To call social action a text is to frame it metaphorically, to make salient its 'textuality', to construct it as, or give it the status of, a set of encoded signifiers, and therefore to present it for analysis as something that is readable, or amenable to interpretation. The danger with this text metaphor is that, like all metaphors, it abstracts certain aspects of the phenomenon and carries the meaning away to the workbench for analysis and dissection, leaving the living reality behind. This approach risks backgrounding, for example, a more commercial view of the gig: who is the promoter, what the takings are, what the split is and how it all works. However, all of these commercial practices can themselves also be read as texts. There is another danger in using the textual metaphor, namely that the brand-text is seen as something static, rather than dynamic and continually changing, in line with social interactions. To guard against this, it is useful to incorporate the notion of performance. By this means, it is possible to consider the sensuous and dynamic aspects of meaning-making, and therefore brand construction. It is possible to speak of brands as being performed dynamically within social interaction. All brand texts are performed, and all performances, commercial and musical, may be read as texts. Music brand texts are produced, circulated and consumed – performed – within the circuits of the band-fan cultural economy. Finally, to counteract the rather literary, and therefore perhaps bloodless, connotations of the term 'text', it is important to remember that brand-texts have 'text-ure'; in other words, brand-signs are not just written or visual, but are multi-sensory, including sound and touch.

As mentioned earlier, Barker (2000) defines text as 'all practices which signify'. One may theorize that the interaction between and amongst band members and fans is textually (discursively) constructed. The kinds of texts which are constructed by bands and fans, or third parties, include lyrics, art, merchandise (T-shirts), tangible packaged products (CDs, vinyl, Blu-ray discs), interviews, documentaries, reviews, tattoos, body piercings, publicity photographs, articles, the music sounds, videos, live performances, website graphics, social media content, and band members' physical features and appearances, footwear and clothing in general. These text categories constitute both objects of analysis in themselves, and sources of data constructing the phenomenon under investigation. They also have their own intertextuality, providing links to texts via other musical performers or brands in other times and places.

The music production-consumption circuit

Figure 2, adapted from O'Reilly (2010) illustrates how brand meanings are constructed and negotiated along cultural circuits between stakeholders in a musical project.

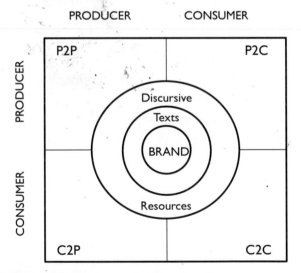

Figure 2: The music production-consumption circuit
Source: adapted from O'Reilly (2010)

The word 'producer' here is being used in the wider cultural sense, rather than the technical sense, and includes any stakeholder working on the 'supply' side of the exchange. Similarly, the word 'consumer' is also being used widely. The producer-to-producer P2P quadrant represents the interaction between stakeholders on the production side of the exchange – for example, during touring, rehearsing, recording or live performance. The bottom right-hand quadrant (consumer to-consumer, C2C) represents the consumption culture in the circuit. It covers interactions between stakeholders on the 'demand' side of the musical exchange relationship. This is where consumers make sense of their response to the music by sharing impressions, and working out their own understanding of the brand. The top-right-hand quadrant (producer-to-consumer, P2C) represents occasions in which producers communicate with consumers, particularly through marketing communications, but also, for example, through radio, television, web, magazine or newspaper interviews, tour announcements, and websites. Finally, the bottom-left-hand quadrant (consumer-to-producer, C2P) consists of actions or communications initiated by music fans, whether positive or negative. At these four sites of social interaction around the brand, meanings are worked out and the sustainability of the brand is decided. These might include, for example, issues to do with the authenticity, credibility or legitimacy of the music artist's claims to cultural distinction and artistic excellence, and the cash in the consumers' bank accounts. Producers and consumers of music-related meanings are always selecting and mobilizing discursive resources to construct texts. These texts go towards making up the meanings of the music brand.

Layered musical and other texts

The relationship between the different kinds of music-related texts in circulation is complex. Figure 3 deals only with the provider side of the exchange. It shows how the different layers of text and meaning are built up in a notional band's artwork. A creative session may result in finding a riff, a hook, a melody or a line that seems to work. This is then built up until a coherent song with lyrics and melody is put together. Stories about these practices make up a large part of music branding.

Layer 1	Layer 2	Layer 3	Layer 4	Layer 5
SONGS Music Lyrics Sounds	**COVER ART/ SLEEVE NOTES** Artwork Text Lyrics Logo Photographs	**MERCHANDISE** T-shirts Sweatshirts Hoodies Hats	**WEBSITE** *News* Newsletters Tour Record News News Archive Talk	**GIGS** Stage design Lighting Instruments Equipment Sound mix Movement Setlist Musical Performance
VISUAL IMAGES Artwork Photographs		**MUSICAL PRODUCT** Vinyl CD Concert DVD Music DVD	*Creative* Lyrics Music Art	**PERSONAL APPEARANCE** Jewellery Tattoos Piercings Clothing
		MARKETING COMMUNICATIONS Interviews Posters Flyers Advertisements Web-site Social media	*Partners* Side Projects	**MERCH BOOTH** Musical Product Merchandise
			Community Noticeboard Links Contact	
			Market The Shop	

Figure 3 : Layering of texts in musical production. *Source:* Adapted from O'Reilly (2010)

The circuit of music culture

It is possible, then, to imagine a circuit of music culture as a frame for the idea of music brands. This idea retains the notion of a circuit of culture (Du Gay et al., 1997), and expands 'representation' by including the use of particular discursive resources (lyrics, melodies, sounds, images) to build texts which signify referents and meanings. Irrespective of which kinds of music texts are under discussion, this framework reminds the analyst that the text must be related to the music provider, as well as the audience members and other stakeholders. It also guides the analyst to examine which discursive resources are being mobilized by whom, and to talk about what meanings might be taken from the discourse/text by its readers. By making explicit these aspects of discursive interaction between music producer and consumer or other stakeholders, the framework promotes reflexivity about language and discourse. Another way of looking at this framework is to consider it as a map of the discursive economy of the band-fan relationship.

Summary

This chapter has proposed a socio-cultural perspective on music brands, building on notions of the circuit of culture and text. This approach places the emphasis on brand meanings in any commercial and cultural analysis of music brands. It also grants a role to all stakeholders in the creation of those meanings. The discussion now moves into the third part of this book, which deals with consumption perspectives. Chapter 7, the next chapter, deals specifically with music consumption. Chapter 8 deals with different framings of people as fans, audience members and consumers, and Chapter 9 addresses music and community.

References

Adorno, T. (2001) *The Culture Industry*, London: Routledge.

Alexander, V. (2003) *Sociology of the Arts: Exploring Fine and Popular Forms*, Oxford: Wiley-Blackwell.

Barker, C. (2011) *Cultural Studies: Theory and Practice*, London: Sage.

Barker, C. (2004) *The Sage Dictionary of Cultural Studies*, London: Sage.

Barker, C. and Galasinski, D. (2001) *Cultural Studies and Discourse Analysis: A Dialogue on Language and Identity*, London: Sage.

Crozier, W. (1997). 'Music and social influence', in: Hargreaves, D.J and North, A.C (ed.) *The Social Psychology of Music*, Oxford, Oxford University Press, 67-83.

Davies, G. and Chun, R. (2003) 'The Use of Metaphor in the Exploration of the Brand Concept', *Journal of Marketing Management*, **19** (1/2), 45-73.

Du Gay, P., Hall, S., Janes, L., Mackay, H. and Negus, K. (1997) *Doing Cultural Studies: The story of the Sony Walkman*, London: Sage.

Elliott, R. and Wattanasuwan, K. (1998) 'Brands as symbolic resources for the construction of identity', *International Journal of Advertising*, **17**, (2), 131-144.

Fonarow, W. (2006) *Empire of Dirt: The Aesthetics and Rituals of British Indie Music*, Middletown, CT: Wesleyan University Press.

Frith, S. (1998) *Performing Rites: Evaluating Popular Music*, Oxford: Oxford Paperbacks.

Geertz, C. (1973) *The Interpretation of Cultures*, London: Fontana.

Gregory, A. (1997) 'The roles of music in society: the ethnomusicological perspective', in: Hargreaves, D and North, A (ed.), *The Social Psychology of Music*, Oxford: Oxford University Press.

Hall, S. (ed.) (1997) *Representation: Cultural representations and signifying practices*, London: Sage.

Hargreaves, D.J. and North, A.C. (ed.) (1997). *The Social Psychology of Music*, Oxford: Oxford University Press.

Hatch, M.J. and Rubin, J. (2006) 'The hermeneutics of branding', *Journal of Brand Management*, **14**, (1/2) 40-59.

Hebdige, D. (1979) *Subculture: The meaning of style*, London: Routledge.

Kruse, H. (2003) *Site and Sound: Understanding Independent Music Scenes*, New York: Peter Lang.

Mansfield, N. (2000) *Subjectivity: Theories of the self from Freud to Haraway*, New York: New York University Press.

Middleton, R. (ed.) (1990) *Reading Pop: Approaches to Textual Analysis in Popular Music*, Oxford: Oxford University Press.

O'Reilly, D. (2005) 'Cultural brands/branding cultures', *Journal of Marketing Management*, **21**, (5/6), 573-588.

O'Reilly, D. and Kerrigan, F. (ed.) (2010) *Arts Marketing: A Fresh Approach*, London: Routledge.

Rouget, G. (1985) Music and Trance: A theory of the relations between music and possession, Chicago: University of Chicago Press.

Sacks, H. 1984. 'On doing "being ordinary"', in: Atkinson M. and Heritage, J. (ed.) *Structure of Social Action: Studies in Conversation Analysis*, Cambridge, UK: Cambridge University Press.

Shuker, R. (2001), *Understanding Popular Music*, London: Routledge.

Titon, J. T. (2003) 'Text', in: Feintuch, B. (ed.) Eight Words for the Study of Expressive Culture, Champaign, Il: University of Illinois Press.

Veblen, T. (1899) *The Theory of the Leisure Class*, New York: New American Library.

Weinstein, D. (2000) *Heavy Metal: The music and its culture*, Cambridge, MA: Da Capo Press.

Part III

Consumption

Perspectives

7 Music Consumption

Introduction

> 'The world is not for beholding. It is for hearing. It is not legible, but audible.'
>
> (Attali 1977/1985: 3)

Music can be heard everywhere, infiltrating our everyday existence. Not only does one choose to listen to music across a range of situations, times and spaces; one is also exposed to music in innumerable day-to-day situations – on public transport, from a passing car, through advertisements. Even prior to the technological advances which have revolutionized the way music is acquired, purchased and used (Elberse 2010; Simun 2009), Merriam noted that 'the importance of music, as judged by the sheer ubiquity of its presence, is enormous... There is probably no other human cultural activity which is so all-pervasive and which reaches into, shapes and often controls so much of human behaviour' (1964: 218). Technological, social and cultural trends have only served to deepen and diversify the ways in which one listens to, or engages with, music.

The marketing and consumer behaviour perspective on music engagement has focused primarily on experiential aspects. Interest in the consumption of music arose on the back of the experiential turn in consumer research, and the associated interest in aesthetic products (e.g. Holbrook and Hirschman 1982). Music is a rich and complex symbolic, social and political product (Larsen et al., 2010), the experience of which can be distinguished from the consumption of other kinds of products. For example, music is the only product which is primarily auditory (Larsen and Lawson, 2010); consumption does not alter its recorded form and it can be consumed actively or passively, with or without ownership, in private and in public (Lacher and Mizerski, 1994). As a result, most of our knowledge about the consumption of music has concentrated on the emotional and aesthetic reasons for listening to music (e.g. Cherian and Jones, 1991; Kellaris and Kent, 1993; Lacher and Mizerski, 1994; North and Hargreaves, 1997; Chien et al., 2007; Lonsdale and North, 2011); the relationship between music and identity, particularly the use of music as a 'badge of identity' (e.g. Holbrook, 1986; DeNora, 1999; North and Hargreaves, 1999; Shankar, 2000; Goulding et al., 2002; Negus and Velazquez, 2002; Nuttall, 2009) and the symbolic function of music (Hogg and Banister, 2000; Larsen et al., 2009, 2010).

There is a broader question, underlying this body of knowledge, which remains unexamined. That is: What does it mean to frame music engagement as consumption and music listeners as consumers, and what are the consequences of doing so for our understanding of music consumption? As conceptualized by Holbrook and Anand (1990) and Lacher and Mizerski (1994), music consumption is the act of listening to a piece of music. Listening to music is, without a doubt, one of the most significant aspects of the act of consuming music; however, it does not entirely capture all that is involved. For example, talking and reading about music are also important activities in consuming music (Larsen et al., 2009). If, in addition, one also acknowledges that the music product can be an artist, venue and associated paraphernalia (see Chapter 3), then the consumption of the music product must necessarily go beyond listening. Finally, this conceptualization does not help us to identify or understand how the experience of engaging with music differs if one does it as an audience member, as a fan, or as a consumer. Thus, a clearer understanding is needed of what one means by consumption in the context of music.

Consumers and consumption

Developing a broader and more nuanced conceptualization of music consumption should be underpinned by a more general understanding of what 'consumption' is and in what situations a person is a 'consumer'. Although consumption infuses many aspects of contemporary life, such as our identity construction, social relations and leisure activities, there is a lack of agreement about the definition and conceptualization of the notions of the 'consumer' and 'consumption', even within the disciplines of marketing and consumer behaviour, which are primarily concerned with consumption. Gabriel and Lang (2006) note that the term 'consumer' is so overused that it has lost any sort of specificity. It can mean all things to all people, and is therefore in danger of collapsing into meaninglessness. Much scholarly work simply assumes that a common understanding exists, but very rarely is it made explicit. Furthermore, when a definition is provided, it is often treated as a given, and not scrutinized in any way (Borgerson, 2005; Wilk, 2004). For example, consumer behaviour is defined by Arnould et al. (2004: 9) in their student textbook '*Consumers*', as 'individuals or groups acquiring, using and disposing of products, services, ideas or experiences'. Examples of each of the components of this definition are provided, and but there is little discussion of where the limits of each of these categories are. For example, at what point does an experience become an act of consumption (Woodward and Holbrook, forthcoming)?

There has also been little consideration paid to the socio-historical embeddedness of such a conceptualization, and how what one means by 'consumption' has changed over the course of history. First appearing in English in the 14th century, the word 'to consume' had a slightly negative connotation, as it meant destroying, using up, wasting or exhausting (Gabriel and Lang, 2006; Graeber, 2011). Gradually, as people like Adam Smith began to use the term in juxtaposition to 'production', the focus of 'consumption' shifted from the object that is destroyed to the human needs that are fulfilled in the process (Williams, 1976). From this perspective, consumption is a cultural universal (Douglas and Isherwood, 1979). Everyone needs to eat, be clothed and have shelter, and mark social rituals in some way, and therefore consumption is a necessary aspect of human existence and a prominent, mundane social practice. It is only in the last century that consumption has begun to broaden beyond simple utilitarian needs to a much wider range of cognitive, symbolic, hedonic, and emotional ones – such as pleasure, enjoyment, freedom and self-expression. Consequently, in consumer societies, consumption is no longer considered a means to an end, but rather is an end in and of itself (Gabriel and Lang, 2006).

These limitations notwithstanding, there are common identifying features across the existing conceptualizations that help us to develop a useful understanding of the consumer and consumption in contemporary society. The first is the notion of 'choice', which is the unchallenged, beating heart of consumption in modern capitalist economies. Gabriel and Lang (2006) note that the universal nature of the experience of choice is what differentiates contemporary consumption from that which came before. This reflects a shift in the status of consumers in the economy, from passive to active agents (Graeber, 2011). From an economic perspective, consumption is the end point of production (e.g. Wilk, 2004). Thus, in economic theories such as those of Adam Smith and John K. Galbraith, the interests of the consumer take precedence over those of the producer in determining production, thus elevating the consumer to the role of 'sovereign'. As productive capacity expanded during the industrial revolution, concerns grew about how to generate sufficient consumer demand to ensure continued economic growth. The key element of the subsequent emergence and growth of consumer culture (see Adam Curtis' (2002) documentary *The Century of the Self: Happiness Machines* for a critical examination of how this was achieved) was the increasing reference to the importance of consumer choice (Smart 2010). The assumptions underlying the rhetoric of choice express a powerful and seductive link between choice, consumption, capitalism and democracy. These assumptions are: the more choice there is for consumers, the better; choice is good for the economy as it is the driving force of efficiency, growth and diversity; a social system based on choice is better than one without; and consumer capitalism means more choice for everyone (Gabriel and Lang, 2006). Thus, the dominant representation of the consumer is that of a 'chooser', while consumption is the enactment of one's right and responsibility to choose.

The act of consumption is also shaped by the consumers' efforts to realize the value they seek to gain and to satisfy the needs, wants and desires that drive their choices. Products serve numerous functions for the people who own or use them (Furby, 1978). Thus, the notion of use-value (compared to exchange value) is the second common identifying feature of contemporary consumption, but it is one that is multifarious and contested. Different interpretations of use-value emerge, depending on underlying assumptions about who or what a consumer is.

Based on the 'economic man' model from classical economics, much early consumer research focused on the functional and utilitarian benefits of products. This approach viewed consumers as rational decision makers who choose and purchase products that maximize the utility they gain from them. With the exception of a period of research into irrational buying needs based on motivation research (e.g. Dichter, 1964), the rational choice model dominated and evolved to logical flow models of bounded rationality (e.g. Howard and Sheth, 1969) and then later into what is commonly referred to as the 'information-processing model' (Bettman 1979). There are, however, a number of limitations to the information processing perspective. For example, it encourages an emphasis on purchase decisions, rather than on the consumption process as a whole. Also, this model is only useful in explaining the purchase of products that are chosen for their tangible and utilitarian benefits, and does not capture any of the other motivations for consumption activities.

Fuelled by an interest in the consumption of aesthetic products, which could not be adequately explained by the rational perspective, Morris Holbrook and Elizabeth Hirschman heralded a new perspective in consumer research. The 'experiential view' regards consumption as primarily subjective, and influenced by fantasies, feelings and fun (Holbrook and Hirschman, 1982). Based on a realization that choice depends on use, and that buying depends on consuming (Holbrook, 1995), experiential consumption moves the scope beyond the focus on purchase to all stages of consumption. Most importantly, this perspective highlights the primacy of emotions, experience and the subconscious over rationality, cognition and the conscious, which are central to the information-processing model (Maclaran, 2009).

Building from the platform of the experiential turn, and captured in consumer culture theory (Arnould and Thompson, 2005), the perspective of 'consumer as communicator' began to gain ground. The symbolic value of products has long been recognized both explicitly (e.g. Levy, 1959; Veblen, 1899) and implicitly through the consideration of brands, however the experiential turn provided fertile ground for these ideas to take root. Contemporary consumer research commonly portrays consumers as active subjects, who negotiate and transform market-mediated meanings in order to construct and communicate their identities and social positions (Karababa and Ger, 2011). Central to this is the idea that the products people consume (both tangible and intangible) embody a system of meaning, which can be used as symbols to express themselves and to communicate with each other (Gabriel and Lang, 2006).

Taking all of these perspective into account, it is now widely recognized that use-value goes far beyond instrumental and utilitarian functions, and reaches into the symbolic, experiential, social and aesthetic (Dittmar, 1992; Gabriel and Lang, 2006). A significant consequence of the broadening of consumption from the functional to the experiential to the communicative is that the boundaries of 'consumption' have become blurred. When a person gains pleasure from listening to music or displaying tickets from the concerts they have attended as part of their personal narrative, are they being a consumer, or a fan, or something else? Attali (1977/1985: 9) says that music provides three simultaneous values of human work: 'joy for the creator, use-value for the listener, and exchange value for the seller'. But exactly how does this use-value manifest in different frames of music engagement?

Consuming music

Music consumption implies a type of engagement with music that is mediated by the market, and which therefore necessitates a view of the consumer as sovereign. Recalling that the music product can take a number of different forms, such as a recording, a concert, a piece of memorabilia (see discussion in Chapter 3 on music as product), in the market for music, the consumer is represented as someone who actively chooses from amongst a number of producers or suppliers of that product type (e.g. an artist or a venue). The music consumer participates in economic exchange in order to take ownership and gain the right to access music. Given the economic value of the music product, acquisition usually requires the consumer to exchange money. Although this is the dominant discourse in understanding the relationship between music and consumption, the sovereignty of the music consumer is challenged. Adorno (1991) and Attali (1977/1985) both argue that musical marketplace offerings are commodities which are controlled, ordered and shaped by capitalism, and which therefore exert power and structure our consumption patterns in ways which transform us into slaves to capital. This counterargument also highlights that although the rhetoric of sovereignty and choice suggests individual autonomy, the representation of the music consumer takes the form of the masses. Music is produced in a multiple-serial form (Laing, 1985) for mass consumption. Implicit in this is that the framing of musical engagement as consumption is only really acceptable in the realms of 'popular' music, where it has been reproduced in a commodity-like form. In contrast, describing engagement with forms of music that are more highly valued on aesthetic grounds, such as avant-garde and classical music, as consumption sits uncomfortably with many.

There are clearly some situations in which music can be consumed instrumentally, such as to enhance performance in running (e.g. Karageorghis and Priest 2008; Terry and Karageorghis 2006), and in such situations the information processing model might provide a sufficient understanding of the consumption of music. However, music is experiential and fundamentally social – it is socially constructed, socially embedded and its nature and value are inherently social (Bowman, 1998). Therefore, the reasons why people consume music primarily reflect the experiential and communicative use-values in consumption. For example, Hargreaves and North (1999), building on Merriam's (1964) work on the functions of music, provide a comprehensive list of the functions music performs for the individual in everyday life. These are: (1) emotional expression, (2) aesthetic enjoyment and entertainment, (3) communication, and (4) symbolic representation.

Music performs other functions at a societal level, such as validating social institutions and religious rituals, and providing continuity and stability of culture (Merriam, 1964; Hargreaves and North, 1999), but these provide little understanding of the sovereign music consumers' behaviour, which is intrinsically individualist. As noted earlier, new digital technologies have transformed the consumption of music, making it cheaper, more accessible, convenient and portable, and thus enabling new music consumption practices. This stimulated Lonsdale and North (2011) to re-examine the reasons for listening to music. Their research does not explicitly ask about the consumption of music, but as it is embedded in a 'uses and gratification research' method which enables the investigation of how people use mass media to satisfy their individual needs, the results provide valuable insight. Thus, it can be said that people consume music to:

1   Cope with, and alleviate negative feelings, and also to create and optimize a positive mood (*mood management*).

2   Construct and/or present a social image to others (*personal identity*).

3   Find out about and learn what is going on in the world (*surveillance*).

4   Distract themselves in order to relieve boredom or pass the time, escape or relax (*diversion*).

5   Engage in music regardless of musical ability, by singing along or dancing (*musical participation*).

6   Remember and reminisce about happy times and loved ones (*reflect on the past*).

The congruence between these uses of music and the use-values underlying the experiential and communicative perspective is evident. It is important to note that the experience of consuming music is often characterized by a complex interplay of these different functions (Larsen *et al.*, 2009, 2010).

The practices of musical engagement that are highlighted by framing it as 'consumption' centre on choosing music and consuming it in a manner that draws out these different and multiple use-values. In response to dynamic and innovative digital technologies, consumers acquire music in increasingly diverse, contentious, and sometimes even deviant ways. We have some understanding of who, what, where and how consumers download music and file-share illegally (Fox and Wren, 2001; Langdenderfer and Cook, 2001; Moore and McMullan, 2004; Dilmperi et al., 2011), but less of an understanding of why. Understanding the consumers' position on the ethics of file sharing seems to be key. Many consumers believe that file sharing is less serious than other forms of stealing, such as shoplifting (e.g. Gopal et al., 2004; Wingrove et al., 2010), because there is no direct harm to anyone (Vitell and Muncy, 1992). Consumers' attitudes towards file sharing are also influenced by their views of the music industry. Downloaders justify file sharing as taking away from corporations who are more interested in profit and exploiting consumers than attending to their consumers' needs (Giesler and Pohlmann, 2003a, 2003b; Denegri-Knott, 2004; Moore and McMullan, 2004) or musicians' interests. Furthermore, many blame the increase in file sharing on the extortionate prices charged for an album (Kwong et al., 2003). Consumers are more likely to illegally download an artist's work if the artist is excessively successful (Ouellet, 2007), as they believe that infringement activity will not greatly affect the profits of the artist or the related large corporations (Moore and McMullan, 2004).

In line with contemporary interest in the communicative perspective in consumer research, the symbolic aspects of music consumption are particularly salient. Music is understood as a special type of symbolic product, which enables people to construct, maintain and communicate their identity (Holbrook, 1986; DeNora, 1999; Hogg and Banister, 2000; Shankar 2000; Goulding et al., 2002; Nuttall, 2009; Larsen et al., 2009, 2010), values, attitudes and distinctive views, through their individual preferences (Hagreaves et al., 2002). When consuming music symbolically, consumers evaluate the congruency between the image of the music and the identity they wish to present, both of which are socially constructed and situated. Rituals, such as singing along with music, dancing to it and discussing it, reinforce the representation of self and support the transition between different identities in daily life (Larsen et al., 2010).

It is clear that framing music engagement as 'consumption' illuminates the range of use-values that motivates consumers. At the same time, the focus on the consumer sovereignty, choice of market-mediated music and experiential and communicative consumption practices averts our gaze from other ways in which people engage with music.

People are framed in addition to, and other than as consumers, when they engage with music. They might, for example, be viewed as audiences, fans or collectors. These frame differs in (1) the representations of the person engaging with music, (2) the reasons for engaging in music (i.e. use-values from a consumption perspective), and (3) engagement practices. While they transcend the scope of the current conceptualization of music consumption, it remains important to briefly examine these different frames, as they highlight other representations, motivations and practices which contribute to a broader understanding of music engagement and the relationship between music, markets and consumption.

Audiences

An audience in the context of music is, simply put, an assembled group of listeners or spectators before whom a performance takes place (*Oxford Dictionaries Online*, 2012). Thus, the prevailing representation of musical engagement that the frame of 'audience' offers is that of a collective or group, rather than an individual. Audiences are complex, in that they take different forms in relation to the type and nature of performance, and are comprised not of a mass of individuals, but a weave of socially interacting groups and individuals (Abercrombie and Longhurst, 1998). As such, they also take on a temporary and transient character. Though many audiences come together in venues with a permanent physical presence, the experience remains only in the memory (Waterman, 1998). This type of musical engagement is ephemeral, experiential and primarily intangible, although often material artefacts are purchased (e.g. official t-shirts, programmes, tickets) or created (e.g. photos, bootleg recordings) as carriers of meaning and memory to mark the experience. Prior to the turn of the 20th century and the introduction of technologies that enabled the reproduction of music, being a member of an audience was the only way of listening to music, and thus audiences are deeply embedded, culturally, socially and historically.

Audiences come together to engage in music for a number of reasons. Of greatest significance is the sense of community and belonging which can be brought about by sharing an intense experience (e.g. Kozinets, 2002). This can result in 'flow' experiences (Csikszentmihalyi, 1990) where people lose themselves through full immersion in an absorbing experience. The pursuit of 'flow' or ecstatic experience in order to escape the everyday is central to rave or dance culture (e.g. Goulding *et al.*, 2002). In addition, the temporary, engaging and co-creative nature of the audience enables people to experiment with utopian possibilities by creating and experimenting with ideal alternative communities, such as at Glastonbury Festival (Larsen and O'Reilly, 2008).

The frame of the 'audience' highlights certain music engagement practices, such as the highly embodied nature of the 'flow' experience. Of these, the ritualistic character of audiences is notable. The ritual practices and social norms of classical music, such as refraining from clapping between the movements of a symphony or concerto, or dressing in the appropriate manner, are widely acknowledged and are so embedded that they act as a barrier to attendance for those not versed in them. Fonarow (2006) illustrates that British indie music audiences are also highly ritualized, organizing forms of participation in gigs in a manner which marks distinctions between different communities in the audience.

Fans

Music fans and fandom are examined in detail in Chapter 8, so the purpose of this section is to briefly identify representations, motivations and practices of music engagement highlighted by the frame of 'fan'. The music fan is someone with a focused interest, who is highly engaged in a particular type of musical product, and who has developed a special type of relation with the object of their admiration (e.g. Thorne, 2011). This conceptualization suggests engagement at an individual level, however the notion of fandom also brings in a collective dimension which is often manifest as a subculture, such as punk, goth or heavy metal. What differentiates music fans from other people engaging with music is the degree to which they are involved – fans often weave their interest in music throughout their daily lives in a very visible way, and consequently music can become central to their identity construction and representation (Shankar, 2000). Fans also tend to engage with a variety of products related to their object of interest; these can be either musical in nature, such as recorded music, memorabilia, concerts; and/or non-musical, but part of the constellation of products symbolic of a particular subculture, such as clothing, leisure activities, body art and so on. The level and type of engagement pursued can be quite extreme, as in the case of groupies who seek personal and intimate interaction with their revered musicians. Groupies are commonly portrayed as dysfunctional or deviant fans, but this is only one of a number of representations of groupies that exist in popular culture (Larsen, 2012).

Fans develop such high levels of involvement for a number of reasons. In more extreme forms of fandom, such as with groupies, fandom is an expression of passion for the object of affection and a desire to become a part of their creative process and output. One famous groupie, Pamela des Barres (2007), likens the role of the groupie to that of the muse, and suggests that the groupie's behaviour is a demonstration of their devotion, appreciation and love for the artistic creations of the musician. Fans are also motivated by a complex interplay of needs to both belong to a particular subculture and, through that membership, mark themselves as different or unique in comparison to the general population (e.g. Hebdige, 1979). Basing their identity on subcultural and social capital can, however, be fraught with tension for fans, especially when the commodification of that subculture threatens to devalue the capital. The mythologization of the 'hipster', for instance, has led to the practice of 'aesthetic discrimination' through which authentic hipsters demonstrate their cultural authority over stereotypical hipsters by selecting aesthetically superior indie music from the marketplace (Arsel and Thompson, 2012).

Communal practices of engagement with music are highlighted by the frame of the 'fan'. Fan clubs have long engaged in what would now be called the co-creation (Vargo and Lusch, 2004) of cultural texts. Historically, these texts commonly took the form of fan magazines, however as a consequence of the diffusion and proliferation of digital technologies and social media, they now take a range of forms, including blogs, unofficial websites, Facebook sites, mashup videos, and so on. These can have great influence on the success of a musical endeavour.

Collectors

An important form of musical engagement can be viewed through the frame of the collector. Two distinct representations of music collectors exist. The first portrays collectors as infantile or nerdy, engaging in behaviour that some might argue they should have grown out of. The second depicts a worthwhile cultural pursuit akin to curatorship, if the objects collected hold a valued status (Longhurst, 2007). Both representations imply an individual pursuit which provides some sort of refuge from the wider world, and there is some evidence to support the male gendering of music collectors (Macdonald et al., 2002). For example, Thornton (1995) and Richards (1998) indicate that males enjoy opportunities to display the quantity and range of their music collections, in part because it enables them to publicly exhibit their economic capital, which in turn affirms a masculine work ethic and identity. Collectors are often viewed as aficionados, and the collections are public displays of knowledge or cultural capital. Thus, record collecting has both public and private dimensions. There is also a hint of the obsessive in representations of music collectors, which can lead to addiction (Cockrill et al., 2011) and/or illegal behaviours such as the recording and trading of bootleg recordings.

Collectors are motivated to collect for a number of different reasons. Gabriel and Lang (2006) note that collecting of any sort is a quest for completeness, consistency and unity, driven by the 'Diderot unity' (McCracken, 1988), where objects communicate only in concert with one another. An implication is that collecting is an investment in cultural capital which positions the collector in social space, communicates their identity and provides a means of self-recording one's own history (e.g. Shankar, 2000). Music collections can be an important means of remembering and connecting with the emotional (DeNora, 2000).

Music collections are usually comprised of recordings, but can also be of or include a range of material items, such as concert tickets or programmes, memorabilia and newspaper articles. One of the most characteristic practices of this form of music engagement, as noted above, is curatorship. In order for a collection to be consistent, unified and therefore meaningful, it must somehow be ordered and organized. Curating may be highly ritualized and this practice is often caricatured, as in Nick Hornby's (1995) novel *High Fidelity*. Different modes of the public use of music collections can be identified, such as Straw's (1997) modes of masculinity, of which he distinguished three types: (1) the dandy who transforms his musical knowledge into an ongoing public performance, which may be seen as superficial; (2) the nerd who has a mastery of knowledge that is of little use in, or even detrimental, to social interaction; and (3) the brute whose persona is of a pure and uncultivated instinctuality or an innate sense of 'hipness'.

Summary

Each of these frames – the consumer, audience, fan and collector – provide different perspectives on how and why people engage with music. The 'music consumer' frame is the most visible in the marketing and consumer research discipline, however each of the frames highlights aspects of musical engagement that should be, and are, of significant interest in understanding the relationship between music, markets and consumption, and which resonate with the experiential and communicative perspectives in contemporary understandings of consumers and consumption. Many marketing- and consumer-related issues are touched on in each of the representations. Just to name a few, the 'audience' frame highlights the social situatedness of consumption, embodied consumption and consumption rituals; 'fans and fandom' draws attention to brand loyalty, brand communities and tribes, co-creative practices, and deviance; and finally, 'collectors' links to connoisseurship, cultural capital, identity expression, symbolic consumption, product constellations and addiction. Thus, limiting our understanding of the relationship between music, markets and consumption to only the 'music consumer' frame narrows our focus onto too few of the important and interesting aspects of people's engagement with music.

It would be more appropriate and fruitful to think of these frames as different spheres of music engagement that people move in and out of, and which interact and interplay with each other within the wider socio-cultural-political space of the contemporary music market. Sometimes, people can be clearly understood as consumers, and, at others, they might be best understood as part of an audience. However, because the majority of people's musical engagement is now mediated by the market, all of these frames are important in developing a full appreciation of the diversity and complexity of music consumption.

References

Abercrombie, N. and Longhurst, B. (1998) *Audiences: A Sociological Theory of Performance and Imagination*, London: Sage.

Adorno, T. (1991) *The Culture Industry*, London: Routledge Classics.

Arnould, E. and Thompson, C. (2005) 'Consumer Culture Theory (CCT); twenty years of research' *Journal of Consumer Research*, **31** (4), 868-882.

Arnould, E., Price, L. and Zinkhan, G. (2004) *Consumers*, Second edition, New York, NY: McGraw-Hill/Irwin.

Arsel, Z. and Thompson, C. (2011) 'Demythologizing consumption practices: how consumers protect their field dependent identity investments from devaluing marketplace myths', *Journal of Consumer Research*, **37** (5), 791-806.

Attali, J. (1977/1985) *Noise: The Political Economy of Music*, Minneapolis: University of Minnesota Press.

Bettman, J.R. (1979) *An Information Processing Theory of Consumer Choice*, Reading: Addison Wesley.

Borgerson, J. (2005) 'Materiality, agency and the constitution of consuming subjects: insights for consumer research', *Advances in Consumer Research*, **32**, 439-43.

Bowman, W.D. (1998) *Philosophical Perspectives on Music*, Oxford: Oxford University Press.

Cherian, J. and Jones, M. (1991) 'Some processes in brand categorizing: why one person's noise is another person's music', *Advances in Consumer Research*, **18**, 77-83.

Chien, L., Zhou, S. and Bryant, J. (2007) 'Temporal changes in mood repair through music consumption: effects of mood, mood salience and individual differences' *Media Psychology*, **9** (3), 695-713.

Cockrill, A., Sullivan, M. and Norbury, H. (2011) 'Music consumption: lifestyle choice or addiction', *Journal of Retailing and Consumer Services*, **18**, 160-166.

Csikszentmihalyi, M. (1990) *Flow: The Psychology of Optimal Experience*, New York: Harper and Row.

Denegri-Knott, J. (2004) 'Sinking the online "music pirates:" Foucault, power and deviance on the web', *Journal of Computer-Mediated Communication*, **9** (4), http://jcmc.indiana.edu/vol9/issue4/denegri_knott.html [Accessed 30 April 2013]

DeNora, T. (1999) 'Music as a technology of the self' *Poetics*, **27**, 31-56.

DeNora, T. (2000) *Music in Everyday Life*, Cambridge: Cambridge Unity Press.

des Barres, P. (2007) *Let's Spend the Night Together: Backstage Secrets of Rock Muses and Supergroupies*, London: Helter Skelter.

Dichter, E. (1964) *Handbook of Consumer Motivations*, New York: McGraw Hill.

Dilmperi, A., King, T. and Dennis, C. (2011) 'Pirates of the web: the curse of illegal downloading', *Journal of Retailing and Consumer Services*, **18**, 132-140.

Dittmar, H. (1992) *The Social Psychology of Material Possessions: To Have Is to Be*, Harvester Wheatsheaf, New York, NY: St Martin's Press.

Douglas, M. and Isherwood, B. (1979) *The World of Goods: Towards an Anthropology of Consumption*, New York: Basic Goods.

Elberse, A. (2010) 'Bye-bye bundles: the unbundling of music in digital channels', *Journal of Marketing*, **74** (3), 107-123.

Fonarow, W. (2006) *Empire of Dirt: The Aesthetics and Rituals of British Indie Music*. Middletown, CT: Wesleyan University Press.

Fox, M. and Wren, B. (2001) 'A broadcasting model for the music industry', *Journal of Media Management*, **3**(2), 112-119.

Furby, L. (1978) 'Possessions: toward a theory of their meaning and function throughout the life cycle', in: Baltes, P.B. (ed.) *Lifespan Development and Behaviour*, Vol 1., New York, NY: Academic Press, 297-336.

Gabriel, Y. and Lang, T. (2006) *The Unmanageable Consumer*, London: Sage

Giesler, M. and Pohlmann, M. (2003a) 'The social form of Napster: cultivating the paradox of consumer emancipation', *Advances in Consumer Research*, **30** (1), 94-100.

Giesler, M. and Pohlmann, M. (2003b) 'The anthropology of file sharing: consuming Napster as a gift', *Advances in Consumer Research*, **30** (1), 273-279.

Gopal, R.D., Sanders, G.L., Bhattacharjee, S., Agrawal, M. and Wagner, S. (2004) 'A behavioural model of digital music piracy', *Journal of Organizational Computing and Electronic Commerce*, **14** (2), 89-105.

Goulding, C., Shankar, A. and Elliott, E. (2002) 'Working weeks, rave weekends: identity fragmentation and the emergence of new communities', *Consumption, Markets and Culture*, **5** (4), 261-284.

Graeber, D. (2011) 'Consumption', *Current Anthropology*, **52** (4), 489-511.

Hargreaves, D.J. and North, A.C. (1999) 'The functions of music in everyday life: redefining the social in music psychology', *Psychology of Music*, **27**, 71-83.

Hargreaves, D.J., Miell, D.E. and MacDonald, R.A.R. (2002) 'What are musical identities, and why are they important?', in: MacDonald, R.A.R., Hargreaves, D.J. and Miell, D.E. (eds), *Musical Identities*, Oxford: Oxford University Press, 1-20.

Hebdige, D. (1979) *Subculture: The Meaning of Style*, London: Routledge.

Hogg, M.K., Banister, E.N. (2000) 'The structure and transfer of cultural meaning: a study of young consumers and pop music', *Advances in Consumer Research*, **27**, 19-23.

Holbrook, M.B. (1986) 'I'm hip: an autobiographical account of some musical consumption experiences', *Advances in Consumer Research*, **13**, 614-618.

Holbrook, M.B. (1995) *Consumer Research: Introspective Essays on the Study of Consumption*, Thousand Oaks, CA: Sage.

Holbrook, M.B. and Anand, P. (1990) 'Effects of tempo on responses to music', *Psychology of Music*, **18**, 150-162.

Holbrook, M.B. and Hirschman, E. (1982) 'The experiential aspects of consumption: consumer fantasies, feelings and fun', *Journal of Consumer Research*, **9**, 132-140.

Hornby, N (1995) *High Fidelity*, London: Victor Gollancz Ltd

Howard, J.A. and Sheth, J.N. (1969) *The Theory of Buyer Behaviour*, New York: John Wiley.

Karababa, E. and Ger, G. (2011) 'Early modern Ottoman coffeehouse culture and the formation of the consumer subject', *Journal of Consumer Research*, **37** (5), 737-760.

Karageorghis, C.I. and Priest, D.L. (2008) 'Music in sport and exercise: an update on research and application', *The Sport Journal*, [online] **11** (3), http://www.thesportjournal.org/article/music-sport-and-exercise-update-research-and-application [Accessed 30 April 2013].

Kellaris, J.J. and Kent, R.J. (1993) 'An exploratory investigation of responses elicited by music varying in tempo, tonality and texture', *Journal of Consumer Psychology*, **2** (4), 381-401.

Kozinets, R.V. (2002) 'Can consumers escape the market? Emancipatory illuminations from burning man', *Journal of Consumer Research*, **29** (1), 20-38.

Kwong, K.K., Yau, O.H.M., Lee, J.S.Y., Sin, L.Y.M. and Tse, C.B. (2003) 'The effects of attitudinal and demographic factors on intention to buy pirated CDs: the case of Chinese customers', *Journal of Business Ethics*, **47** (3), 223-235.

Lacher, K.T. and Mizerski, R. (1994) 'An exploratory study of the responses and relationships involved in the evaluation of, and in the intention to purchase new rock music', *Journal of Consumer Research*, **21** (September), 366-380.

Laing, D. (1985) 'Music video: industrial product, cultural form', *Screen*, **26** (2), 78-83.

Langenderfer, J. and Cook, D.L. (2001) 'Copyright policies and issues raised by A&M Records v. Napster: "The Shot Heard 'Round the World" or "Not with a Bang but a Whimper?"' *Journal of Public Policy & Marketing*, **20** (2) (Fall), 280-288.

Larsen, G. (2012) 'Music groupies: challenging co-creation?' *11th International Colloquium of the Academy of Marketing SIG on Arts, Heritage, Nonprofit and Social Marketing*, 19 September, London.

Larsen, G. and Lawson, R. (2010) 'Evolving Perspectives on Music Consumption', in: O'Reilly, D. and Kerrigan, F. (ed.) *Marketing the Arts: A Fresh Approach*, Abingdon, Oxon: Routledge, 190-204.

Larsen, G. and O'Reilly, D. (2008) 'Festival tales: utopian tales', *Academy of Marketing Annual Conference*, 8-10 July, Aberdeen, Scotland.

Larsen, G., Lawson, R. and Todd, S. (2009) 'The consumption of music as self representation in social interaction' *Australasian Marketing Journal*, **17** (3), 16-26.

Larsen, G., Lawson, R. and Todd, S. (2010) 'The symbolic consumption of music', *Journal of Marketing Management*, **26** (7/8), 671-685.

Levy, S (1959) 'Symbols For sale', *Harvard Business Review*, (July/August), 117-124.

Longhurst, B. (2007) *Popular Music and Society*, Cambridge: Polity Press.

Lonsdale, A.J. and North, A.C. (2011) 'Why do we listen to music? A uses and gratifications analysis', *British Journal of Psychology*, **102**, 108-134.

Macdonald, R., Hargreaves, D. and Miell, D. (2002) *Musical Identities*, Oxford: Oxford University Press.

Maclaran, P. (2009) 'Postmodern marketing and beyond', in Parsons, E. and Maclaran, P. (ed.) *Contemporary Issues in Marketing and Consumer Behaviour*, Oxford: Butterworth-Heinemann, 37-54.

McCracken, G. (1988) *Culture and Consumption: New Approaches to the Symbolic Character of Consumer Goods and Activities*, Bloomington, IN: Indiana University Press.

Merriam, A.P. (1964) *The Anthropology of Music*, Chicago: Northwestern University Press.

Moore, R.M. and McMullan, E.C. (2004) 'Perceptions of peer-to-peer file-sharing among university students', *Journal of Criminal Justice and Popular Culture*, 11 (1), 1-19.

Negus, K. and Velázquez, P. (2002) 'Belonging and detachment: musical experience and the limits of identity' *Poetics*, **30**, 133-145.

North, A.C and Hargreaves, D.J. (1997) 'Music and consumer behaviour', in: Hargreaves, D.J. and North, A.C. (ed.) *Social Psychology of Music*, Oxford: Oxford University Press.

North, A.C. and Hargreaves, D.J. (1999) 'Music and adolescent identity', *Music Education Research* 1(1): 75-92.

Nuttall, P. (2009) 'Insiders, regulars and tourists: exploring selves and music consumption in adolescence', *Journal of Consumer Behaviour*, **8** (4), 211-224.

Ouellet, J.F. (2007) 'The purchase versus illegal download of music by consumers: the influence of consumer response towards the artist and music', *Canadian Journal of Administrative Sciences*, **24**, 107-119.

Oxford Dictionaries Online (2012) 'Audience', http://oxforddictionaries.com/definition/english/audience?q=audience [Accessed: 30 April 2013].

Richards, C. (1998) *Teen Spirits: Music and Identity in Media Education*, London: UCL London.

Shankar, A. (2000) 'Lost in music? Subjective personal introspection and popular music consumption', *Qualitative Market Research: An International Journal*, **3** (1), 27-37.

Simun, M., (2009) 'My music, my world: using the MP3 Player to shape experience in London', *New Media & Society*, **11** (6), 921-941.

Smart, B (2010) *Consumer Society: Critical Issues and Environmental Consequences*, London: SAGE Publications

Straw, W. (1997) 'Sizing up record collections: gender and connoisseurship in rock music culture', in: Whiteley, S. (ed.) *Sexing the Groove: Popular Music and Gender*, London: Routledge, 3-16.

Terry, P.C. and Karageorghis, C.I. (2006) 'Psychophysical effects of music in sport and exercise: an update on theory, research and application', in: Katsikitis, M. (ed.), *Psychology Bridging the Tasman: Science, Culture and Practice – Proceedings of the 2006 Joint Conference of the Australian Psychological Society and the New Zealand Psychological Society*, Melbourne: Australian Psychological Society: 415-419.

The Century of the Self (2002), documentary film, Adam Curtis (Director), BBC Four, United Kingdom

Thorne, S. (2011) 'An exploratory investigation of the theorized levels of consumer fanaticism', *Qualitative Market Research: An International Journal*, **14** (2), 160-173.

Thornton, S. (1995) *Club Cultures: Music, Media and Subcultural Capital*, Cambridge: Polity Press.

Vargo, S. and Lusch, R. (2004) 'Evolving to a new dominant logic for marketing', *Journal of Marketing* **68** (January), 1-17.

Veblen, T. (1899) *The Theory of the Leisure Class*, New York: Macmillan.

Vitell, S.J. and Muncy, J. (2005) 'The Muncy-Vitell consumer ethics scale: a modification and application' *Journal of Business Ethics*, **62**, 267-275.

Waterman, S. (1998). 'Carnivals for élites? The cultural politics of arts festivals', *Progress in Human Geography* **22** (1), 54-74.

Wilk, R. (2004) 'Morals and metaphors: the meaning of consumption', in: Ekstrom, K. and Brembeck, H. (ed.) *Elusive Consumption*, London: Berg, 11-26.

Williams, R. (1976) *Keywords: A Vocabulary of Culture and Society*, London: Fontana.

Wingrove, T., Korpas, A.L. and Weisz, V. (2010) 'Why were millions of people *not* obeying the law? Motivational influences on non-compliance with the law in the case of music piracy', *Psychology, Crime & Law*, **1477-2744**, 1-16.

Woodward, M. and Holbrook, M. (forthcoming) 'Dialogue on some concepts, definitions, and issues pertaining to "consumption experiences"', *Marketing Theory*.

8 Music, Fans and Fandom

Introduction

Fans and fandom have been studied in a variety of different contexts, from soap operas to novels. Although there is a lot one can learn from studies about the characteristics of fandom and the behaviour of fans in general, research into music fans and fandom remains relatively scarce, with only a handful of works in the fields of popular music, marketing and consumer behaviour. Yet understanding music fans is crucial if one is to comprehend the production and consumption of music. For so many avid music consumers, the pleasures derived from music allows them to make sense of their everyday lives and experiences (Willis, 1990), 'letting other people know who we are, or would like to be, what group we belong to, or would like to belong to' (Shankar, 2000: 28). Music consumption is a very rich source of symbolic resources that can be drawn on by music fans to construct their individual and social identities. The purpose of this chapter is to explore fans and fandom in the context of music consumption and production. It builds on the earlier discussion in Chapter 7 on music consumption, where the frame of the music 'fan' was introduced. The chapter begins, therefore, with an attempt to provide a historical context for fans and fandom, and then outlines our understanding of fans and their behaviours and motivations. This is followed by an overview of fandom, its intensity and social organization. The chapter concludes with some observations on the material productivity of fans.

Historical background

Most of us associate music fans with enthusiastic crowds following musical icons like Elvis Presley, the Beatles, or many boy- and girl-bands of the last 20 years. But in fact, behaviours typical of contemporary music fans have been traced back as far as the 19th century (Cavicchi, 1998, 2007). Music fans from as long ago as the times of Chopin and Paganini expressed their appreciation by throwing parts of their garments on stage, and the Hungarian piano virtuoso Liszt was regularly followed around Europe by an ecstatic group of female fans (Lebrecht, 1997; Parker, 1994). Across the Atlantic, in mid-19th-century America, a tour of Swedish opera singer Jenny Lind turned her into a celebrity (with a significant contribution, which needs to be acknowledged here, from the marketing machine designed by P.T. Barnum (Waksman, 2011)).

The 19th and 20th centuries brought some significant changes to the production and consumption of music. Although, as seen above, music fandom as a collective behaviour focusing on the appreciation of a musical act is not a new phenomenon, it has recently taken on a completely new dimension. With the increasing professionalization of musicians and the industrialization of musical cultures through, for example, the commercial publishing of sheet music and increasing numbers of concerts, music gradually became a passive activity requiring very little engagement from ordinary people in the production of sounds in order to be able to listen to them (Fishzon, 2012). In the 20th century music was becoming a commodity, and a new class of people emerged who can be described as music fans and who devoted themselves to following and enjoying the music made by professional musicians. One example of such changes in musical culture is 'Club Crosby', which was established in 1936 and remains the longest-running fan club in the world (Theberge, 2005). The burgeoning 20th-century music industry developed professional music-makers into celebrities, and music consumers into fans. Nowadays, in the contemporary, money-driven music industry, fans' market power and influence can make or break an artist, and with the emergence of more and more studies into fandom as a consumption phenomenon one can begin to see the richness and diversity of fans' behaviours (Baym, 2000; Hills, 2002). There is a growing body of research into fans and fandom, with studies focusing on fans of artists including Elvis Presley (Harrison 1992; Duffett 2003; Doss 2004), Bruce Springsteen (Cavicchi, 1998), and David Bowie (Stevenson, 2009).

Fans

Although there are no universal definitions of fans and fandom, as different musical genres require different forms of engagement from audience members for them to be perceived as fans, the word 'fan' implies a special type of relationship between a person and the object of their admiration. Early understanding of the fan-celebrity relationship focused on its stereotypically parasocial character, where one side (fans) have a substantial knowledge of the musician, and the other (musicians) know very little – or indeed nothing – about the individual lives of their fans (Horton and Wohl, 1956). Stever (2011), however, highlights the fact that although this kind of unidirectional relationship has often been presented in the literature in a negative light, it is important to recognize that it has a real influence on fans and their lives. More recent studies have moved away from seeing fandom as a parasocial form of interaction that is dangerous; pathological behaviours of fans are indeed rare and insignificant when considering the diversity and richness of the fan experience (Horton and Wohl, 1956). This chapter will discuss fans and fandom as a normal form of cultural behaviour, although it is acknowledged that, at its extreme, it can lead to deviant or even dangerous behaviours, like the murder of John Lennon by Mark Chapman, or of Selena by the president of her fan club, Yolanda Saldívar. Although these kinds of tragedies are far less common than one might think, unruly behaviour of fans, such as stalking, or verbally threatening and abusing artists during live performances, is often a cause of concern for musicians. Our focus is, nevertheless, on what one would describe as the normal, rather than criminal or deviant, consumption behaviours of fans.

With the emergence of online communities, fans acquired a new virtual tool. Traditionally, music critics held the key to musicians' futures in the music business. Highly respected for their knowledge and experience, critics can be credited for the success of many musicians. But while their influence still remains significant in jazz and classical music, their heyday in popular music is long gone thanks to the rising importance of 'users' reviews' and the emergence of social networking websites such as Myspace.com, Last.fm and Facebook. Organized in online and offline communities, fans have become important partners in cultural practice, creating, reproducing and eliminating competing discourses surrounding the production and consumption of music.

To be a fan, one does need to engage in a form of music consumption which may differ from that of ordinary music consumers. Ordinary consumers go to a concert, but fans follow their favourite group around the country; consumers buy one album, while fans have all of them; consumers recognize a song, yet fans memorize its lyrics and study their meaning; consumers post comments online, and fans write reviews. The degree of fans' engagement with musical texts is expressed through their greater attention to detail (De Vries, 2004), for example comparing the same songs played at different concerts, or finding contradictions in interviews given by artists at different times or published in different media. When Guzetti and Yang (2005) asked punk rock fans how they enacted their fandom, the answers they received focused on examples of personal displays, such as genre-appropriate dress and behaviour, constant self-education and learning about punk rock, and advocacy through teaching others about punk and sharing their enjoyment of the music and punk culture. The need to become an integral part of the musical experience, which is rejected by the commodification of music, is common across different genres. For example, a study of opera fans in Russia showed their struggle to accept the commercially imposed role of spectators, which was required by the standardized format of live opera performance (Fishzon, 2012) that separated production from consumption, and professional musicians from passive spectators. These spectators strived to engage with the experience on a different level, and co-produced the experience beyond the actual performance by collecting paraphernalia, and corresponding with – or even stalking –

musicians. As fans, they searched for a more meaningful connection with music that stretched beyond a simple market exchange, and would allow them to bring their emotions to the music.

Fans: behaviours and motivations

Fans can be attracted to musicians for a variety of reasons. The most obvious include the musicians' talent, personal qualities, and physical attractiveness (Stever, 1991), but one cannot forget that being a fan is, by and large, a social activity, and therefore friendship with other fans and a sense of acceptance and belonging to a fan community also have an important role to play. Like Grossberg (1992), one needs to distinguish between ordinary music consumers and music fans. However, these terms are what Williams (2001: 225) calls 'discursive constructs', employed to 'position people, rather than as real social positions'. Being a fan goes beyond buying an album or going to a concert when a favourite band is in town; it is a much more engaged and demanding form of consumption. A fan is an individual who is knowledgeable about a particular artist or a music genre, experiences an emotional attachment to them/it, and is prepared to display their obsession in social situations. For music fans, music is woven into their daily lives in a much stronger and more visible way than for an average occasional consumer of music. To be a fan, people need to express their attachment even in ordinary and mundane situations, as their passion is not only an ephemeral sensation in the form of satisfaction from consumption, but a constant quasi-religious devotion to the object of their admiration, which affects every domain of the fan's life (Löbert, 2012). Fans engage in the same activities as ordinary consumers – they listen to the music, buy albums, talk about concerts they have been to, or even post comments online. But the main difference stems from the degree of their engagement – they do it to the point of obsession and become what Fiske (1992) calls 'excessive readers', who are not satisfied by simple participation and consumption. Fans are a very specific type of audience, who are much more active and engaged in the consumption and production of music: 'fans are consumers who also produce, readers who also write, spectators who also participate' (Jenkins, 1992: 214).

Löbert (2012) distinguishes between four main types of interaction between fans and the object of their admiration: primary interaction rituals, secondary interaction rituals, special rites, and cult of the individual. Primary interaction rituals are the most important rituals performed in the presence of musician(s) and other fans. They include live events such as concerts, public interviews, and meetings with fans, where both artists and fans co-produce musical experiences. All other activities performed in the presence of other fans but without musician(s) are called secondary interaction rituals. They include all communal acts and interactions within a group of fans, for example fan club meetings and other gatherings, journeys to and from primary interaction rituals and joint preparations for them, online discussion boards and forums, etc. Special rites are the most treasured form of interaction, as they include individual interactions between the fan and the musician(s) that give the fan private access to the object of their admiration, for example meetings backstage after a concert, and other accidental encounters in public spaces. Finally, cult of the individual includes the most personal and private rituals when neither musician(s) nor other fans are present. They are the backbone of being a fan, when one listens to their favourite artists on their own, establishes a very private meaning for different songs, albums or music videos, reads and listens to interviews, or enjoys their collection of paraphernalia.

Fandom

Fandom refers, in principle, to the cultural and social milieu within which fans develop and practise their rituals (Harris, 1998). Fishzon (2012: 101), for example, describes fandom as a 'set of socially and historically located tastes, interpretative strategies, and consumption practices', yet the abundance of those tastes, strategies and practices means that studies of fandom often explore them in their local contexts. Fandom is indeed a uniquely complex phenomenon (Pullen, 2000). Different fans use music in different ways for different purposes; individual genres are associated with specific consumption behaviours and require varying levels of engagement with music as a social practice.

There are many inherent differences between punk rock fans and opera fans, Black Sabbath fans and Jacques Loussier fans; they express their attachment and interests differently, follow different rituals and practices, and, even within the same broad category of fans, for example jazz aficionados, may produce different meanings from musical texts. Hence, it is practically impossible to treat all fans in the same way by attempting to find a common denominator, as it is often those differences between various groups of fans that makes them unique and interesting. Yet, as Jenson (1992) observed, fans are often differentiated in terms of the status of the musicians or genre they admire, which is assigned by the wider society. While heavy metal fans or punks might be seen by some as dangerous deviants, classical music concert-goers are often presented by the mainstream media as more valuable members of society.

Fandom can be looked at from a wide range of angles: one can study the relationship between fans and musical acts, the motivation of fans to commit an important part of their lives to fandom, and interactions between fans in fan communities. Jenkins (1992: 209-212) suggested four levels of fandom:

1 *Fans adopt a distinctive mode of reception*: fans' consumption of musical texts is a social and interactive process which goes beyond that of ordinary consumers, who may simply just listen to the music. Fans engage in the process, produce their own meanings from the texts, and translate these into other activities like discussions with other fans, posting messages online, and membership in fan clubs and fan communities.

2 *Fandom constitutes a particular interpretive community*: the social orientation of fans' practices is such that the meanings of musical texts produced by individual fans are debated, negotiated and contested in fan communities.

3 *Fandom constitutes a particular Art world*: using Howard Becker's (1982) understanding of 'Art world' as a network of stakeholders and activities involved in the production, distribution, consumption, interpretation and evaluation of art works, fandom can be seen as one of the elements of that system, and as being focused on the creation and distribution of knowledge.

4   *Fandom constitutes an alternative community*: Fandom is a form of
    community where more traditional differences like gender, age
    or physical location (in terms of online communities) are only a
    background to shared interests.

Fandom can express itself in a variety of solo activities, for example
playing and singing songs, watching music videos, sending letters to
favourite artists, or attending concerts alone (Rhein, 2000). But fandom
becomes a different, more powerful and self-defining form of experience
when individual desires of fans are incorporated into shared experiences
by participating in communities such as fan clubs. Fans, unlike ordinary
followers, develop social identities around the objects of their desires
(Tulloch and Jenkins, 1995). Membership in a fan club allows individual
fans to meet like-minded people, participate in consumption rituals
appropriate for the object of their admiration, share and develop their
knowledge, and use it as a form of cultural capital in exchange for
social status and esteem. Fandom is, therefore, highly contextual and
performative (Hills, 2002). The cultural uniqueness of fans is described in
the next section through the prism of the intensity, social organization
and semiotic/material productivity of the fandom (Hills, 2002).

Intensity of fandom

The representational properties of music mean that it can be used
to communicate complex ideas and emotions. Musical texts, such
as a band, album or concert, can become a semantic representation of
fans' individual and social identities. In fact, for fans, their engagement
with musical texts acts as a basis for the construction of their identities.
It is an intensive and emotional investment which affects their whole
lives, and is a participatory culture requiring commitment and passion,
which integrates fans into musical texts and allows them to become
an integral element of musical brands. 'Punk rock fan' or 'Cliff Richard
fan' are labels used to describe a bundle of characteristics, where both
elements are equally important and defining: there is no punk rock
culture without fans, and no fans without punk rock; Cliff Richard would
never have become an iconic music star without his fans, but his fans
would not have anything to worship without Cliff Richard. This is a

reciprocal process through which fans and the intensity of their fandom co-produce musical texts, which in return offer distinctive fan identities. And, as is the case with impersonators or tribute bands, the boundaries between fan identities and music idols can become blurred (Stever, 2011).

Being a fan also changes the course of one's life, marking new stages and important events in one's biography (Harrington and Bielby, 2010). The life of a fan becomes dotted with facts, the meaning and purpose of which can only be interpreted through one's emotional attachment to the object of their admiration: first album, first concert, and first disappointment. It is also influenced by important people – those who introduce a fan to the music and guide them through their learning, and those who follow them to their own journey through fandom and development of their cultural capital. However, the initial lack of specific cultural capital, as illustrated by Kerrigan and Dennis (2011), can also act as a deterrent to participation in music consumption and fan communities. The engagement in fandom and its practices can have an empowering effect on individuals, when the intensity of their engagement, which sets them apart from ordinary consumers, is seen as a form of desirable and valued cultural capital. Empowerment of fans takes place through social interactions between fans and the production of their own interpretations of musical texts (Harris, 1998). Actively participating in media, either through that production of meanings, or via interaction with media (e.g. by posting comments on the Internet or giving interviews), creates opportunities for fans to challenge the dominant interpretations using their own voice. Acting collectively, fans can become a significant power in the music industry, and when they speak with a unified voice the media naturally take an interest in what the fans have to say (Baym, 1998; Clerc, 2000; Pullen, 2004).

Social organization of fandom

Being a fan is a social experience, even if one does not desire to socially interact with other fans. As a minimum, fandom requires some form of engagement with an interpretive community. The meanings of musical texts (regardless of whether it is a band, live concert, interview, album review, or indeed lyrics) are co-produced between musicians and fans within their culturally constructed and limited assumptions. Therefore, even if one opposes the dominant interpretations preferred by the community of fans, one needs to engage in discourses opposing it. But for the majority of fans, a fan community offers structures for collective experience and engagement with the object of their desires, saving them from isolation and loneliness by providing ready-made social identities and a collective mind (Cowie, 2001).

Groups of fans are often referred to as fan communities. Yet traditional understanding of the concept of community focuses on 'locality based communities, including people living in close proximity and having something in common, such as similar daily routines or interests' (Queralt, 1996: 223). Since the development of the Internet, and in particular over the last 20 years, the traditional notion of community has had to be re-examined. With the rapid spread of new communication technologies, including smartphones, tablets and social media, communities are no longer attached to a particular location. Online (or virtual) fan communities, where physical distance is less relevant and a shared interest becomes the crucial factor defining membership, have mushroomed all over the Internet. The migration of fandom to the Internet has further helped to change its focus from individual activities to communal ones (Wall and Dubber, 2009). Online environments offer fans a plethora of different ways to enact their fandom, and include: unofficial websites, mailing lists, e-mails, discussion boards and forums, blogs (including micro-blogging on Twitter), Facebook sites, and video streaming on YouTube. Online social interactions with large numbers of other fans have become easier and less demanding. There is evidence to suggest that the online environment encourages more frequent fan socialization, thereby increasing the number of interactions and expanding their social networks (Baym, 2000; Clerc, 2000). The Internet provides an additional avenue through which fans can 'perform their fandom' (Garrity, 2002: 177). Online fan clubs create a more direct and regular avenue of communication between artists and fans, as well as between fans themselves. They are two-directional – channelling fans' desires to contact the artists and providing them with information about artists' activities (Theberge, 2005). Any online conversations between fans can develop over time into a more organized form of community, where fans start forming relationships by discussing their shared interests, and eventually, when they become familiar with their online personas, move on to other topics that reveal more about themselves, and forming stronger social bonds (Baym, 1998) and hierarchies.

MacDonald's (1998) study of fans of the TV series *Quantum Leap* distinguished five different dimensions in the hierarchy of fans: hierarchy of knowledge, fandom, access, leaders, and venue. Her findings can be extrapolated to better understand the hierarchical status of music fans. The relatively straightforward hierarchy of knowledge defines the position of fans within a fan community using the amount of knowledge they possess about their favourite musicians, musical act and genre – the more knowledgeable the fan is, the higher their status in the community. The hierarchy of fandom is directly relevant to the intensity of the fandom and their contribution to the community. The hierarchy of access is influenced by fans' direct access to musicians and other individuals involved in the production of musical products. The hierarchy of leaders identifies leaders among smaller groups of fans within the wider fan community. The final type of hierarchy, the hierarchy of venue, gives some fans more administrative power through control over mailing lists, message boards, online communities or other virtual or real spaces for conversation between fans.

One can observe among hierarchically organized fan communities what John Fiske (1992) refers to as a 'cultural economy', where knowledge is the most important and valuable currency (Hunt, 2003; Bennett, 2011). The knowledge of admired musicians and their music becomes a cultural currency that is traded among hierarchically organized groups of fans for peer respect and position within a group, generating an impressive amount of collective knowledge, a distinctive culture of appreciation (with a unique understanding of what being a fan means) and individual and social identities, all of which reinforce emotional ties between fans and musicians and among fans themselves. Even mentioning just a few consumption behaviours creates a long list that cuts across many academic disciplines, for example: autograph-hunting, poster-collecting, musical tourism, stalking, blogging, exchanging MP3 files, and piracy.

Knowledge is therefore one of the most sought-after forms of capital among fans. The most devoted fans spend significant amounts of time and money studying their favourite musicians and learning every detail of their life and music so as to be able to share their wisdom with less knowledgeable fans in exchange for status, prestige, esteem, reputation and power within the fan community (Jenkins, 1992). Fans who are higher up in the hierarchy of knowledge become opinion leaders, educating others and allowing them access to new assets of fandom (Wall and Dubber, 2009). For fans, being able to tell a relevant story is an important marker of their status and knowledge. Those stories often involve one's journey to becoming a fan (Cavicchi, 1998; Kibby, 2000; Bennett, 2011), and identification of crucial moments and other fans, all of which are influential in shaping one's identity as a fan. The stories also play other roles – they establish and reinforce the hierarchy of fandom. More experienced fans, through their self-narrative, set out the rules for new adepts and introduce them to the hierarchy in the fan community. The sharing and exchange of knowledge can often have a ritualistic character (Kibby, 2000).

A successful initiation into a fan community involves an acquisition of the beliefs and assumptions shared within that community (Hills, 2004). Beliefs and behaviours which attract positive reactions from other fans are seen as an acceptance of one's membership in the community. The expected and desired fan identity needs to be constantly reaffirmed and reinforced. The process of initiation is crucial for the collective production and circulation of meanings (Jenkins, 2002), which draw boundaries, albeit fluid, around the fan community. The process of acquiring information is the cornerstone of fandom (Fiske, 1992), and communication is the key element of that process. For example, in her ethnographic study of soap opera fans Baym (1998) distinguished four types of communicative practices: informing, speculating, criticizing and reworking, which can be applied to better understand the knowledge creation and exchange behaviours of music fans. Informing refers to circulating information about the topics of fans' interest, and is used to advance the knowledge of others, often new fans, who can learn factual information about their favourite musicians or genre and understand the rituals and practices in place within the fan community.

Speculating, which is usually performed by fans who already have significant knowledge, is about making predictions about future events. For example, music fans may speculate about new albums, music videos, tours, and the various meanings of song lyrics. Criticizing is about fans' engagement with the dominant interpretations of musical texts in the mainstream media. It allows them to challenge those interpretations and propose alternative understandings. Reworking includes fans' own production of musical texts and meanings, and is referred to by Hills (2002) as the semiotic/material productivity of fans. This is a channel for the creative productivity of the most knowledgeable and skilful fans, who may design their own graphics, write songs, impersonate their favourite artists or start a tribute band. Speculating, criticizing and reworking are usually reserved for fans who are higher in the hierarchy, as they need to have significant knowledge and commitment to the fan community for the other fans to listen to their opinions and respect them.

Semiotic/material productivity of fans

But the intensity of the attachment between a fan and the object of their admiration, and the social organization of fans, are not the only elements that distinguish fan cultures from other forms of cultural consumption. Looking at the relationships between fans and musicians as a one-way avenue through which musicians create products and fans consume and exchange them within socially organized structures would be simplistic and reductionist. As cultural theorist John Storey (1996) argued, fans are indispensable to the production of cultural texts traded in their social networks. Those texts include fanzines, videos, songs or even full DVDs. For example, in 2008 the American industrial rock band Nine Inch Nails invited its fans to submit all HD footage of their concert in Webster Hall, New York City (Cosgrove, 2009). Within two months fans had sent in all the concert footage they could track down and a DVD had been prepared for free distribution online. This DVD is an example of fans going beyond a typical co-production of meaning. It is a musical text, and a commodity, which was co-produced by fans.

All music texts are produced through a continuous and multi-directional interaction between fans themselves, musicians, the media and all other stakeholders. In reaction to the professional media industry, fans engage with musical texts by taking the emphasis away from the production of musical texts to the production of social knowledge and discourses (Alvermann and Hagood, 2000). Their contribution to the process depends on the level of intensity of their fandom, and its outcome is disseminated using the social structures of the community of fans.

The most popular example of material productivity from fans is fanzines. Many early fanzines were produced by only the most committed and loyal fans, often in very primitive conditions, using any available photocopying machines, in a back room or a garage. But in the last 20 years they have appeared all over the Internet thanks to the unparalleled growth in the popularity of the World Wide Web and easy access to cheap IT equipment and software. Using a computer or an iPad, and with something interesting to say about their favourite musician, anyone can start a fanzine or Facebook page, post messages on relevant forums, or simply 'tweet' their thoughts.

Fanzines, as one form of fans' material productivity, have been described as having some unique characteristics which distinguish them from more traditional forms of publishing (Atton, 2001). There are usually fans behind them who are also amateur writers. They might be students, or have other jobs providing them with income, while they spend every moment of their spare time producing or soliciting content for their fanzine. As publishing fanzines requires a diverse type of expertise, from writing good text to website design, even small publications need contributions from wider groups of fans with broader sets of skills in order to grow and be successful over time. New contributors are often recruited from readers who want to share knowledge and experience relevant to the object of their admiration, and in this way advance their own status within the social structures of fans. Readers can create content in the form of album and concert reviews, their own research into a topic of interest, interviews, and so on (Atton, 2001). In the case of online fanzines many barriers associated with print publishing are removed – readers can be writers and contribute in real time to content creation using Internet forums, posting videos on websites such as YouTube, and participating in social networking via Facebook and Twitter. Live updates can be posted before, during and shortly after a concert, creating a sense of participation and belonging to the community for those who cannot be a physical part of the event.

As most fanzines stem from a lot of enthusiasm and passion but very limited resources, they share a strong not-for-profit ethos (Atton, 2001), which nevertheless may develop into a commercial undertaking when a publication acquires sufficient commercial potential, for example in the form of large numbers of readers or an ability to influence opinions. Due to their cost constraints, most fanzines now start their life on the Internet, thereby bypassing more commercially driven and traditionally audience-focused media such as television, radio and press, and allowing the fans to fill in the cultural space with their anti-expert discourse (in the case of early fanzines of the '70s and '80s) or, more recently, creating an avenue for expression within the community of fans. Fanzines in the 21st century have become cultural spaces that empower communities of fans; they are forms of cultural enactment, reproduction and development (Rau 1994; Duncombe 1997; Atton, 2001). They have been compared to 'ideological magazines' (Frith, 2002), which act as a glue holding a community of fans together, and define its boundaries, rules of engagement, acceptable and unacceptable behaviours, and dominant discourses. New fans learn the codes of being a respected fan within the community from existing fans. Fanzines, therefore, organize the relationship between fans, their community, the object of their admiration, and the external world (Atton, 2010).

Summary

This chapter has provided a discussion on the understanding and roles of fans in the production and consumption of music. Taking as its starting point the discussion on music consumption from Chapter 7, our argument has been that fandom in music is an old and complex phenomenon, in which the behaviours and motivations of fans play a pivotal role in terms of co-producing musical texts, which can have both positive and negative meanings. In fan cultures, marketers are just one of many sources of meanings that surround music, and our attempt to understand the productivity of fans needs to go well beyond traditional marketing tools and techniques, and stem from a thorough understanding of fan cultures and their social organization.

References

Alvermann, D.E. and Hagood, M.C. (2000) 'Fandom and critical media literacy', *Journal of Adolescent & Adult Literacy*, **43** (5), 436-446.

Atton, C. (2001) '"Living in the Past"?: value discourses in progressive rock fanzines', *Popular Music, 20* (1), 29–46.

Baym, N.K. (1998) 'Talking about soaps: communicative practices in a computer mediated fan culture', in: Harris, C. and Alexander, A. (ed.), *Theorizing Fandom: fans, subculture and identity*, Cresskill, NJ: Hampton Press, pp. 111-129.

Baym, N. (2000) *Tune in, Log on: Soaps, Fandom, and Online Community*, Thousand Oaks, CA: *Sage*.

Becker, H. (1982) *Art Worlds*, Berkeley: California University Press.

Bennett, L. (2011) 'Music fandom online: R.E.M. fans in pursuit of the ultimate first listen', *New Media Society*, **14** (5), 748-763.

Cavicchi, D. (1998) *Tramps Like Us: Music and Meaning among Springsteen Fans*, Oxford: Oxford University Press.

Cavicchi, D. (2007) 'Loving music: listeners, entertainments, and the origins of music fandom in the nineteenth century', in: Sandvoss, C., Gray, J. and Harrington, C.L. (ed.) *Fandom: Identities and Communities in a Mediated World*, New York: New York University Press.

Clerc, S. (2000) 'Estrogen brigades and "big tits" threads: media fandom on-line and off', in: Bell, D. and Kennedy, B.M. (ed.), *The Cyberculture Reader*, London: Routledge.

Cosgrove, L. (2009) '"The Downward Spiral: Live at Webster Hall" fan-produced DVD', nin.com, available at: http://ninblogs.wordpress.com/2009/10/23/the-downward-spiral-live-at-webster-hall-fan-produced-dvd/ [Accessed 30 April 2013].

Cowie, J. (2001) 'Fandom, faith and Bruce Springsteen', *Dissent Magazine*, **48** (1), Winter.

De Vries, P, (2004) 'Listen to the fans', *Music Educators Journal*, **91**, 25-28.

Doss, E. (2004) *Elvis Culture: Fans, Faith and Image*, Lawrence, KS: University of Kansas Press.

Duffett, M. (2003) 'False faith or false comparison? A critique of the religious interpretation of Elvis fan culture', *Popular Music and Society*, **26** (4), 513-522.

Duncombe, S. (1997) *Notes from Underground: Zines and the Politics of Alternative Culture*, London: Verso.

Fishzon, A. (2012) 'Confessions of a *Psikhopatka*: opera fandom and the melodramatic sensibility in *Fin-de-Siècle* Russia', *The Russian Review*, **71**, 100-121.

Fiske, J. (1992) 'The cultural economy of fandom', in: Lewis L.A. (ed.) *The Adoring Audience: Fan Culture and Popular Media*, London: Routledge, pp. 30-49.

Frith, S. (2002) 'Fragments of a sociology of rock criticism', in: Jones, S. (ed.) *Pop Music and the Press*, Philadelphia, PA: Temple UP, pp. 235-246.

Garrity, B. (2002) 'Online fan clubs emerge as potential profit centres', *Billboard*, 114 (33), 17 August, 1-2, 3c.

Grossberg, L. (1992) 'Another boring day in paradise: rock and roll and the empowerment of everyday life', *Popular Music*, **4**, 225-258.

Guzetti, B. and Yang, Y. (2005) 'Adolescents' punk rock fandom: construction and production of lyrical texts', *Yearbook – National Reading Conference*, **54**, 198-210.

Harrington, C.L. and Bielby, D.D. (2010) 'A life course perspective on fandom', *International Journal of Cultural Studies*, 13, 429-450.

Harris, C. (1998) 'Introduction theorizing fandom: fans, subculture and identity', in: Harris, C. and Alexander, A. (ed.), *Theorizing Fandom: fans, subculture and identity*, Cresskill, NJ: Hampton Press, pp. 3-8.

Harrison, T. (1992) *Elvis People – The Cult of the King*, London: HarperCollins.

Hills, M. (2002) *Fan cultures*, London: Routledge.

Horton, D. and Wohl, R. (1956) 'Mass communication and parasocial interaction: observation on intimacy at a distance', *Psychiatry*, **19**, 215-229.

Hunt, N. (2003) 'The importance of trivia', in: Jancovich, M., Reboll, A.L., Stringer J., Willis, A. (ed.) *Defining Cult Movies: The Cultural Politics of Oppositional Taste*, Manchester: Manchester University Press, 185-201.

Kibby, M.D. (2000) 'Home on the page: a virtual place of music community', *Popular Music*, **19** (1), 91-100.

Jenkins, H. (1992) '"Strangers no more, we sing": filking and the social construction of the science fiction fan community', in: Lewis, L.A. (ed.), *The Adoring Audience: Fan Culture and Popular Media*, London: Routledge, pp. 208-236.

Jenson, J. (1992) 'Fandom as pathology: The consequences of characterization', in: Lewis, L.A. (ed.), *The Adoring Audience: fan culture and popular media*, London: Routledge, 9-29.

Kerrigan, F. and Dennis, N. (2011) 'The secret jazz fan: a tale of sublimation featuring film and music', *Arts Marketing: an international journal*, 1 (1), 56-69.

Lebrecht, N. (1997) *When the Music Stops… Managers, Maestros and the Corporate Murder of Classical Music*, London: Simon & Schuster.

Löbert, A. (2012) 'Fandom as a religious form: on the reception of pop music by Cliff Richard fans in Liverpool', *Popular Music*, 31 (1), 125-141.

MacDonald, A. (1998) 'Uncertain utopia: science fiction media fandom and computer mediated communication', in: Harris, C. and Alexander, A. (ed.), *Theorizing Fandom: Fans, Subculture and Identity*, Cresskill, NJ : Hamption Press, pp. 131-152.

Parker, B. (1994) *Building a Classical Music Library*, Minneapolis, MN: Jormax Publications.

Pullen, K. (2000) 'I-love-Xena.com: creating online fan communities', in: Gauntlett, D. (ed.) *Web Studies: Rewiring media studies for the digital age*, London: Arnold, pp. 52-61.

Queralt, M. (1996) 'Communities', in: Queralt, M. (ed.), *The Social Environment and Human Behavior*, Boston: Allyn and Bacon, pp. 222-258.

Rau, M. (1994) 'Towards a history of fanzine publishing: from APA to zines', *Alternative Press Review*, **Spring/Summer**, 10-13.

Rhein, S. (2000) 'Being a fan is more than that: fan-specific involvement with music', *The World of Music*, 42 (1), 95-109.

Shankar, A. (2000) 'Lost in music? Subjective personal introspection and popular music consumption', *Qualitative Market Research*, 3 (1), 27-37.

Stevenson, N. (2009) 'Talking to Bowie fans: Masculinity, ambivalence and cultural citizenship', *European Journal of Cultural Studies*, 12, 79-98.

Stever, G. (1991) 'The celebrity appeal questionnaire', *Psychological Reports*, 68 (3), 859-866.

Stever, G. (2011) '1989 vs. 2009: a comparative analysis of music superstars Michael Jackson and Josh Groban, and their fans', *Journal of Media Psychology*, 16 (1).

Storey, J. (1996) *Cultural Studies and the Study of Popular Culture*, Athens, GA: University of Georgia Press.

Théberge, P. (2005) 'Everyday fandom: fan clubs, blogging, and the quotidian rhythms of the Internet', *Canadian Journal of Communication*, **30**, 485-502.

Tulloch, J. and Jenkins, H. (1995) *Science Fiction Audiences: Watching Doctor Who and Star Trek*, London: Routledge.

Waksman, S. (2011) 'Selling the nightingale: P.T. Barnum, Jenny Lind, and the management of the American crowd', *Arts Marketing: an International Journal*, **1** (2), 108-120.

Wall, T. and Dubber, A. (2009) 'Specialist music fans online: implications for public service broadcasting', *The Radio Journal*, **7**, 1, 1-32.

Williams, C. (2001) 'Does it really matter? Young people and popular music', *Popular Music,* **20** (2), 223-242.

Willis, P. (1990) *Common Culture*, Milton Keynes: Open University Press.

9 Music and Collectivity

Introduction

The purpose of this chapter is to explore issues of music and collective consumption by using notions such as consumer culture, consumer tribes, brand communities and scenes. This is not intended to be an exhaustive analysis of music and community or collectivity. Rather, this chapter focuses specifically on a number of ideas which have potential implications for the analysis, interpretation and understanding of music markets. Part of the contribution of this book is to examine what they buy us in terms of understanding exchange relationships, what their limitations are, and how these limitations might be remedied by combining them with social identity and consumer culture theory. The discussion of brand community builds on the earlier discussion of branding in Chapters 5 and 6. The focus of consumer tribes builds on the discussion in Chapter 7 about music consumption by focusing on collective aspects of consumption. The notion of scenes is one which has emerged within music studies.

Consumer culture

In his well-known book entitled *Consumer Culture and Postmodernism*, Featherstone (2007: 12 ff.) argues for a focus on the 'growing prominence of the culture of consumption' (emphasis in original). He identifies three ways of looking at consumer culture: (a) pleasures, dreams and desires associated with consumption; (b) a sociological view on the 'ways in which people use goods in order to create social bonds or distinctions'; and (c) the idea that capitalist production drives consumption and ideologically seduces consumers. He sees consumer culture (2007:27) as using 'images, signs and symbolic goods which summon up dreams, desires and fantasies', and these 'suggest romantic authenticity and emotional fulfilment'. Consumer behaviour is defined by Arnould *et al.* (2004: 9) as: 'Individuals or groups acquiring, using and disposing of products, services, ideas or experiences'. In older consumer behaviour textbooks, the individual consumer is treated as a rational economic individual. The thrust of the applied research is the description and analysis of consumers and potential customers in terms of their behaviour and attitudes. There is a heavy emphasis on cognitive psychology, as well as borrowings from sociological theory. Consumers are analysed in terms of their choice criteria, buying process, buying involvement, influences from peers on the buying decision, and roles occupied in the buying centre. Despite this treatment of the consumer as an individual, in general, marketers understand the benefit of getting people together in groups as both a recruitment and retention strategy. It enables resources (marketing spend) to be focused economically and relationships to be 'managed'. However, in their monograph entitled 'The Unmanageable Consumer', Gabriel and Lang (2006) explore characterizations of the consumer in different literatures as chooser, communicator, explorer, identity seeker, hedonist, artist, victim, rebel, activist, citizen. Their conclusion is that in the 'twilight of consumerism':

> the fragmentation of images of consumption is itself a symptom of the malaise of contemporary consumerism … The same fragmentation of the consumer may keep academics busy, since each tradition can claim the consumer for itself, exaggerating those features which fit its arguments, while blatantly disregarding the rest … and in a world where everyone claims the consumer for her- or himself, the consumer must now be deemed unmanageable, claimed by many, but controlled by few, least of all by consumers themselves (2006: 189-190).

The culturalist approach to popular music identified by Middleton (1990) constructs the consumption of popular music brand texts as an active rather than passive process. Consumption is conceived as a process of meaning-making, and the notion of 'active' or 'creative' consumption recognizes that consumers are reflexive about their consumption activities, actively interpreting or judging, appropriating or resisting the texts offered for consumption. De Certeau et al. (2002) argue that meaning is produced by consumers as they use and experience consumption offerings in the context of their everyday lives. Earlier interpretive consumer research work by Hirschman (1983) envisaged consumers as having intelligence, creativity, and consciousness. In her paper on consumer subjectivity, Schau (2000) proposed that 'imagination provides a critical link between identity and consumption. Furthermore, through the dynamic force of imagination consumers: 1) make sense of sensation, 2) construct and express individual and group level identities and realities by manipulating signs, accumulating possessions, and developing consumption practices'. Beck (1992), Rose (1996), Giddens (1991, 1998) and Fairclough (2000) argue that there has been a fundamental shift in Western society toward neo-liberal rationalities which encourage people to fulfil themselves as free individuals and be linked to society through their consumer choices. Musical preferences offer rich opportunities for individuals to forge social identities and experience the solidarity, security and sense of belonging attached to identification with like-minded peers (see e.g. Larson 1995).

Elliott and Wattanasuwan (1998) suggest that in conditions of postmodernism the self is 'something which the person actively creates, partially through consumption'. They quote Thompson (1995) who describes the self as a symbolic project, which the individual must actively construct out of the available symbolic materials, materials which 'the individual weaves into a coherent account of who he or she is, a narrative of self-identity'. They note that the relationship between individual self-identity and collective is one of tension.

Elliott and Wattanasuwan (1998) also suggest that consumers will consume things with particular meanings and for what these things may enable them to say about themselves. The lived and mediated experiences (actual or communicated) serve as symbolic resources for self-construction. Lived experience has stronger value for the consumer than mediated experience. Applying this framework, one might then say that a fan experiences a band at a gig (lived experience) and through the media (mediated experience). The fan then relates these experiences of the band to their own life history and situation, and discursively elaborates the meanings of these in social interaction with others. This e-labor-ation is important work in the figuring out of the fan's own subject positions and meanings of themselves; in other words, it is identity work.

In Chapter 6, it was pointed out that in terms of cultural production and consumption, consumers may be cultural producers, and producers can also be cultural consumers. A paper by Meamber (2000) speaks of the artist as both producer and consumer, for example. Therefore, in addition to saying that brands are symbolic resources for the construction of consumer identity, one may also (a) say that bands are symbolic resources for the construction of fan identity, and (b) reverse the polarity in the framework and say that fans may equally be symbolic resources for the construction of a band's identity. For example, bands 'consume' fans through lived experience (at gigs or in personal interactions), or through mediated experience of them (e.g. by reading the fans' comments about the band on a website). The band members make sense of these encounters with fans in certain ways, and this enables them to construct their own identity, using statements such as 'we are a cult band', or 'we have a passionately loyal following'.

Musical culture and subculture

An enduring construct within the fields of cultural studies and popular music studies is the notion of 'subculture'. As far as a more collective than individual dimension of consumption is concerned, there has been an extensive amount of literature on subcultures (usually traced back to Hebdige, 1979), but for some time the value of subculture as an analytical construct has been seriously challenged (Hesmondhalgh, 2005).

There is a considerable amount of academic writing on popular music subcultures, for example punk, goth (Hodkinson, 2002), extreme metal (Kahn-Harris, 2007), and heavy metal (Walser, 1993). In their critical reassessment of the notion of subculture, Bennett and Kahn-Harris (2004: 11) state that this concept has 'dominated the study of youth, style, music, and leisure in the related fields of sociology and cultural studies since the 1970s'. According to the authors there is now a move towards 'post-subcultural' theory. According to Weinzierl and Muggleton (2003: 4), 'the era seems long gone of working class youth subcultures "heroically" resisting subordination through "semiotic guerrilla warfare"'. They argue that:

> certain contemporary 'subcultural' movements can still express a political orientation, the potential for style itself to resist appears largely lost, with any 'intrinsically' subversive quality to subcultures exposed as an illusion.

Weinzierl and Muggleton (2003) name Pierre Bourdieu, Judith Butler and Michael Maffesoli as key thinkers whose work can be drawn on to shape post-subcultural studies. Maffesoli is of particular interest, because writers in marketing and consumer studies often draw on his work on neo-tribes. Maffesoli's importance to the post-subcultural studies project is his emphasis on the fluidity and mobility of subcultures (Weinzierl and Muggleton, 2003: 11), although Weinzierl and Muggleton note his lack of a political dimension. In any case, in a move which appears to have escaped the notice of marketing and consumer studies scholars, popular musical sociological and cultural theorists have been developing a new construct, namely 'scene', to talk about related issues (see below). Kahn-Harris (2007:15) suggests that the use of the word 'scene' frequently 'takes as its starting point a rejection of the competing concept of subculture' (see also Kruse (2003: 145)).

Brand communities

Since the late 1990s, there has been a considerable growth in the body of theory which deals with collective consumption, or consumer groups. A wide range of terms has emerged to talk about consumer 'groupness', including user group, brand culture, tribe, neo-tribe, brand tribe, user community, brand community, cult, scene, microculture, subculture and so on. Examples of the kinds of groups concerned include musical subcultures such as goths, punks and metalheads; skydivers; bikers; gay and lesbian subcultures; skateboarders;

fantasy and science fiction fans; and yuppies. For those seeking conceptual clarity in this field, the proliferation of academic constructs does not help matters. However, these groups have certain issues in common, for example, their boundaries with the outside; membership criteria and assessment; group composition; intra-group hierarchies; group values; group identity; the tension and/or fit between group and individual identities; spirituality/religiosity; and heritage.

The original paper in the brand community strand of literature is by Muñiz and O'Guinn (2001). This constructs a brand community as 'a form of human association situated within a consumption context' (p.426), separate from geographical proximity, in which members share a social bond around a branded, mass-produced commodity. These 'brand communities' have three key characteristics: a consciousness of kin, rituals and a sense of moral responsibility. Members have 'a shared knowing of belonging' (p. 413) and see themselves as being similar to each other and different from other people. They exhibit signs of 'oppositional brand loyalty', in other words they seek to differentiate themselves by comparing other groups unfavourably to themselves on certain key values. As far as community rituals are concerned, members of the community adhere to conventions that set up 'visible public definitions' (p. 413) between themselves and other groups, e.g. waving or flashing lights to drivers of the same make of car. They celebrate brand heritage and tell stories about their experiences of consuming the brand. Members show a desire to ensure community survival by integrating and retaining members. They also assist each other by providing advice, assistance, and information.

Key themes in the brand community literature include religiosity (Muniz and Schau, 2005, 2007), the role of the brand in relation to the wider community, the instrumental imperative to build stronger brands and successful brand communities (McWilliam, 2000; McAlexander et al., 2002; McAlexander et al., 2003), the dangers of brand communities which become too powerful, online brand communities (Kim, 2006) and community typologies (Devasagayam and Buff, 2008). Schau et al. (2009) develop the brand community notion further by pointing to ways in which brand community practices create value. These include social networking, community engagement, impression management and use of the brand. Through these practices, the authors argue, consumers 'realise value beyond that which the firm creates or anticipates' (2009: 30). What marketers call consumer 'value', the benefits of product consumption, can therefore be related to the idea of cultural or subcultural capital. Schau et al.'s (2009) paper provides a list of practices which help consumers to realize this value.

Given the information presented above from the work of Fonarow (2006) on Puritan ideology in indie music, it is interesting to note that religiosity appears as quite an important topic in the brand community literature. In fact, it appears to be the only aspect of ideology that is mentioned. Muñiz and Schau (2005, 2007) point to what they see as the presence of religiosity in brand communities. In their account of the Apple Newton community (2005), they show that religiosity is a feature of the tales told to each other by member of the community whose Newton brand was abandoned by its creator, Apple Inc. The work on religiosity is helpful in indexing religiosity or spirituality as a dimension of meaning in social groups. However, in their account of a popular music 'brand community', namely Tom Petty and the Heartbreakers, they appear to be suggesting that religiosity is also a feature of a mainstream brand (Petty being considered 'mainstream'). From a culturalist point of view, religious discursive resources are always already available to consumers and citizens, whatever their culture.

Another way of reading this is to to say that it is not so much a question of religiosity being an attribute of a reified brand community, but rather of religious discursive resources being contextually and strategically mobilized in consumer accounts of people's experiences in relation to certain offerings. 'Brand community' is an apolitical project which seeks to work up old notions of community in the service of capital. Muniz and O'Guinn (2001) assert that the brand is the social 'tie that binds', yet are careful to say that the 'felt sense of duty' of the brand community members to each other goes only so far. The questions remain, however, as to whether consuming one of their musical offerings makes one a member of e.g. the Warner Music Group brand community, and what it means to be a member of a 'community' along with a multi-billion-dollar corporation.

From a business or marketing management point of view, the brand community literature is helpful in pointing to the sociality of brands, to the importance of rituals in collective consumption, and to the peer-to-peer axis of social interaction which had hitherto largely been ignored in the focus on the brand-customer dyad. It also reminds us that the customer base or fan base, when framed as a social entity, can also be used as a source of identity.

Consumer tribes

In contrast to the brand community literature, there is another line of thinking about consumer 'groupness', namely the idea of consumer tribes. This is perhaps most readily associated with the work of Bernard Cova (Cova and Cova, 2001, 2002; Cova et al., 2007), who argues that what binds a consumer group is not so much the brand but the emotional tie or shared passion of group members about the consumption activity, and not necessarily any set of shared or common attributes. As is the case with the brand community literature, this switches the attention of the marketer from the brand-to-consumer relationship towards the consumer-to-consumer relationship.

Tribal marketing proponents, as well as other commentators, like to quote Michael Maffesoli, the French postmodern sociologist, in support of their notion of tribe. For example, Maffesoli (1996: 76) states that 'in contrast to the stability induced by classical tribalism, neo-tribalism is characterized by fluidity, occasional gatherings and dispersal'. It has to be asked whether such fluidity offers good market opportunities. Maffesoli describes tribes in different ways, such as 'networks of solidarity' (1996: 72), a 'communion of saints (1996: 73)', 'electronic mail, sexual networks, various solidarities including sporting and musical gatherings' (1996: 73), 'youth groups, affinity associations, small-scale industrial enterprises' (1996: 75), and 'small community group[s]' (1996: 94). It is interesting that tribes are not necessarily made up only of consumers. The willingness to include enterprises suggests that Maffesoli sees producers as also having a tribal role. In a band-fan relationship or community, then, one might regard both the band members and the fans as part of a single tribe, though separated by their roles of performer/audience, artist/art-lover or musician/fan.

Maffesoli's book *The Time of the Tribes* (1988/1996) is frequently referenced by a range of scholars interested in communities and consumption. Where authors mention Maffesoli's book, it is usually either to associate it with the concept of 'neo-tribes', or to emphasize the ephemeral nature of consumer groups. For example, Arnould and Thomspon (2005) speak about 'ephemeral collective identifications'. Kozinets (2002) says that 'it remains to be explored whether marketers can engineer experiences that offer and deliver a sense of instant, caring, and judged-to-be-authentic community'. But Maffesoli's work really just functions as a shorthand for the notion of neo-tribes, which are ephemeral gatherings of consumers. In contrast, Maffesoli's lack of a political dimension is noted in post-subcultural music studies (Weinzierl and Muggleton, 2003: 11). His idea of a neo-tribe is not based on any empirical research.

Maffesoli sees experiencing the other as the basis of community, and suggests that it is 'the feeling or passion which, contrary to conventional wisdom, constitutes the essential ingredient of all social aggregations' (1996: 36). He believes that the undirected being-together is 'a basic given of tribes' and that 'Before any other determination or qualification, there is this vital spontaneity that guarantees a culture its own *puissance* and solidity'. The 'religious model' is a key point in his argument: 'the use of the religious metaphor can then be compared to a laser beam allowing the <u>most complete reading</u> of the very heart of a given structure' (1996: 82, emphasis added). He also invoked the notion of the 'social divine' (1996: 38) – the aggregate force which is the basis of any society or association, and of demotheism (1996: 41) – the people as god. He also makes the point that there has always been a heavy religious aspect to revolutionary phenomena. In using the term 'elective sociality', he is referring to something which, he suggests, has always existed – the choice to be with other people. Finally, he uses 'the law of secrecy' to refer to a 'protective mechanism with respect to the outside world'; a secrecy which allows for resistance (1996: 90, 92).

In the end, while it has led to some interesting case analyses, consumer tribal theory ignores the central ideas of Maffesoli, by whom it says it is partly inspired (Cova et al. 2007:5). It also neglects, as O'Reilly (2012) has argued, to develop any theoretical roots, or indeed political awareness. Its usefulness as a facilitator of insights into collective consumption of music is therefore open to question. Maffesoli's ideas, on the other hand, remain useful for an exploration of ideas of resistance and religiosity in music (e.g. with reference to Fonarow, 2006).

Music scenes

The word 'scene' has many meanings (Moberg, 2011). In our everyday life, outside of the arts or musical contexts, it is often used to describe a socio-spatial situation in a geographically defined location, for example the 'political scene' in London, or the 'social scene' in Sydney. In the performing arts, it is most commonly used to denote a space in any performing arts venue where artists perform their music. However, when the word 'scene' is used in the context of musical life, its meaning is rather broad. 'Music scene' is a concept that has been increasingly used in popular music literature since the early 1990s to capture the complexity and diversity of all musical practices, including both production and consumption, in a particular place. Since the term was proposed by Straw in 1991 as a useful unit of academic analysis of musical activities, its meaning is still being widely debated. It is usually presented as a cultural space, which includes a network of organizations, venues, events, situations and a community of artists and audiences which is organized around music (Straw, 1997; Futrell et al., 2006; Knowles, 2008). Cisar and Koubek (2012), in their review of different definitions of 'scene', identified some common attributes, namely the interconnectedness of political and cultural activities, a link to a certain space (social, geographic or virtual), and ties to a given music or artistic genre. Scenes may also be looked at as discursive spaces created through internal and external discourses, as well as aesthetic construction (Kahn-Harris, 2007). Internal discourses refer to discursive practices among members of the scene, through which they construct it as a distinctive space which new members can recognize and identify with. External discourses are discursive practices among non-members of the scene, who construct it as a distinctive space, for example by presenting it as a music scene in media. Kahn-Harris (2007: 100) also argues that 'scenes are constructed through the development of particular aesthetics, musical and otherwise, that become both internally and externally visible'. It is important, however, to note the difference between the concepts of scene and genre. The latter concept is used to represent a more rigidly defined set of musical characteristics, something resembling a musical style, for example jazz or progressive rock. Most often, both concepts are used together to describe all musical activities within a particular location and style, as in the case of the New York jazz scene or the Russian ballet scene.

In studies prior to the late 1980s, the terms 'community' and 'subculture' were either used interchangeably with the term 'scene' (Polsky, 1967), or were used to describe, in a much narrower way, what is now meant by scene – i.e. the entirety of musical practice in a particular place. Scene as a theoretical concept has been often described as a holistic and anti-essentialist category (Moberg, 2011), which means it attempts to capture musical activities in their entirety, and as such is devoid of any pre-determined and unique characteristics that are essential for its existence. Following wide criticism and rejection of 'community' and 'subculture' theoretical frameworks (Bennett, 1999), they have been replaced by music 'scenes' as a central unit of academic analysis. Music scenes, it has been argued, are less stringent and allow for more heterogeneity and dynamism in musical spaces; loose relations have been established between all of their constituents, and they have been presented as a type of context for all musical production and consumption (Harris, 2000) – a musical universe. The phrase 'music scene' is also often used in everyday conversations to describe networks of music-makers and consumers with reference to a type of music or genre and the geographic location of the musical activities, for example the 'jazz scene' in New Orleans, or the 'cabaret scene' in Paris. One can safely assume that regardless of whether one wants to use the term 'scene' to describe a unit of academic analysis, or just to describe musical activities in a particular location, it is, in most cases, used to capture the totality of musical activities, from going to a gig at a local pub, through watching a busker on a high street, to buying a CD. Unlike communities and subcultures, participation in music scenes is not limited by gender, class or ethnicity (Straw, 1991).

According to Kahn-Harris (2007), scenes consist of five main dimensions: infrastructure, stability, relation to other scenes, scenic capital, and production and consumption. The infrastructure of each music scene consists of a group of organizations, such as venues, record labels, management companies, the media, and festivals, which collaborate closely to encourage and maintain musical activities and reproduce the meaning and social character of the scene. The stability of a scene represents the ability and strength of the scene to develop its own infrastructure, which will support its existence and reinforce its unique characteristics. Every music scene exists in a network of other scenes, defined by geography and genre, and the relation to other scenes will define its nature. Different scenes share different elements of their infrastructure, from musicians playing in different bands, through venues hosting an eclectic portfolio of artists, to record labels signing a diverse group of musical acts. Scenic capital is a form of cultural capital similar to that created by subcultural groups in a form of unique hierarchy (see, for example, Chapter 8), knowledge and resources, physical appearance and dress, behavioural code, and rituals. Last but not least, every scene develops different modes of production and consumption. For example, the majority of music consumed within a local scene may be produced elsewhere, within a larger national or global scene.

The broad understanding of the phrase 'music scene' locates all of the related musical activities within a larger context of cultural life, without artificially separating it from all other human activities of daily life, and at the same time creating constant fluidity of the scene. All of these daily activities coexist and interact with each other (Straw, 1991), loosely connecting consumers, who 'enter' the music scene through the most mundane acts. For example, listening to a local radio station while driving to work or exercising in a gym, catching a glimpse of a band playing in a local pub, going to a Lady Gaga concert, taking a child to music classes, buying a musical instrument with every intention of learning to play it, rehearsing with a band in a garage, or giving a few spare coins to a musician busking on the street are all small acts of participation in a music scene. Various music scenes – local, regional, national, transnational, global and virtual – coexist at the same time, and their boundaries are constantly redrawn by participants' acts in terms of engaging and disengaging in different activities. When local scenes, as the smallest analytical units among all scenes, establish sufficient connections between one another, they form regional scenes, which develop over time into national scenes, and may then become part of a larger transnational or global scene (Moberg, 2011). For example, the Northern soul scene in the UK, which developed in the late 1960s from the British mod scene, started as a constellation of local scenes and popular venues in various towns and cities of Northern England: Twisted Wheel in Manchester, Blackpool Mecca, Wigan Casino and Stoke-on-Trent's Golden Torch. Together they formed the Northern soul scene, which, along with other UK-born artists such as Tom Jones and Dusty Springfield, formed the British soul scene of the 1960s and 1970s. The British soul scene was then obviously a part of large global phenomenon connecting a large number of regional scenes (e.g. Motown soul, Chicago soul, Memphis soul, blue-eyed soul). Nowadays, in a globalizing music world even a simple act such as going to a Michael Bublé concert on a Friday evening in Manchester represents an engagement in multiple music scenes: a Manchester music scene (for example if the concert takes place at the Manchester Evening News Arena), a virtual music scene (buying the ticket online from Ticketmaster), a New York music scene (Naturally 7, who toured with Michael Bublé and opened for his Crazy Love Tour, is a New York-based group), and a Canadian and international music scene (Michael Bublé is Canadian, as well as being an international artist). Most likely, a person planning to attend a concert will also follow some news in the media regarding the concert as well (a UK national music scene). Therefore, through their actions, individuals engage in different music scenes at the same time without being closely attached to any one of them. The smaller local and national music scenes are in constant dialogue with larger international and virtual music scenes, and through their interconnections they reposition each other, thereby shaping each other's meaning. As a consequence, various music scenes are often difficult to distinguish. The same local musicians may participate simultaneously in a local jazz scene as well as a classical music scene, which is differentiated by venues, promoters and booking agents, yet connected through musicians and some members of the audience.

Following Peterson and Bennett's (2004) suggestion, music scenes can be divided into three categories: local, translocal and virtual. These categories, although having some distinct characteristics, often overlap, and therefore can be studied from three different perspectives, putting local, translocal or virtual at the centre of musical activities (Bennett *et al.*, 2008). Local music scenes are those traditionally defined geographical spaces in which various stakeholders interact to co-create a local music culture. The focus of academic studies of local music scenes range from pub rock (Bennett, 1997) to karaoke (Drew, 2004), and from Liverpool (Cohen, 1991) to Austin, Texas (Shank, 1994). However, in a globalizing world, local music scenes cannot always capture the complexity of relations between musical activities that are unbound by geography, culture and social relations. Most people, including both musicians and music fans, although connected to their local music scene, simultaneously participate in other music scenes through global media or travels, thereby creating translocal links between local music scenes, the products of which are translocal music scenes (Peterson and Bennett, 2004). Some examples of translocal music scenes include the goth music scene in England (Hodkinson, 2002), and dance music scenes (Laing, 1997). The popularity of the Internet, and more recently the emergence of online communities and social networking websites, have opened up new, virtual spaces to the creation of virtual music scenes. Musicians, fans and ordinary people can exchange information, music files, and opinions without coming into face-to-face contact with each other, and these interactions can span cities, countries and continents. Myspace, Facebook, Twitter, blogs, musicians' websites and chat rooms facilitate these exchanges, at the same time creating a virtual geography of new music scenes. An example of such scenes, as examined by Bennett (2002, 2004), is the Canterbury scene.

The existence of any music scene requires a group of participants (Crossley, 2008), which is a social and economic network consisting, for example, of musicians, fans and venues, who are capable of generating musical activities which allow the scene to be differentiated from all other scenes. This minimum number of participants may vary from a music-friendly village pub with a couple of musicians, to a very diverse group of stakeholders in a large-city music scene. The scene also requires some connection between participants, such as through taking part in the same activities. For example, musicians need to find a venue they feel comfortable performing in, and audiences need to be aware of musical performances and the venue. The existence of a music scene requires collective actions among its participants (Crossley, 2008). This is where marketing and marketers enter the scene to become an integral element of it. Broadly speaking, marketing's role within a music scene is to facilitate the connection between various members of the scene. In the next section of this book, the many ways in which marketing can be used to promote live music and interaction between members of the music scene will be discussed.

Before closing, it is worth noting that Hesmondhalgh raises arguments (2005) about all three terms (subculture, scene, tribe). This position is tied up with his view that 'the privileging of youth in studies of music has actually become an obstacle to a more fully developed understanding of music and society' (ibid.: 21).

Summary

This chapter has focused on a range of ideas about music and community. Although, from a marketing point of view, the ideas of brand community and tribe have something to offer in understanding the social dimension of brands, and the idea of music scene can to some degree act as a helpful frame for a broader view of music-making practices, none of these notions by themselves offer more than a partial insight. Nevertheless, taken together, they point to elements which marketers could usefully consider alongside their traditional focus on exchange relationships and deal flow, including the importance of rituals, a sense of kinship, shared passion, ethical responsibility, the ideological and geographical dimensions of musical collectivities, the realization of value (or 'capital') by consumers, the importance of musical practices in a specific cultural space, and so on.

References

Arnould, E., Price, L. and Zinkhan, G. (2003) *Consumers*. London: McGraw-Hill Higher Education.

Arnould, E. and Thompson, C. (2005) 'Consumer Culture Theory (CCT): twenty years of research', *Journal of Consumer Research*, **31**, (4), 868-882.

Beck, Ulrich. 1992. *Risk Society: Toward a New Modernity*. London, UK: Sage.

Bennett, A. (1997) 'Going down the pub: the pub rock scene as resource for the consumption of popular music', *Popular Music*, **16** (1), 97-108.

Bennett, A. (1999) 'Subcultures or neo-tribes? Rethinking the relationship between youth, style and musical taste', *Sociology*, **33** (3), 599-617.

Bennett, A. (2002) 'Music, media and urban mythscapes: a study of the Canterbury sound', *Media, Culture and Society*, **24** (1), 107-120.

Bennett, A. (2004) 'New tales from Canterbury: the making of a virtual music scene', in: Bennett, A. and Peterson, R.A. (ed.) *Music Scenes: Local, Translocal and Virtual*, Nashville, TN: Vanderbilt University Press, pp. 205-220.

Bennett, A. and Kahn-Harris, K. (2005) *After Subculture: Critical Studies in Contemporary Youth Culture*. Basingstoke: Palgrave Macmillan

Bennett, A., Stratton, J. and Peterson, R.A. (2008) `The scenes perspective and the Australian context?', *Continuum: Journal of Media & Cultural Studies*, **22** (5), 593 - 599.

Cohen, S. (1991) *Rock Culture in Liverpool: Popular Music in the Making*, Oxford: Clarendon Press.

Cova, B. and Cova, V. (2001) 'Tribal aspects of postmodern consumption research: The case of French in-line roller skates'. *Journal of Consumer Behaviour*, **1** (1), 67-76.

Cova, B. and Cova, V. (2002) 'Tribal marketing: The tribalisation of society and its impact on the conduct of marketing'. *European Journal of Marketing*. **36** (5/6), 595 – 620.

Cova, B. Kozinets, R. and Shankar, A. (2007) *Consumer Tribes*. Oxford: Butterworth-Heinemann.

Crossley, N. (2008) 'The man whose web expanded: network dynamics in Manchester's post/punk music scene 1976–1980', *Poetics*, **37**, 24-49.

De Certeau, M., Luce, G. and Mayol, P. (2002) *The Practice of Everyday Life*. Berkeley, CA: University of California Press.

Devasagayam, P.R. and Buff, C.L. (2008) 'A Multidimensional Conceptualization of Brand Community: An Empirical Investigation'. *Sport Marketing Quarterly*, 17 (1), 20-29.

Drew, R. (2004) 'Scenes' dimensions of karaoke in the US', in: Bennett, A. and Peterson, R.A. (ed.) *Music Scenes: Local, Translocal and Virtual*, Nashville: Vanderbilt University Press, pp. 64-79.

Elliott, R. and Wattanasuwan, K. (1998) 'Brands as symbolic resources for the construction of identity.' *International Journal of Advertising*, 17 (2), 131-144.

Fairclough, N. (2000) 'Language and neo-liberalism', *Discourse & Society*, 11 (2), 147-148.

Featherstone, M. (2007) *Consumer Culture and Postmodernism*. Second edition. London: Sage.

Meamber, L.A. (2000) Artist Becomes/Becoming Artistic: The Artist as Producer-Consumer, *Advances in Consumer Research*, 27 (1), p44-49

Fonarow, W. (2006) *Empire of Dirt: The aesthetics and rituals of British indie music*. Middletown, CT: Wesleyan University Press.

Futrell, R., Simi, P. and Gottschalk, S. (2006) 'Understanding music in movements: the white power music scene', *Sociological Quarterly*, 47, 275-304.

Gabriel, Y. And Lang, T. (2006) *The Unmanageable Consumer*. Second edition. London: Sage.

Giddens, A. (1991) *Modernity and Self-Identity: Self And Society In The Late Modern Age*. Cambridge, UK: Polity Press.

Giddens, A. (1998) *The Third Way: The Renewal of Social Democracy*. Cambridge, UK: Polity Press.

Harris, K. (2000) '"Roots"?: the relationship between the global and the local within the Extreme Metal scene', *Popular Music*, 19 (1), 13-30.

Hebdige, D. (1979) *Subculture: The meaning of style*, London: Routledge.

Hesmondhalgh, D. (2005) 'Subcultures, scenes or tribes? None of the above', *Journal of Youth Studies*, 8 (1), 21-40.

Hirschman, E.C. (1983) 'Consumer Intelligence, Creativity, and Consciousness: Implications for consumer protection and education', *Journal of Public Policy & Marketing*, 2 (1), 153-170.

Kruse, H. (2003) *Site and Sound: Understanding Independent Music Scenes*. New York, NY: Peter Lang.

Hodkinson, P. (2002) *Goth: Identity, Style and Subculture*, Oxford: Berg.

Kahn-Harris, K. (2007) *Extreme Metal: Music and Culture on the Edge*, Oxford: Berg.

Kim, J. (2006) 'Advances Toward Developing Conceptual Foundations of Internet Brand Community'. *Advances in Consumer Research*, **33** (1), 300-301.

Knowles, J.D. (2008) 'Setting the scene: developments in Australian experimental music since the mid-1990s', in: Priest, G. (ed.) *Experimental Music: Audio Explorations in Australia*, Sydney: UNSW Press, pp. 6-25.

Kozinets R. (2002) 'Can consumers escape the market? Emancipatory illuminations from Burning Man'. *Journal of Consumer Research*, **29** (1), 20-38.

Laing, D. (1997) 'Rock anxieties and new music networks', in: McRobbie A. (ed.) *Back to Reality: Social Experience and Cultural Studies*, Manchester: Manchester University Press., pp. 116-132.

McAlexander, J.H., Schouten, J.W. and Koening, H.F. (2002) 'Building Brand Community', *Journal of Marketing*, **66** (1), 38-54.

McAlexander, J., Kim, S. and Roberts, S. (2003) 'Building Brand Loyalty: The influences of satisfaction and brand community integration', *Journal of Marketing Theory and Practice*, **11** (4), 1-11.

McWilliam, G. (2000) 'Building Stronger Brand through Online Communities'. *Sloan Management Review*, **41** (3), 43-54.

Maffesoli, M. (1996) *The Time of the Tribes: The Decline of Individualism in Mass Society.* London: Sage.

Meamber, L.A. (2000) 'Artist Becomes/Becoming Artistic: The Artist as Producer-Consumer', *Advances in Consumer Research*, **27** (1), 44-49.

Moberg, M. (2011) 'The concept of scene and its applicability in empirically grounded research on the intersection of religion/spirituality and popular music', *Journal of Contemporary Religion*, **26** (3), 403-417.

Muniz, A.M. and O'Guinn, T. C. (2001) 'Brand Community', *Journal of Consumer Research*, **27** (4), 412-432.

Muñiz, A.M. and Schau, H.J. (2005) 'Religiosity in the Abandoned Apple Newton Brand Community', *Journal of Consumer Research*, 31 (4), 737-747.

Peterson, R.A., and Bennett, A. (2004) 'Introducing music scenes', In: Bennett, A. and Peterson, R.A. (ed.) *Music Scenes: Local, Translocal and Virtual*, Nashville: Vanderbilt University Press, 1-15.

Polsky, N. (1967) *Hustlers, Beats, and Others*, Chicago: Aldine.

Rose, N. 1996. *Inventing Our Selves: Psychology, Power and Personhood.* Cambridge, UK: Cambridge University Press.

Schau, H.J. (2000) 'Consumer Imagination, Identity and Self-Expression', in Hoch, S.J. and Meyer, R.J.) (ed.) *NA-Advances in Consumer Research*, 27, 50-56.

Schau, H.J. and Muñiz, A.M. (2007) 'Temperance and Religiosity in a Non-Marginal, Non-Stigmatized Brand Community', in Cova, B., Kozinets, R. and Shankar, A. (ed.) *Consumer Tribes: Theory, Practice and Prospects*. Oxford: Elsevier-Butterworth-Heinemann, pp. 144-162.

Schau, H.J., Muñiz, A.M. and Arnould, E.J. (2009) 'How Brand Community Practices Create Value'. *Journal of Marketing*, **73** (5), 30-51.

Shank, W. (1994) *Dissonant Identities: The Rock'n'Roll Scene in Austin*, Hannover, CT: Wesleyan University Press.

Straw, W. (1991) 'Systems of articulation, logics of change: communities and scenes in popular music', *Cultural Studies*, **5**, 368–388.

Straw, W. (1997) 'Communities and scenes in popular music', in: Gelder, K. and Thornton, S. (eds) *The Subcultures Reader*, London: Routledge, pp. 494-505.

Walser, R. (1993) *Running with the Devil: Power, Gender and Madness in Heavy Metal Music*. Middletown: Wesleyan University Press.

Weinzierl, D. and Muggleton, R. (2003) *The Post-subcultures Reader*, London: Berg.

Part IV
Live Music

10 Live Music and Festivals

Introduction

The purpose of this chapter is to explore the importance of live music, music venues, music festivals and live music promotion in the production and consumption of music. As shown in Chapter 3, music is a complex product which can be enjoyed in a wide range of social situations, from listening to music in one's own home or car, through enjoying a concert in a large music venue like an opera house or stadium, to spending several days at a music festival attended by over a million people. This chapter therefore begins with an attempt to provide an understanding of some of the historical developments of live music, its main characteristics, and the reasons behind its growing popularity. Music festivals are an important variant of live music, and the chapter also includes a discussion of the nature, form and function of music festivals, their multiple impacts and the marketing issues which they present.

Live music

Live music was the only form of music consumption up until the invention of the gramophone by Thomas Edison in 1877. The invention marked a new era in the consumption and production of music, allowing audiences to enjoy the beauty of sounds from the privacy of their own homes, and separating the process of production from consumption. From the middle of the 20th century recorded music was becoming easily available, and radio stations and bars were replacing live music with recordings and jukeboxes (Thornton, 1995). While, throughout the 20th century, the increasing importance of recorded music and the domestication of musical activities were negatively affecting live music and opportunities for musicians to perform live (Frith, 2007), the most recent years have bucked the trend. During the last decade it has become common for music journalists and researchers to comment on the increasing importance of live music at the expense of the record industry (Frith, 2007). There are more live music events now than ever before, and more and more bands come back from retirement to capitalize on the prosperity of the live music industry. Although it seems as though live music has acquired a cultural value and importance that is unprecedented since the beginning of the music industry, there is still surprisingly little research into the market for live music (Holt, 2010; Oakes, 2003).

The history of live music venues and public concerts began hundreds of years ago. The first opera house open to the public was Teatro San Cassino in Venice, which opened in 1637 and fully relied on the box office; it also sparked an emergence of travelling opera companies and other opera houses all over Italy (King, 2001). The first public concert in London was given by violinist John Bannister in 1672, and this was followed by regular public concerts in Paris from 1683, in Germany from 1743 and in Vienna from 1772 (Tschmuck, 2012). From the perspective of music production and consumption, live music is an interesting element of any music scene. It brings together musicians and music consumers, and often all of the relevant stakeholders, into a physically and socially defined space such as a concert hall or stadium. Most cities and towns around the world offer some form of live music to their residents and visitors, and often become famous for the quality of their live music provision, as in the case of New Orleans, London and Vienna. Vibrant music scenes are a hugely important part of the cultural life of these places, attracting large numbers of tourists, and offering employment as well as entertainment opportunities to local residents. Young and up-and-coming musicians perform in pubs, restaurants and nightclubs to reach their audiences, while more established acts perform in traditional venues designed for live performances, like concert halls and theatres, and global music stars attract thousands to large music arenas and stadiums. It is also necessary to recognize that in some music genres, like folk, jazz and rock, live music remains the benchmark of quality and the most important rite of passage for young musicians. For jazz or rock fans, it is the live performance that ultimately reveals the authenticity of their music idols. And, according to Frith (2007), such fans recognize live performance as something that enables them to witness the extraordinariness and uniqueness of musical talent and hard work. The value of live music lies in experiencing the performance and authenticity of creative musicianship.

Music can be broadly divided into two categories: recorded and live. Although many venues offer both of these, in this chapter the discussion focuses on live music. This is not to say that one is more important than the other, but live music is a unique form of musical experience spontaneously co-created by musicians and their audience. While live music was traditionally treated by the music industry as a tool to stimulate sales of recorded music (Cluley, 2009), nowadays recorded music is increasingly being treated by artists not as a revenue stream, but as an avenue for promotion and an opportunity for recognition. Increasingly, for many musicians live concerts have become the main source of income (Connolly and Krueger, 2006); a broad range of ancillary products, such as t-shirts and programmes, can also be sold to fans at live performances, thereby generating additional income. Therefore, while recorded music can be described as a product consumed through a tangible medium such as a CD or MP3 player, live music is part of a service industry, and as a product relies heavily on the five key characteristics of services (Fisher et al., 2010): intangibility, inseparability, variability, perishability and non-ownership. Live music performance is intangible; it cannot be touched or stored and its consumption is predominantly an experience. Although there is a significant market for live music recordings, their value lies mainly in documenting the experience, rather than exactly recreating it. Indeed, musical performances cannot be precisely recreated as they are produced through the interaction between musicians, audiences and the environment, and the experience itself cannot be separated from the music. The ephemeral nature of live music experience makes it unique, but also variable in terms of quality. Two concerts from the same artist are never identical, as they are spontaneously created 'in the moment' through interactions between all present and through the physicality of their environment. They are also perishable – once performed and experienced, a concert is gone forever – and while the same set of songs performed by the same band, but at a different venue or with a different audience represents the same service, it does not provide the same service experience every time. Finally, music performance cannot be owned by a member of the audience, as by buying a ticket one acquires access to the experience, but not the service itself.

But live music is first and foremost a big business. While digitalization brought to recorded music the threat of piracy and copyright infringement, live music has been largely immune to those problems, and therefore could continue growing undisturbed. The commercial potential of live music has been spotted by the entertainment industry, which was quick to enter the live music market to take a share of revenues generated by live performances. Although most small and medium inner-city and suburban music venues are run as independent businesses by local entrepreneurs, many large venues become jewels in the crown of international corporations (Frith, 2007). In the UK, the market leaders among such corporations are Live Nation and AEG Live (both US-based entertainment companies), Irish MCD Productions and SJM Concerts. Live Nation and AEG Live are also the world's two biggest live music promoters. The role of these companies goes well beyond traditional roles of booking agents or promoters, since they also act as middlemen between artists and venues and organize live music events. Their aggressive expansion in recent years has focused on vertical integration and a gradual acquisition of different elements of the live music value chain, from venues, through organization and management of tours, ticket sales, merchandise, and sponsorship deals, to recordings (Holt, 2010).

Live music performances attract audiences for a variety of very diverse reasons. Although live music is often up to ten times more expensive than recorded music, and can be enjoyed only once – during the performance – it remains one of the most important forms of music consumption. Earl (2001) identified a long list of reasons behind the popularity of live music. For example, infrequent concert-goers attend live concerts as they are curious to see musicians that they have seen on TV or heard on the radio, while devoted fans are motivated by the opportunity to experience familiar music being performed live, often in new arrangements. Live music also encourages a sense of shared experience among members of the audience, where other listeners are as important as the music itself. Live performance offers spontaneity and the thrill of things which may go wrong during the performance, for example an artist forgetting lyrics, and a chance to experience music in a way that differs from the perfection of its recorded version. The most loyal fans can manifest their devotion to the artists, while in the case of lesser-known musicians consumers can sample their music without having to make a commitment to them by buying an album. Concerts also have a unique social dimension: the audience can behave in a way that would not be allowed in other situations, for example dancing, shouting or singing loudly. However, it is also important to note the many barriers that discourage people from attending live music performances (Earl, 2001). Many large venues are located out-of-town, and childcare and travel-related costs such as parking and petrol, and long commuting time, may be a problem for some consumers. Once inside the venue, attendance at any live performance brings other risks such as problems with sound quality, high volume, and undesired supporting acts, and many inconveniences associated with social consumption, for example overcrowded spaces, limited ability to see the performers, or unruly behaviour of other fans. Many venues have exclusive contracts with food and drink suppliers, which reduce the options available to consumers to products offered by only a small number of companies. Live music venues have a very important influence on the audience's enjoyment of music and the quality of their experience. Dobson's (2008) research, for example, emphasized good acoustics and sight lines, and physical comfort.

When it comes to consumer satisfaction with a live music performance, Grove *et al.*'s (1992) model of service experience as a drama has been used in previous research. It distinguishes between participants (personnel and audience), physical evidence (venue) and process of service assembly (performance). In the centre of the model is the relationship between participants (musicians and audience). Minor *et al.* (2004), for example, when measuring the importance of the many dimensions of live music performance, concluded with the following list of factors, in order of importance: sound quality and volume, musical ability, musician's creativity, temperature, seating facilities, audience enthusiasm, song interpretation, stage lighting, song familiarity, parking facilities, background lighting, social compatibility, musician's movements, physical appearance and clothing, stage decoration and background decoration.

Live music promotion

Music scenes come to life through live music. Musical concerts create spaces in which all members of the music scene come together to enjoy musical experiences. Yet all types of live music require appropriate music promotion. Promotion entails a wide range of communication activities. For example, popular music brands, such as Lady Gaga, Justin Bieber and One Direction, rely on the quality of their professional mass marketing communications to appeal to the social identities of their fans. On the other hand, groups like symphony orchestras, opera companies and jazz ensembles live off their audience's loyalty and devotion, which is developed through highly targeted niche marketing. Any piece of marketing communication aims to inform music consumers about the musical brand and its values, meaning and activities, and persuade them to try new musical experiences, or even remind them of old and forgotten music. Communication in live music promotion is also about the process of reaching a shared understanding of cultural texts – that is, music brands. Within a particular music scene, marketing communications employed to promote music brands and live performances become part of the wider music discourse, where their meaning is co-produced by musicians, marketers, audiences and other members of this music scene. The content of marketing communications is locally contextualized by various audiences, and therefore live music marketers need to understand their target audiences' knowledge of the music brand, their previous level of experience with the brand or genre, acceptable social and cultural norms within the community of music fans, and assumptions held by the target audiences about the brand. Live music promotion fulfils a wide range of functions within a particular music scene: beyond its traditional role in the marketing mix, live music promotion plays a social role in the diffusion of information among fans, influencing the decision-making processes of consumers. For different types of audiences, live music promotion can help consumers conceptualize their wants (engaging previously disinterested consumers in live music), develop their wants (increasing their participation in live music), focus their wants (creating an attachment to a genre or particular venue), and satisfy their wants (creating reassurance).

A wide range of promotional tools can be used to reach audiences and achieve communication objectives, including advertising, public relations, direct marketing, sales promotion, personal selling, sponsorship, e-marketing, guerrilla marketing, viral marketing, exhibitions, merchandising, packaging, word-of-mouth and word-of-mouse. The marketing role in the process of communication focuses on the management, coordination and integration of these various communications tools (so-called integrated marketing communication (IMC)) to deliver coherent, clear and consistent messages to the music scene, engaging with user-generated content (such as blogs, reviews, fanzines, fan pages, Facebook pages, etc.) to facilitate the creation of a shared understanding of cultural texts. Apart from the musicians themselves, there are several marketing roles in the promotion of live music. Venue owners and managers will often take responsibility for some of the communication activities, utilizing their own communication channels such as the venue's website, Facebook page, posters and leaflets. Music promoters, often operating within a city or a region to develop good relations with venues, are responsible for booking bands and organizing concerts. They act like middlemen between bands and their agents and venues, often promoting the concerts themselves, making sure everything in the venue is ready for musicians and audiences (including equipment), and even handling all the financial aspects of the organization of concerts. The responsibility of the band manager is to oversee all business affairs of musicians, from booking gigs, through promotion, to administration and accounting. While music promoters work for themselves, managers work for musicians. Sometimes music agents (or booking agents) can be involved in the organization of live music, and they may be responsible for the organization of a tour, working with local music promoters and band managers.

The first and primary objective of any marketing communication is to increase awareness of the musical brand among members of the target audience. First, a much wider dimension of awareness is brand recognition, which is most commonly created through mass-marketing communication tools such as advertising and public relations and mass media such as television and radio. When the name of the band is mentioned in the media it increases consumers' aural and visual recognition of the band. Using marketing communications to create awareness is crucial, as in most cases consumers' awareness of the musical brand is a prerequisite to all other consumption behaviours. Marketing communication tools are used to stimulate brand recognition, but one of the desired outcomes of communicative activities is brand recall. This is much harder to achieve, however, as it requires the musical brand to be recalled by consumers in the right circumstances, when they are not stimulated by any marketing communications. In other words, brand recognition is about the passive familiarity of consumers with the brand, while brand recall is the ability of music consumers to remember the brand in a situation when they might be able to consume it. For example, good brand recognition is achieved when a jazz fan comes to London and, while walking around town, notices a poster promoting jazz gigs at Ronnie Scott's. From this stimuli, the fan recognizes the legendary jazz club and considers going out to a concert. On the other hand, brand recall is much harder to achieve as it requires consumers to be active in their search: good brand recall would be achieved when the same consumer comes to London and, knowing they have a free evening, decides to investigate (using other communication tools like a website or concert programs) as to whether there is anything on that evening at Ronnie Scott's.

When it comes to live music promotion and effective marketing communications, one may make use of Sayre's (2008) classification of audiences into three distinctive groups: passive spectators, focused experiencers, and absorbed identifiers, each of which require a different communication approach.

Passive spectators are people who display minimum or no loyalty to any music. They are infrequent concert-goers and might come along to a free concert in the park, or listen to a band in the background when they are already in a pub to meet up with friends. As their involvement and identification with live-music experiences is very low, they normally need to get free tickets or have someone else take them to a concert. With passive spectators, the main objective of marketing communications is to educate them about the benefits of live music in order to increase their engagement and participation. This can be achieved through educational and outreach programmes (as is often the case with symphonic orchestras), providing background information and additional resources on the Internet, or videos of live concerts and venues on YouTube.com, which can educate audiences about the benefits of participation in live music, as well as addressing any doubts passive spectators may have about the appropriateness of the experience for them. Advertising and public relations messages need to be placed in non-musical media such as mainstream newspapers and magazines, outdoor billboards and posters, or even through giving away free tickets via radio contests. The communication messages should also focus on the enjoyment of the overall experience, rather than the music itself. For example, each year Queensland Symphony Orchestra (QSO) in Brisbane, Australia, performs a free concert inaugurating the new season; it aims to educate and engage new audience members with extensive talks and various introductions to musical instruments, composers and regularly performed pieces. In 2012, the QSO's inaugural concert was also streamed live online.

The second type of audience members, **focused experiencers**, are characterized by much more active engagement in live musical experiences, compared to passive spectators. They already have some knowledge of music, and score higher on both aspects of brand awareness: recognition and recall. Focused experiencers are frequent consumers of live music, but hardly ever remain loyal to one particular musician, band or venue. Rather, they might have some preference for specific genres, such as jazz and classical music (Oakes, 2003), and will regularly attend, for example, various orchestral concerts, operas and jazz gigs. They plan their live music consumption and are frequently the people who take passive spectators to live music concerts. Sayre (2008) suggested that it is these consumers that should be targeted with promotional messages. They are aware of the value of live music, and as regular consumers of music do not need to be educated about its value or the rituals surrounding their favourite genre. From the communication perspective, long-term sales promotions encouraging consumer loyalty, such as season tickets and multi-concert packages, are most effective. The above-mentioned QSO, for example, offers a wide range of subscription packages to suit different levels of loyalty. Further, direct marketing is also often used to maintain the focused experiencers' regular engagement through social media (Facebook pages, Twitter accounts) and more traditional newsletters containing reviews and updates about concerts, events and promotions.

The highest level of engagement in live music is displayed by so-called **absorbed identifiers** (Sayre, 2008), who can be simply described as fans. These are the most loyal and regular group of music consumers, and as fans they identify themselves with different musical genres and brands such as bands and venues. As discussed in Chapter 8, fans distinguish themselves through much more intensive consumption practices and unique identities centred on their music life. Some of the most important aspects of their engagement are knowledge and community, and therefore they are very receptive to communication that provides them with information and encourages the existence of the community. Absorbed identifiers engage in the musical life of their community, often running fan clubs and fanzines, or organizing musical events and festivals.

Music festivals

Music festivals are a particular and significant case of live music, both historically and in contemporary times. They are spaces where music, markets and consumption come together and intersect with culture, society, and politics in ways that produce rich and engaging experiences for the musicians, organizers, audiences, and all those involved. An estimated 485 music festivals, covering every genre of music, were held in 2007 in the UK. Despite not including any free festivals, this figure still represents a staggering 38% growth in the number of festivals in just seven years (Mintel, 2008). This phenomenal growth has, however, slowed down since the UK recession began in 2009. A number of festivals have been dissolved (Music Week, 2011), but, on the other hand, major festivals such as the Glastonbury Festival of Contemporary Performing Arts continue to sell out in record times (BBC News, 2012). This begs the question of why music festivals are of such significance.

Festivals are special celebrations involving a range of artistic performances, which usually occur over a number of days. With roots in the first Olympic games in Greece, several hundred years BC (Sadie, 2001), festivals have been of cultural importance for millennia. Contemporary music festivals are an important variant (Shuker, 1998), not only culturally, but also economically and socially. Music festivals are diverse in nature and, as such, the study of them is thinly spread across a range of disciplines such as human geography, sociology and business. Across this literature, three characteristics emerge which help in defining their form and highlight the complex range of social, cultural, economic, and political functions they perform. First, festivals transform places from everyday settings into temporary, unique, and spectacular spaces (Connell and Gibson, 2003; Waterman, 1998). They are not necessarily bounded by place, and they are all ephemeral. Second, festivals can create and maintain cultural meaning and social structure, reinforcing popular music personas and creating icons and myths in the process (Shuker, 1998). Last, festivals facilitate the formation of communities of audiences, performers and/or organizers. Some communities last beyond the spatial and temporal boundaries of the festival, but most are considered to be temporary (Connell and Gibson, 2003). These characteristics are apparent in both commercial and non-commercial festivals, and also underpin the significance of music festivals.

The significance of festivals

Music festivals are significant in numerous ways, and have a great impact on the communities and regions in which they take place. Although the large majority of contemporary music festivals are explicitly commercial, with various 'stakeholders' seeking to benefit financially from them, both commercial and free festivals provide recognized economic benefits to their host locales. This economic impact can be measured in a number of ways. For example, UK Music (2011) analysed the contribution of music festivals and large-scale live concerts to the tourism economy, and found that they attract at least 7.7m attendances by domestic and overseas music tourists who collectively spend £1.4bn during the course of their trip.

Larsen and Hussels (2011) analysed the sparse economic data that is available for commercial festivals in the UK and found that they have not only grown in number, but also in terms of scale as measured by attendance and repertoire. There have also been substantial increases in ticket prices across the festivals. For example, between 2000 to 2010 ticket prices for Glastonbury, V Festival, and Reading Festival increased by 213%, 234% and 225% respectively, which means, on average, more than 20% per annum. These price increases have not, however, slowed sales, as the large commercial festivals continue to sell out in record times. In 2013, the Glastonbury Festival of Contemporary Performing Arts sold out in 90 minutes, despite technological difficulties. The largest single stream of income for festivals continues to be the box office (Larsen and Hussels, 2011). However, the greatest economic impact on the local economy from any cultural activity generally arises through spend on hospitality, accommodation, retail and travel. A survey of 3000 UK festival fans in 2009 estimated average ticket spends of £140 per head, plus a further £130 on drinks, £60 for food and £100 on travel (Canizal Villarino et al., 2009). A lot of big festivals outsource food and drink provision; thus, festivals indirectly create additional employment – the equivalent to 19,700 full-time jobs in 2009, according to UK Music (2011). Altogether, the Association of Independent Festivals (2010) estimates that the music festival market is booming and that it contributes more than £1bn each year to the UK economy.

The significance of festivals is not only economic. Festivals, like live music generally, are a form of experiential production and consumption comprised of cultural, symbolic, social and emotional dimensions (Botti, 2000) in addition to the political and economic. Thus, drawing on a range of these perspectives, an enriched view of the impact of music festivals is developed (O'Reilly et al., 2010).

First, music festivals are integral in producing, consuming and preserving culture. As a form of cultural activity, music festivals are carriers of culture and important vehicles by which humans construct and interpret their own culture (e.g. Bowman, 1998; Drummond et al., 2009). The temporal and spatial concentration of festivals (Waterman, 1998) creates an intense and immersive cultural experience for participants (Dowd et al., 2004) which in turn creates, shapes and even contests the meaning of both the festival, and culture more generally. Cultures naturally develop and change; however, as they do, certain cultural activities, such as music, dance, language, folk art and even history, can be lost. Music festivals can, however, contribute to the preservation of culture, as in the case of the blues festivals of the Mississippi Delta, which have revived and preserved the blues (King, 2004). In keeping valuable forms of music alive, festivals may also enhance the community's exposure to, and therefore awareness and experience of culture (Gibson and Connell, 2005), thus contributing to an increased appreciation of the arts.

Music festivals can also play an important role in the creation and strengthening of communities. Early festivals were often as much about establishing and strengthening social bonds as they were about celebration and thanksgiving (e.g. Sadie, 2001). Participants in music festivals, whether they are audiences, performers or organizers, form temporary communities, although sometimes these communities do last beyond the spatial/temporal boundaries of the festival itself if, for example, a network develops during a single festival or on the festival circuit (Connell and Gibson, 2003). Consequently, music festivals facilitate the creation, maintenance and expression of group/community identity (e.g. Shuker, 1998; Connell and Gibson, 2003; Waterman, 1998). Groups and communities can celebrate the shared mythologies, values and meanings that are integral to their identity. Thus, the music festival is a cultural framework that enables communities to reify their group identity (Rao, 2001) and distinctiveness. At the same time, music festivals enable a lessening of difference or distinction by encouraging social integration and community cohesion (Crespi-Vallbona and

Richards, 2007). King (2004) shows that even in a highly segregated and fragmented society such as the Mississippi Delta, blues festivals have the power to unite people and create a sense of community, as people from different groups in society develop important connections with one another

Finally, music festivals can also be a site of social change, transformation and the contesting of culture. The raison d'être of the counter-cultural music festivals of the 1960s was social change (e.g. Partridge, 2006). Music festivals provided spaces where people could express themselves differently and experiment with alternative ways of living that were not permissible in everyday life (Gibson and Connell, 2005). The carnivalesque nature of festivals encourages questioning of the status quo, and an imagining and temporary enactment of a better future. Bakhtin's (1965/1984) 'carnival' refers to a specific space and time in which all normal barriers are broken down, hierarchical structures are challenged and the rules that underpin those structures are suspended. In this way, festivals are oppositional. At the Glastonbury Festival of Contemporary Performing Arts, many examples of the inversion of the normal order and of the grotesque can be seen both in the organized art performances and in the spontaneous creative activities of the people who attend (Larsen and O'Reilly, 2008). The intense experiences that facilitate such communities were arguably at their height in the rock and pop festivals of the 1960s, such as Woodstock (Tiber, 1994). However, echoes of these counter-cultural sentiments can still be heard in contemporary commercial music festivals. For example, Yazicioglu and Firat's (2007) study of commercial rock festivals showed how both choices to attend and the consumption practices at the festival are ideologically informed and motivated by the contested nature of the meaning of rock music itself. Thus, a valuable contribution of music festivals is in raising cultural political questions about the relationship between aesthetics, style, taste and power, inequality and oppression, for those who attend, observe and study them. For example, Waterman (1998) explains how elites establish social distance through their support for certain kinds of music festivals.

Sponsorship and music festivals

The phenomenal growth and wide-reaching significance of music festivals has not gone unnoticed by businesses who see the potential marketing and commercial opportunities in gathering tens of thousands of 'consumers' in one place for a few days. Consequently, in recent years music festivals of all kinds have become increasingly commercial, corporate, regulated and organized, on the principles of business and marketing (Anderton, 2011; Brennan, 2010). For example, there has been a growing interest in and use of branding to differentiate festivals and thus provide a means for ensuring success in an increasingly competitive market. Festivals now cater to different segments of the market on a number of criteria, such as the genre of music (e.g. Newport Folk Festival, Download Festival (rock music)), and often festivals sell different packages to reflect the level of service provision and comfort provided (e.g. standard camping tickets versus luxury camping accommodation). However, one of the most notable marketing activities to emerge from the commercialization of music festivals is that of sponsorship.

In the arts generally, sponsorship is a way of bridging the gap between the income that can be gained through ticket prices and the actual costs sustained in staging an event. This gap can be significant, especially in the public arts sector where there is often little income by way of ticket sales. Companies will sponsor particular arts activities in return for publicity and promotion amongst the arts audience (Hill et al., 2003). From a company's point of view, sponsorship is usually thought of as a promotional activity, and thus a number of marketing issues are taken into consideration, such as the congruency between the target segments of both the sponsoring and sponsored organization. Sponsors seek a range of benefits, such as increasing visibility, enhancing their brand image, raising their profile, growing their customer base, and fulfilling social and philanthropic agendas. Similar benefits are sought by the sponsored organization, in addition to an increase in financial resources.

Sponsorship of music festivals of all different kinds is increasingly common, primarily as a result of the escalating costs and risks associated with staging a festival. As noted by Anderton (2011), these costs include meeting the requirements and fees of licensing, security, policing, surveillance, insurance, rising artists' fees, and increasingly complex on-site technologies and stage shows. The lump sum of money provided through sponsorship enables festival organizers to plan ahead and book many of the essential elements, such as the headline acts, before cash flows in from ticket sales – thus reducing risk (Anderton, 2009). The sponsor of a music festival doesn't necessarily expect to benefit from a high level of sales of their product at the festival, except where they are the sole provider of a specific type of concession, such as with Carling's sponsorship of the Reading and Leeds Festival from 1998-2007. Rather, the real benefits accrue for the sponsor in the long term, through enhanced attitudes towards the sponsor brand (Roberts, 2009; Skinner and Rukavina, 2003).

Festival sponsorship is however, not without caution, challenge and critique. As with any form of sponsorship, there are challenges in managing the relationship in a manner that ensures the benefits are delivered for all parties involved. For example, if multiple sponsors are sought for a festival, policies should be developed that will disallow competing organizations to become sponsors, as there is likely be a conflict of interest (Hill et al., 2003). In the case of music festivals, a significant critique of sponsorship is that its inherently commercial nature clashes with the counter-cultural ethos of the earlier free festivals which still echo in many contemporary large-scale music events. If sponsorship activities are too overt and excessive, they may be regarded as exploitative (Anderton, 2011), and therefore detrimental to the objectives of the sponsorship agreement. A response to this has been for sponsors and music festival organizers to work together to develop creative, surprising, engaging and memorable activities which actually enhance the festival-goers' experience, and thus create a meaningful, long-term connection with the brand (Lainer and Hampton, 2009). For example, the motor vehicle brand Toyota AYGO wished to leverage their broadcast sponsorship of the T4 On the Beach festival by developing a 'brand activation experience', as research indicated that the festival audience comprised a number of potential first-time car buyers. They converted an AYGO into a state-of-the-art DJ set-up, commissioned a second stage at the event and obtained access to T4's main-stage talent, who then played DJ sets from the AYGO stage. Toyota also created AYGO slot car races and staged a competition between McFly (a pop band) and the band's fans (Brand Activation, 2012).

Anderton (2011) concludes that as a result of these potential tensions and challenges, two broad trajectories of music festival sponsorship can be identified. The first trajectory is rooted in the counter-cultural ethos of the free festivals of the 1970s, and is manifest in the non-corporate, ethical, environmental and sustainable approach of mostly small, boutique festivals such as the Green Man Festival. However, as Larsen and O'Reilly (2008) note, this kind of ethos is also part of the large and commercially successful Glastonbury Festival of Contemporary Performing Arts where festival organizers and attendees are reluctant to engage in any kind of corporate sponsorship. The second trajectory is overtly commercial, where there is an active engagement with and use of multiple corporate sponsors and co-branding partners. These are two extreme points, and therefore many music festivals lie somewhere along the continuum between the two, where there is some involvement with corporate sponsors, but perhaps not to the extent of full co-branding and sponsorship.

Summary

This chapter explored a number of issues facing the production and consumption of live music, including those relating to music venues, music scenes and the promotion of live music. Live music has been gaining prominence in the 21st century, from both socio-cultural and economic perspectives. Contemporary live music promotion needs to be sensitive to social and cultural norms within the community of music fans. As places where live music, markets, marketing and consumers come together in significant ways, music festivals are complex events with many layers of meanings. There are clear market dynamics within the festivals themselves, but they deliver social and aesthetic value beyond their economic and exchange value.

References

Anderton, C. (2009) 'Commercializing the carnivalesque: The V Festival and image/risk management' *Event Management*, **12** (1), 39-51.

Anderton, C. (2011) 'Music festival sponsorship: between commerce and carnival' *Arts Marketing: An International Journal*, **1** (2), 145-158.

Arnould, E., Price, L. and Zinkhan, G. (2003) *Consumers*. London: McGraw-Hill Higher Education.

Association of Independent Festivals (2010) 'Festivals Remain Number One Entertainment Choice For Britons This Summer' http://www.aiforg.com/ [Accessed at 17 July 2010].

Bakhtin, M. (1965/1984) *Rabelais and His World*, translated by Iswolsky, H., London: John Wiley and Sons.

BBC News (2012) 'Glastonbury Tickets Sell Out in Record Time' 7 October 2012 http://www.bbc.co.uk/news/entertainment-arts-19861686 [Accessed 19 December 2012].

Botti, S. (2000) 'What role for marketing in the arts? An analysis of arts consumption and artistic value', *International Journal of Arts Management*, **2** (3), 14-27.

Bowman, W.D. (1998) *Philosophical Perspectives on Music*, Oxford: Oxford University Press.

Brand Activation (2012) 'Festival Activity' http://www.brandactivation.co.uk/our-work/festival-activity/ [Accessed 20 December 2012].

Brennan, M. (2010) 'Constructing a rough account of british concert promotion history' *Journal of the International Association for the Study of Popular Music*, **1** (1), 4-13.

Canizal Villarino, M., Whitehall, B. and Mecke, B. (2009) 'Music festivals: music and food for the masses', *Food Service Europe & Middle East*, Verlagsgruppe Deutscher Fachverlag, 21 August, 8-17.

Cluley, R. (2009) 'Engineering great moments: the production of live music', *Consumption Markets & Culture*, **12** (4), 373-388.

Connell, J. and Gibson, C. (2003) *Sound Tracks: Popular Music, Identity and Place*, London: Routledge.

Connolly, M. and Krueger, A.B. (2006) 'Rockonomics: the economics of popular music', *The Milken Institute Review*, **9** (3), 50-66.

Crespi-Vallbona, M. and Richards, G. (2007) 'The meaning of cultural festivals: stakeholder perspectives in Catalunya', *International Journal of Cultural Policy*, 13 (1), 103-122.

Dobson, M. (2008) 'Exploring classical music concert attendance: The effects of concert venue and familiarity on audience experience', in: Marin, M.M., Knoche, M. and Parncutt, R. (eds) *First International Conference of Students of Systematic Musicology: Proceedings* (SysMus08), Graz, Department of Musicology, University of Graz, 27-34.

Dowd, T., Liddle, K. and Nelson, J. (2004) 'Music festivals as scenes: examples from serious music, womyn's music and skate punk', in: Bennett, A. and Peterson, R. (eds) *Music Scenes: Local, Translocal and Virtual*, Nashville: Vanderbilt University Press, pp. 149-167.

Drummond, J., Kearsley, G. and Lawson, R. (2008) *Culture Matters: A Report for the Ministry of Research, Science and Technology*, Dunedin, New Zealand: University of Otago.

Earl, P.E. (2001) 'Simon's travel theorem and the demand for live music', *Journal of Economic Psychology*, 22, 335-358.

Fisher, C., Pearson, M. and Barnes, J. (2002) 'A study of strength of relationship between music groups and their external service providers: impacts on music group success', *Services Marketing Quarterly*, 24 (2), 43-60.

Frith, S. (2007) 'Live music matters', *Scottish Music Review*, 1 (1), 1-17.

Gibson, C. and Connell, J. (2005) 'Music and tourism: on the road again', *Aspects of Tourism* 19, London: Channel View Publications.

Grove, S.J., Fisk, R.P. and Bitner, M.J. (1992) 'Dramatizing the service experience: a managerial approach', in: Schwartz, T.A., Bowen, D.E. and Brown, S.W. (eds) *Advances in Services Marketing and Management*, San Francisco, CA: JAI Press, pp. 91-121.

Hill, L., O'Sullivan, C. and O'Sullivan, T. (2003) *Creative Arts Marketing* 2nd edn, Oxford: Butterworth Heinemann.

Holt, F. (2010) 'The economy of live music in the digital age', *European Journal of Cultural Studies*, 13 (2), 243-261.

Kahn-Harris, K. (2007) *Extreme Metal: Music and Culture on the Edge*, Oxford: Berg.

King, S. (2004) 'Blues tourism in the Mississippi Delta: the functions of blues festivals', *Popular Music and Society*, 27 (4), 455-475.

King, T. (2001) 'Patronage and market in the creation of opera before the institution of intellectual property', *Journal of Cultural Economics*, **25**, 21-45.

Lalner, C. and Hampton, R. (2009) 'Experiential marketing: understanding the logic of memorable customer experiences', in: Lindgreen, A., Vanhamme, J. and Beverland, M. (eds) *Memorable Customer Experiences: A Research Anthology*, Farnham: Gower Publishing, pp. 9-23.

Larsen, G. and Hussels, S. (2011) 'The significance of commercial music festivals', in: Cameron, S (ed.) *Handbook on the Economics of Leisure*, Cheltenham, UK: Edward Elgar, pp. 250-270.

Larsen, G. and O'Reilly, D. (2008) 'Festival tales: utopian tales' *Academy of Marketing Annual Conference*, 8-10 July, Aberdeen, Scotland.

Minor, M.S., Wagner, T., Brewerton, F.J. and Hausman, A. (2004) 'Rock on! An elementary model of customer satisfaction with musical performance', *Journal of Services Marketing*, **18** (1), 7-18.

Mintel (2008) *Music Festivals and Concerts – UK – August 2008*. Mintel International Group Ltd

Music Week: The Business of Music (2011) 'Record Number of Festivals Being Dissolved' August 1 2011 http://www.musicweek.com/news/read/record-numbers-of-festivals-being-dissolved/046352 [Accessed 19 December 2012].

O'Reilly, D., Kerrigan, F. and Larsen, G. (2010) 'Re-orienting arts marketing: the new textbook generation', *Academy of Marketing Annual Conference*, 6-8 July, Coventry.

Oakes, S. (2003) 'Demographic and sponsorship considerations for jazz and classical music festivals', *The Services Industries Journal*, **23** (3), 165-178.

Partridge, C. (2006) 'The spiritual and the revolutionary: alternative spirituality, british free festivals, and the emergence of rave culture', *Culture and Religion*, **7** (1) 41-60.

Rao, V. (2001) 'Celebrations as social investments: festival expenditures, unit price variation and social status in rural India', *The Journal of Development Studies*, **38** (1), 71-97

Roberts, J. (2009) 'Music Festival Sponsorship', *Marketing Week*, 9 July, http://www.marketingweek.co.uk/music-festival-sponsorship/3002146.article Accessed 2 May 2013.

Sadie, S. (ed.) (2001) *The New Grove Dictionary of Music and Musicians*, London: Macmillan

Sayre, S. (2008) *Entertainment Marketing & Communication*, Upper Saddle River, NJ: Pearson.

Shuker, R. (1998) *Key Concepts in Popular Music*, London: Routledge.

Skinner, B.E. and Rukavina, V. (2003) *Event Sponsorship*, Hoboken, NJ: John Wiley and Sons.

Thornton, S. (1995) *Club Cultures*, Cambridge: Wesleyan University Press.

Tiber, E. (1994) *Knock on Woodstock*, New York: Festival Books.

Tschmuck, P. (2012) *Creativity and Innovation in the Music Industry*, Heidelberg: Springer.

UK Music (2011) *Destination: Music: The Contribution of Music Festivals and Major Concerts to Tourism in the UK*, http://www.ukmusic.org/news/post/147-music-tourists-contribute-at-least-864m-a-year-to-the-uk-economy Accessed 1 May 2013

Waterman, S. (1998) 'Carnivals for élites? The cultural politics of arts festivals', *Progress in Human Geography*, **22** (1), 54-74.

Yazicioglu, E.T and Firat, A.F (2007) 'Glocal rock festivals as mirrors into the future of culture(s)', in: Belk, R.W and Sherry, J.F (ed.) *Consumer Culture Theory: Research in Consumer Behaviour*, 11, Bingley, UK: Emerald Group Publishing, pp. 101-117.

11 Conclusion

Mainstream managerial marketing relies on models and theories that prioritize rational behaviours and decision-making, yet the power of music goes beyond attempts to measure it and escapes a standard cost-benefit analysis. Music is an important aspect of emotional life, for both creators of music and its consumers; it is something that most of us engage with habitually, and often unreflectively, turning to it to satisfy our emotional needs. Music is part of our culture, and as such is every bit as complex as the culture itself. Culture influences what kind of music is produced and consumed, what purpose it serves and in what situations. The pace of changes in the music world over the last 20 years has made it impossible to fully understand its complexity through a lens of mainstream marketing theories and concepts, such as the marketing mix. As the production and consumption of music evolves, our understanding must evolve as well. The traditional or classical marketing approach presents musicians as producers and operatives, yet their relationship with their music is deeply personal and intimate. The same goes for music consumers, who, through their commitment and love of sounds, play a far more important role than the word 'consumer' brings to mind. They are active participants in the creation of musical experiences, from live concerts to b(r)ands.

Throughout the process of writing this book we have been concerned with moving beyond the mainstream view of marketing in order to explore other perspectives. It is not the end, but rather the beginning of a journey for us, and hopefully for other academics, practitioners and students that are interested in music, markets and consumption. The content of this book has been chosen to encourage other such interested parties to venture beyond what the traditional marketing toolkit and its simple modifications can offer, and to help us better understand what other disciplines have to say about our common interest in the production and consumption of music. By critically reflecting on music as product (Chapter 3), musicians and their role in the music business (Chapter 4), the social construction of music brands (Chapters 5 and 6), music consumption and engagement (Chapter 7), musical fandom (Chapter 8), the role of collectivities in music (Chapter 9), and festivals and music venues (Chapter 10), we attempted to challenge the boundaries of music marketing. These chapters serve to illustrate some of the depth and breadth of knowledge that multiple disciplines and approaches can offer to each of the issues we decided to include in this book. For example, there has been a very limited amount or research into music as a product; musicians; fandom as a form of consumption; and marketing of live music in mainstream marketing – yet a wide range of research into those areas exists in popular music, psychology, sociology, philosophy, cultural studies and other disciplines.

This book acknowledges the importance of the economy, policy and technology for the production and consumption of music, yet it also attempts to shift the focus by exploring the social and cultural aspects of the music business and music marketing. The role of music in the marketplace stretches far beyond that of a simple product; it is an important part of our culture, and culture as a theme can be identified throughout most of the chapters of this book, be it in cultural reproduction systems such as music education (Chapter 4), cultural branding and cultural economy (Chapters 5 and 6), fan cultures (Chapter 8), or the socio-cultural role of music festivals (Chapter 10).

Another important theme running through many discussions in this book is that relating to how the use and mass-adoption of new technologies in the music business have affected both production and consumption practices. Such technologies have shifted the power in the music industry away from record labels towards music consumers and musicians themselves, fuelling innovation and creativity among both. Musicians are now able to market their products directly to consumers via the Internet, and market themselves using social media, thereby bypassing many traditional music industry distribution channels . In addition, music consumption is being redefined through downloading, file sharing and online streaming (Chapters 2 and 7), thereby creating massive variety in music consumption practices and experiences. Technological changes have also led to a large shift in the online behaviour of fans (Chapter 8), who have been given unprecedented access to information opportunities that allow them to communicate and create virtual communities, despite physical distance.

Last but not least, any discussion of music and marketing has to touch on the art vs. commerce debate, which influenced much of the thinking about music production and consumption in the 20th century (Chapters 3 and 4). This is a very sensitive theme that provokes many heated debates amongst academics (see, for example, Bradshaw et al., 2006; Holbrook, 2005, 2006), and some strong divisions amongst musicians themselves (Kubacki and Croft, 2004). Music is a very diverse art form, and its relationship with the marketplace does not always need to be full of tension, since various members of the music business bring different values to the discussion. What the marketing perspective can offer is a fusion of these different perspectives. Music is a diverse art form, and it is impossible to identify one set of theories to understand the complexity of its relationship with marketing and the market. As argued elsewhere, music marketers need to be situationists (Kubacki and O'Reilly, 2009) when trying to facilitate the production and consumption of music. Music marketing needs to take into account the technological changes, policies and economic structure of the music business (Chapter 2), the mainstream marketing toolkit (Chapter 1), the complexity of musical products (Chapter 3), artistic conventions and ideologies (Chapter 4), the social construction of music brands (Chapters 5 and 6), the wide range of music consumption behaviours (Chapter 7), music fandom (Chapter 8), the role of music in the formation of communities (Chapter 9), and spaces in which the production and consumption of music come together (Chapter 10).

We began this book with an overview of the traditional marketing management tools (marketing mix, branding and services marketing) which have been most frequently used to study the relationship between marketing and music. However, they allow us to capture only some of the layers involved in the production and consumption of music, and many of its complexities have completely escaped the attention of marketing academics involved in researching the music industry. Chapter 1 introduced classical marketing theory in order to position the mainstream approach to the subject. This was followed, in Chapter 2, by an analysis of some of the most influential forces shaping the music business: economy, policy and technology. The second chapter also examined the historical development of the music industry and its current structure, as well as the implications of cultural policy and technological changes for music in the marketplace.

Part II – *Production Perspectives* – considered some of the crucial elements of the music production system: product (music), producers (musicians) and production processes, leading to an interpretation of the cultural meaning in music offerings (branding). Chapter 3 discussed the consequences of looking at music as a product in the marketplace, and what actually comprises the music product. Directly related to the problem of framing music as a product is the discussion of its nature and value, especially its economic value in exchange. Chapter 4 presented a discussion about musicians and their roles in the music business. It revealed a very complex system of music production, showing that musicians are not mere producers, but also products of the music industry. Both formal and informal music education serve as an important economic activity, as well as a platform for social engagement, especially among young people. The music education industry is a cultural production system that shapes the attitudes and behaviours of future music-makers and leads the way in the development of musical identities and hierarchies among artists. Chapters 5 and 6 considered the important symbolic aspects of music production and consumption, and attempted to craft a socio-cultural view of branding, which took account of useful notions such as the circuit of culture and text, and offered a view of brands as being produced and consumed by all of the relevant stakeholders.

In Part III – *Consumption Perspectives* – provided an overview of the most pressing issues in the consumption of music, via a discussion of the various types of engagement in music in the marketplace, and the social consumption of music. Chapter 7 considered different understandings of how people engage with music – as consumers, audiences, fans and collectors – to better elucidate the diversity and complexity of music consumption. Chapter 8 introduced one of the most fascinating aspects of the consumption of music – fandom and the behaviour of music fans. Yet, surprisingly, there has been very little interest in music fans among marketing academics. As consumer loyalty is the ultimate goal of marketing, fans are arguably the most loyal consumers. Throughout this chapter the discussion focused on a wide range of consumption behaviours by fans, whose behaviours co-produce musical brands. Chapter 9 dealt with a range of constructs or ideas relating to music collectivities.

Part IV focused on one of the most unique forms of music production and consumption – live music. Chapter 10 considered the role of music venues and festivals in the music business. Both of these sites are music marketing microcosms, where all aspects of music marketing interact with each other within a clearly defined socio-spatial environment, thereby creating musical experiences for all members of the music business.

We hope that by writing this book we will encourage other academics, practitioners and students to look at music, markets and consumption through the marketing lens, yet fuse the range of interdisciplinary perspectives into a more holistic approach to understanding the relationship between music and the marketplace. The sheer amount of music in contemporary societies, and the variety of ways it is produced and consumed, as well as the complexity and diversity of its discourses across multiple academic disciplines with an interest in music, warrant a lasting interest in it. It is also high time that the marketing discipline attempted to clearly articulate its own role in helping to develop an understanding of music in the marketplace. The music business is still undergoing dramatic changes, and this book has demonstrated some of the key areas that are thought to be of interest to music marketing researchers. We strongly believe that further study of music through a marketing lens, suitably complemented by perspectives from other disciplines, is both worthwhile and capable of offering new and original thoughts about the role of music in our lives. Further extensive empirical and conceptual work will help us illuminate those insights.

As we said in the Preface, this book does not formally develop a new theory of music marketing. However, we trust that it lays some of the foundations which would be essential for such a project.

References

Bradshaw, A., McDonagh, P. and Marshall, D. (2006) 'Response to "Art versus Commerce as a Macromarketing Theme"', *Journal of Macromarketing*, **26** (1), 81-83.

Holbrook, M.B. (2005) 'Art versus commerce as a macromarketing theme in three films from the young-man-with-a-horn genre', *Journal of Macromarketing*, **25** (1), 22-31.

Holbrook, M.B. (2006) 'Reply to Bradshaw, McDonagh, and Marshall: turn off the bubble machine', *Journal of Macromarketing*, **26** (1), 84-87.

Kubacki, K. and Croft, R. (2004) 'Mass marketing, music and morality', *Journal of Marketing Management*, **20** (5-6), 577-590.

Kubacki, K. and O'Reilly, D. (2009) 'Arts Marketing', in Maclaran, P. and Parsons, E. (eds) *Contemporary Issues in Marketing and Consumer Behaviour*, Oxford, UK: Elsevier, 55-71.

Index